Verbal Workout for the

GRE

Third Edition

Yung-Yee Wu

PrincetonReview.com

Random House, Inc. New York

The Princeton Review, Inc.
2315 Broadway
New York, NY 10024
E-mail: editorialsupport@review.com

ISBN: 978-0-375-76573-5
ISSN: 1559-8640

Permission has been granted to reprint portions of the following:

"The Self-Reproducing Inflationary Universe," by Andrei Linde. *Scientific American*, Nov.
1994, pp. 48–49.

Compulsive Beauty, by Hal Foster. MIT Press, Cambridge, MA, © 1993 Massachusetts
Institute of Technology, pp. xi–xiii.

Death Comes to the Maiden: Sex and Execution, 1731–1933, by Camille Naish. Routledge,
a division of Routledge, Chapman and Hall Inc., NY, © 1991, pp. 5–6.

Free Soil, Free Labor, Free Men: The Ideology of the Republican Party Before the Civil War,
by Eric Foner. Oxford University Press, NY, © 1970, pp. 2–4.

The Perils of Humanism, by Frederick C. Crews. Princeton University Press, Princeton, NJ,
© 1962, pp. 3–6.

Gender Differences at Work: Women and Men in Nontraditional Occupations, by Christine
L. Williams. University of California Press, Berkeley and Los Angeles, CA, © 1989, pp. 3–6.

"Cerebral Meningitis Epidemics," by Patrick S. Moore and Claire V. Broome. *Scientific
American*, Nov. 1994, pp. 44–45.

City of Women: Sex and Class in New York, 1789–1860, by Christine Stansell. University of
Illinois Press, Chicago, IL, © 1982, pp. xi–xiii.

California Indian Shamonism, edited by Lowell John Bean. Ballena Press, Menlo Park, CA,
pp. 15–16.

Editor: Rebecca Lessem
Production Editor: Katie O'Neill
Production Coordinator: Kim Howie

Printed in the United States of America.

10 9 8 7 6 5 4 3 2

Third Edition

ACKNOWLEDGMENTS

My first thank you's must go to the people at The Princeton Review who helped me put together this tome. Thank you, Jeannie Yoon, for helping me and for always listening. Thank you, Amy Zavatto, for providing me with critical feedback and for actually reading every word. Thanks also to Melody Marcus, Briana Gordon, Rebecca Lessem, Katie O'Neill, M. Tighe Wall, Stephen White, Suzanne Barker, and Kim Howie.

Finally, three personal thank you's: Thank you, Fritz Faerber, for feeding me while I wrote. Thank you, thank you, thank you, Lin, Shi-yu, Yung-Hsing, and Mie-Mie (a.k.a. my family) for keeping me sane. And last, but not least, thank you, Woobie, (a.k.a. Huckleberry, a.k.a. Muffin Man, a.k.a. Budgie) for being you.

—*Yung Yee Wu*

Special thanks to Adam Robinson, who conceived of and perfected the Joe Bloggs approach to standardized tests and many of the other successful techniques used by The Princeton Review.

ABOUT THE AUTHORS

Yung-Yee Wu joined The Princeton Review in 1993. She began as an instructor and later worked in research and development as the director of high school, graduate, and international courses.

CONTENTS

Introduction

THE GRE AND YOU

So you've finally decided what to do with your post-college life. You're not going to pursue the vaunted M.D., nor are you going to chase the lucrative J.D. Rather, the initials you desire to follow your name are M.A., M.S., or Ph.D. In short, you want to go to graduate school. However, since you can't simply sign up for grad school, you're going to have to tackle the application process. That means writing essays, soliciting recommendations, gathering transcripts, and taking the Graduate Record Examination, otherwise known as the GRE. Nearly all graduate programs require the GRE, so no matter what field you intend to pursue, the GRE probably lies in your future. The GRE is written by the Educational Testing Service (ETS), the same folks who inflicted the SAT upon you during your high school days.

WHAT DOES THE GRE MEASURE?

That's an excellent question. According to ETS the GRE measures "analytical writing, verbal, and quantitative skills that have been acquired over a long period of time and that are not related to any specific field of study." Let's think about that for a moment. What seems to be missing from this statement? If you said, "Something directly related to how successful I will be as a grad student," you're on the right track. Notice that even ETS doesn't claim that the GRE measures how well you'll perform in a program of anthropology, or psychology, or religious studies, or art history, or physics. The GRE is not a test of intelligence or of your aptitude for graduate study. Despite this, graduate schools use it because it gives them an objective way to compare applicants whose other qualifications are often quite subjective.

SO WHAT DOES THE GRE *REALLY* MEASURE?

The GRE tests how well you solve GRE problems. It's true that in order to do that, you need some basic math skills, basic reading skills, basic writing skills, and a good vocabulary, but, perhaps most important, you need good test-taking skills. Many people (including those at ETS) view the GRE as some kind of general assessment of your ability. They believe that you either have what it takes, or you don't. But in reality the GRE tests very specific information and skills. You can learn that information and you can develop those skills. The key is to approach the GRE as a *specific* task, like learning to play the piano or hitting a golf ball. The same two things that will help you become a better piano player will help you become a better GRE test taker: 1) Instruction, and 2) Practice. And both of those are what you will get with this book.

REGISTERING FOR THE TEST

The GRE is a computer-based test that you will take in a designated testing center. You can take the test year-round, on almost any day, morning or afternoon, weekday or weekend, subject to the availability of test appointments at the test center you want to use. The earlier you register, the more likely you are to get your preferred appointment. You can only take the GRE once per calendar month, and a maximum of five times in any 12-month period. In order to schedule a test, call 1-800-GRE-CALL. If you're taking the test in the U.S., Puerto Rico, or most U.S. territories, the GRE currently costs $130, and you have to pay by credit card. The test costs $160 from most other locations. There's a $40 fee if you need to reschedule. These prices may change, so for up-to-date information, visit **www.gre.org**.

HOW IMPORTANT IS THE GRE?

The definitive answer to this important question is: It depends. How much weight the GRE is given will vary from school to school, and from program to program. Some schools consider the GRE very important, while others tend to view it as a formality. Some don't use it at all for admissions, but only in awarding scholarships. Schools may also give different weight to the different sections of the GRE. If you're applying to a masters program in English Literature, for example, they might not care too much about your Math score, and focus instead on your Verbal and Analytical Writing scores. The best way to find out how important your GRE score will be is to contact the schools you're interested in and ask them. Most graduate programs are happy to talk about the application process and can let you know how they evaluate GRE scores.

In any case, there is always much more to a graduate school application than GRE scores. Your grades, undergraduate institution, recommendations, personal statement, research or work experience, and interview are all part of the process. The GRE can be important, but it's never the whole story.

THE STRUCTURE OF THE GRE

Let's take a moment to review the basic structure of the GRE.

THE SCORED SECTIONS

The GRE contains three scored sections:

- One 30-minute Verbal section, which contains 30 questions
- One 45-minute Math section, which contains 28 questions
- One 75-minute Analytical Writing section, which contains two essay questions

All of the Verbal and Math questions are multiple-choice, while the Analytical Writing section requires you to write two essays. The Analytical Writing section will always be the first section presented to you, followed by the multiple-choice sections.

You will be able to see your Verbal and Math scores immediately upon completion of the test, but you will have to wait about two weeks before your Analytical Writing section is scored.

THE EXPERIMENTAL SECTION

In addition to the two scored multiple-choice sections listed above, you will also have an unscored experimental section. This section will look exactly like either your Math or Verbal section, but it won't count at all toward your score. ETS administers the experimental section to gather data on questions before they appear on real GREs.

Thus, after your Analytical Writing section you will actually see three multiple-choice sections: either two Verbal and one Math, or two Math and one Verbal, depending on whether you get a Math or Verbal experimental section. The multiple-choice sections can come in any order; your experimental section could be first, second, or third. You will have no way of knowing which section is experimental, so you need to do your best on all of them. Don't waste time worrying about which sections count and which don't.

Here is how a typical GRE might look:

Analytical Writing – 75 minutes
10-minute break
Verbal – 30 minutes
Math – 45 minutes
Verbal – 30 minutes

Remember, the Analytical Writing section will always be first, and it will never be experimental—the essay section always counts. In this example, the Math section was real, and one of the Verbal sections was experimental, though we don't know which one. Of course, on your actual GRE you might see two Math sections instead of two Verbal sections, and they might come in a different order. Be flexible, and you'll be ready for the test no matter what order the sections come in. You get a 10-minute break after the Analytical Writing section, so make sure to visit the bathroom, refresh your mind, and get ready for the rest of the exam.

RESEARCH SECTION

The GRE will occasionally include an optional research section. This section will always be the final section of the test and will be clearly identified. ETS uses this section to test out new oddball questions. Nothing you do on the research section will change your score in any way.

HOW IS THE GRE SCORED?

You receive three separate scores for the GRE, corresponding to the three scored sections:

- A Verbal score from 200 to 800, in 10-point increments
- A Math score from 200 to 800, in 10-point increments
- An Analytical Writing score from 0 to 6, in half-point increments

The average scores for the GRE are approximately 470 Verbal, 610 Math, and 4.5 Writing.

THE GRE VERBAL SECTION UNMASKED

Let's look in more detail at the Verbal section. As we said before, the GRE Verbal section contains 30 questions for which you are given 30 minutes to answer. Let's examine what types of questions we have to deal with.

The GRE Verbal section contains four types of questions:

- Antonyms
- Analogies
- Sentence Completions
- Reading Comprehension

These questions appear in no particular order, and will be distributed in a roughly equal way. Thirty doesn't divide evenly by four, so the number of questions can't be exactly equal for each question type, but you'll probably see something close to a 7-7-8-8 split. Sentence completion questions tend to be the least common question type and antonyms the most common, so you might see a 6-7-8-9 split as well. In the coming chapters, you will learn how to tackle each of these question types.

SCORE PERCENTILES FOR THE VERBAL SECTION

Let's take a look at the percentile rankings for GRE Verbal scores. A percentile ranking tells you what percent of test takers scored beneath a given score. For example, a 560 in Verbal corresponds to the 76th percentile, which means that 76 percent of test takers scored below 560 on the Verbal section.

Score	Verbal Percentile	Score	Verbal Percentile	Score	Verbal Percentile
800	99	600	85	400	31
790	99	590	83	390	28
780	99	580	81	380	25
770	99	570	78	370	22
760	99	560	76	360	20
750	99	550	72	350	18
740	99	540	70	340	15
730	99	530	67	330	12
720	98	520	65	320	10
710	98	510	63	310	7
700	97	500	60	300	5
690	96	490	56	290	4
680	95	480	54	280	3
670	94	470	50	270	2
660	93	460	48	260	1
650	92	450	45	250	1
640	91	440	43	240	1
630	90	430	40	230	1
620	88	420	37	220	1
610	87	410	34	210	1
				200	1

Here's a look at the average GRE Verbal scores for some general graduate fields.

Intended Graduate Field	Approximate Number of Test Takers	Average Verbal Score
Life Sciences	117,577	462
Social Sciences	101,085	487
Engineering	56,368	468
Physical Sciences	55,910	486
Humanities and Arts	49,882	545
Education	43,844	449
Business	8,357	442

Note that these averages are based on all the people who took the GRE between October 2002 and June 2005 and indicated an intended field, without consideration of whether they actually applied to graduate school or were admitted.

THE ANALYTICAL WRITING SECTION DEMYSTIFIED

In the Analytical Writing chapter, you'll learn all you need to know about writing high-scoring essays. But in the meantime, we'll examine a few of the basics of this section.

The Analytical Writing section requires you to write two essays:

- One Issue essay in 45 minutes
- One Argument essay in 30 minutes

You are given two prompts for the Issue essay, and you must choose one. For the Argument essay you are only given one prompt.

How the Essays Are Scored

Each essay is read by two readers, who give it a score from 0 to 6. The scores from the two readers are averaged for each essay, and then the scores for the two essays are averaged and rounded to the nearest half-point.

The only number that schools ever see is the final score. They don't see how you scored on the individual essays. However, ETS plans to eventually make the individual essays themselves available to schools, so that they could read them if they choose.

ANALYTICAL WRITING PERCENTILES

Essay Score	Percentile
6	96
5.5	87
5	71
4.5	52
4	32
3.5	17
3	7
2.5	2
2	1
1.5	0
1	0
.5	0
0	0

These are the most recent percentiles ETS has published, however the current percentiles may be slightly higher or lower.

HOW TO USE THIS BOOK

There are probably two categories of people who have purchased this book. See if you belong in one of these.

1. People who have also bought a book that covers the whole GRE (such as, perhaps, the excellent *Cracking the GRE*) and are simply looking for some more verbal practice.

2. People who are very comfortable with the math on the GRE and want to focus their preparation mostly or exclusively on the Verbal section.

If you fit into the first category, then you will already know much of the information in this book. However, it's still worth reading all of it. First, doing so will reinforce the points and techniques that you've already studied. Also, the material is presented in a slightly different way in this book, and you will benefit from seeing the same techniques described in different words.

If you fit into the second category, then you obviously will want to study all the material carefully to learn how to approach each type of question. Make sure to practice the techniques when you do the practice sets, and read the explanations carefully to ensure that you pick up both the big picture and the details of our methods.

If you fit into a third category, well, we're sure you'll be able to figure out how to use the book to your advantage.

Whatever your situation, one thing you definitely must do is obtain as much real GRE material as you can to practice on. In particular, there are two items you should get hold of. The first is the book *Practicing to Take the GRE General Test, 10th Edition*. This book is published by ETS and contains a retired pool of real test questions from seven paper-and-pencil GREs. This is the only source of printed real GRE questions available. You can buy it (or order it online) at any large bookstore or directly from ETS at **www.gre.org**.

The second thing you need is GRE *POWERPREP®* software. *POWERPREP* contains two computer-based GREs, sample writing topics, sample essays with commentary, a math review, and some tutorials. The most important part is the practice tests. The GRE is a computer-based test, so part of your preparation must include practice on a computer. By taking the *POWERPREP* computer tests, you'll become familiar with the layout of the buttons and the feel of the computer format, and have the opportunity to practice our techniques in a realistic setting. We recommend taking the computer tests only after you've completed all the material in this book. *POWERPREP* software is automatically sent to you on CD-ROM when you register for the GRE. You can also download it for free from the GRE website at **www.gre.org**.

The most important thing you need to do is work hard. No GRE book can help you if you don't put in the time to learn the techniques, practice the techniques, and then use the techniques on the actual exam. As in many other situations, the results you get out of your GRE preparation will be largely determined by the amount of effort you put into it.

So let's get to work!

1
Strategies

STRATEGIZE

Before we get into the specific techniques for tackling the verbal questions, we need to discuss some of the overall strategies that are important on the GRE. Some of these will make perfect sense, but others may seem counterintuitive. Trust us that everything we recommend here has been tested, refined, and proven through a great deal of experience. Stick with it, and practice until it all becomes automatic and second-nature.

We'll have a lot to say about the computer shortly, but before looking at that, we're going to discuss a few things that are crucial to scoring your best on the Verbal section.

BE METHODICAL

One reason many people particularly despise the Verbal section of the GRE is that there is a specific disadvantage to verbal questions that doesn't exist on math questions. Math questions always have answers that are exact and provable, whereas the answers to verbal questions are always debatable. They involve shades of meaning and nuance that you simply don't have to deal with in math questions. When $x = 7$, you just look for the 7 in the answer choices, but you can never have the same certainty that the answer you choose for a verbal question is correct.

Unfortunately, what many people take from this is the idea that answering verbal questions is a matter of groping your way toward the right answer and picking the one that smells/tastes/feels right. If that's the way you approach verbal questions, it's going to be hard for you to improve. The key to becoming better at solving verbal questions is to adopt a systematic approach. You need a step-by-step method for attacking each part of the Verbal section, and you need to apply that method consistently. Not surprisingly, we will be showing you these techniques in the subsequent chapters.

MEET YOUR NEW BEST FRIEND: POE

This POE is not related to Edgar Allan, but is rather the Process of Elimination. You should use the Process of Elimination on every question in the Verbal section. To understand why POE is so important, we need to look at several elements of the GRE. The first is that the GRE is a multiple-choice test. All the correct answers are given to you on the GRE Verbal section, but each one is surrounded by four incorrect answers. Because there are four times as many wrong answers on the Verbal section as right ones, the wrong ones are easier to spot. And when we spot them and eliminate them, we narrow the range of options we have to choose from, even if we end up guessing.

Another important reason is based on the nature of verbal questions themselves. As we mentioned above, the correct answer to a verbal question is never correct in an absolute, mathematical sense. It's correct because it's the best of the available options. This is why ETS refers to the right answer as the "credited response." Even ETS doesn't claim that one answer is "correct," merely that there's one answer for which you get credit. The point you need to take from this is that the right answer to a verbal question will sometimes be pretty bad. Nevertheless, it will be the least bad of your options. Therefore, what you're really looking for on verbal questions is not an answer choice you like. You're looking for the least objectionable answer, the one that stinks less than all the others.

It's important to understand that POE is not just a matter of crossing off answer choices as you go. It's not simply a physical process. Rather, it's an active mental process that evaluates answer choices by looking for flaws, looking for reasons to get rid of them. Nothing is more frustrating than looking at a few answer choices and not liking any of them, or liking more than one and being unable to decide between them. Get in the habit of making the best case you can *against* each answer choice, and you'll be much more successful.

Watch Out for Traps

ETS has given the GRE to hundreds of thousands of students, and because of all this data and experience you can believe one thing: They know how you think. Don't feel bad about this. They know how you think because most of us think in very similar ways. We all share many of the same associations and tendencies. It's simply part of our nature. ETS has learned how to take advantage of this by writing trap answers, sometimes called "distractors," because they distract you from the right answer. For example, on a killer antonym or analogy question, they love to include an answer choice that contains words that remind you of the stem word. Say you get an analogy that contains the stem words SUN : ZENITH. They know that if they write an answer choice that says, for instance, stars : perihelion, many people will choose it because stars remind them of the sun, and it seems like the best thing they can find. Don't fall for it. If the answer could be found that way, it wouldn't be a hard question.

Scratch Paper

The GRE is a computer-based test, so you can't write on the problems themselves. (The test center employees get very unhappy if you write on their computer screens.) All your work must be done on scratch paper. Since that's how the actual test works, you need to start practicing that way. All GRE practice work should be done on scratch paper. As you study the techniques for the verbal questions, you'll learn what kind of information you should be writing down, but one thing you will always write down is A, B, C, D, and E vertically on your scratch paper so you can cross off answer choices as you apply POE. (There are no actual letters next to the answers on the computer screen, just bubbles, but we'll use letters to represent the answers from top to bottom. You should, too.) Learning to use your scratch paper effectively is one of the keys to scoring well on the GRE. Avoid the temptation to write on the problems as you practice. You can't give yourself a crutch in your preparation that you aren't going to have on the real exam.

At the test center you'll be given about six sheets of scratch paper. If you need more you can request it, but the proctor will take away all your old paper at the same time. Also, if you run out in the middle of a section you'll need to put your hand in the air and wait for a proctor to notice, collect the paper, and bring it in to you. You don't want to waste your precious time waiting for the proctor to attend to you. Time is ticking away! So even though your scratch paper is technically unlimited, don't be extravagant. Try to make it last.

Vocabulary

It might seem odd to think of vocabulary as a strategy, but learning vocabulary is one of the most important things you must do to maximize your score on the GRE Verbal section. The Analogies and Antonyms sections are hugely vocabulary-dependent, and sentence completion questions also often turn on vocabulary. Only the reading comprehension questions give you a respite from this vocabulary obsession.

This means that you have to tackle the vocabulary issue directly. The techniques we'll be showing you are strong, but at some point vocabulary will put a ceiling on your score. The more words you know, the higher that ceiling is. Studying words is unquestionably dull, but you'll know how serious you really are about raising your GRE Verbal score by how diligently you work to expand your vocabulary.

To assist you with this, we have included Chapter 7, which contains lists of words that commonly appear on the GRE. This chapter contains the GRE Hit Parade (which also appears in *Cracking the GRE*) and additional word lists (that do not). Furthermore, there are drills, quizzes, sample questions, and advice for building your vocabulary. Study these words assiduously, and you'll give yourself a big advantage on test day. But don't wait until you've worked through the rest of the book to turn to the vocabulary chapter. Start working on vocabulary from the very beginning. You need to spread it out over the whole period of your GRE preparation for it to be effective.

Ultimately, the most successful way to a higher GRE Verbal score is the combination of better technique and better vocabulary. Either one alone will help raise your score, but truly high scores and stellar improvements require both.

COMPUTER STRATEGIES

Now we're ready to tackle the computer. Taking a test on a computer is strange. If you haven't taken one before, you'll probably discover that it's stranger than you anticipated. This is one reason why it's so important to take the *POWERPREP* tests mentioned in the previous chapter. You will not be comfortable taking the real GRE unless you have some experience with the computer format.

In addition to experience, however, you need to have knowledge about how the computer test works and strategies that take advantage of it. Here we'll be looking at the details of the computer format. Let's start with a look at the computer screen itself and a quick explanation of what the various buttons do.

BASIC FORMAT

00:44	GRE - Section 3	8 of 28

Given the number of hours that he devoted to preparing for his final examination, Mark's reaction to receiving a top grade was surprisingly _____.

- ○ studied
- ○ nonchalant
- ○ industrious
- ○ measured
- ○ earnest

| Test / Quit | Section / Exit | Time | | Help | Answer / Confirm | Next |

As you see, the question will be in the middle of the screen, and the answers will be below it with bubbles beside them. To select one of the five answers, you click on the bubble next to that answer choice. The test time is displayed at the top of the screen, as well as the number of questions in the section and which question you're working on.

The bottom of the screen contains the following buttons, from right to left:

- **Next**: After you select your answer by clicking on the appropriate bubble, you need to click this button to move on to the next question.

- **Answer Confirm**: After you click on the Next button (see above) the Answer Confirm button lights up. You must click it to confirm your answer before the computer will give you the next question. The computer does this to make sure that you don't accidentally pick an answer you didn't intend.

- **Help**: This button will bring up a brief tutorial on what the different buttons do. Don't waste your time with this on the actual test. It won't help you solve problems, and you should already know how the buttons work anyway.

- **Time**: This button allows you to hide the onscreen timer. Generally, we don't recommend doing this, because you need to keep track of your pacing (more on that coming up), and without the timer you might go way too fast or way too slow. However, some people find that they just can't concentrate with the timer counting down in front of them, and they need to hide it in order to focus on the questions. In any case, when the section is almost over, the timer reappears (if it was hidden) and you can't hide it any longer.

- **Section Exit**: Clicking this button will allow you to exit the section you're working on and move on to the next one. There's no real reason ever to use it because you should be answering all the questions in the section (more on this later), and the section will end automatically when you've finished. Even if you finish one of the essays with time to spare, you would be best served by reviewing and proofreading your work instead of exiting early.

- **Test Quit**: This button will end your test. Don't use it unless you're so ill you have to leave the test center. Otherwise, even if you've decided that you're going to cancel your score at the end, continue taking the test if you can. You may change your mind at the end, and even if you don't, the extra practice and experience will be helpful.

ADAPTATION: MEET THE CAT

One of the most important things to know about the GRE is that it is a computer-adaptive test, or CAT. What does this mean? A CAT is a test in which the computer selects questions for you based on your response to prior questions. This is very different from a paper-and-pencil test such as the SAT. On a paper-and-pencil test everyone sees the same questions, and there is a roughly equal number of easy, medium, and hard questions. All this goes out the window on a CAT.

Here's basically how it works. At the beginning of the exam, the computer knows nothing about you, so it begins by giving you a mid-level question. If you get this question right, two things happen. First, the computer raises your score. Second, the computer gives you a harder question. Suppose that you also get this second, harder question right. Again, the computer raises your score and gives you a tougher problem. Next, let's say that you get the third question wrong. The computer now lowers your score and gives you an easier question. And so on.

The goal of the computer is to pinpoint your exact ability level by adjusting the difficulty of the questions until it finds an equilibrium for you. To calculate your final score, the computer considers the number of questions you answer correctly, the difficulty of those questions, and the total number of questions you complete. Thus the GRE is designed to be hard for everyone, because it tailors itself to you. In order to achieve a higher score, you will need to spend most of your time during the CAT answering difficult questions.

Don't Overanalyze

One of the common mistakes that people make, once they learn about the adaptive nature of the GRE, is to try to figure out whether the question they're working on is harder or easier than the one before. This is a very natural temptation, but you want to avoid it. First of all, difficulty is not an exact science. Just because *you* find a question harder or easier does not mean that ETS has made the same judgment.

Second, there are factors that influence the question selection other than whether you got the previous question right or wrong. The GRE has certain statistical requirements and also certain content requirements. For example, the Verbal section must contain the appropriate balance of antonyms, analogies, sentence completions, and reading comprehension.

Finally, even if you were able to discern whether you got the previous question right or wrong, the information is largely useless to you. Your approach to a GRE question will not be affected by what happened on the previous question. You need to keep focused on what you're doing and not worry about past questions.

No Skipping

One of the consequences of the CAT is that you can't skip any questions. That was one of the nice things about paper-and-pencil tests: If you didn't like the question in front of you, you could just skip it and work on something else. But you can't do that on the CAT because the computer doesn't know what to give you until you answer the question in front of you. The whole idea of an adaptive test is that it takes into account how you answered the previous question. You can ponder a question for as long as you like, but the computer will not give you the next question until you choose an answer for the current one.

A corollary to this point is that you can't go back to any question after you answer it. Once you hit the Answer Confirm button and move on to the next question, it's gone. You can't go back and change your answer later. Some people become a little paralyzed by this. They're done with the problem, but they're afraid to move on because they know they can't change their minds later. If you notice this tendency in yourself, learn to get past it. Work each question carefully, yes. But when you're done working the question, move on. Don't second-guess yourself.

Guessing

Since you can't skip any questions, sooner or later you will be forced to guess. The test is adaptive, so the more successful you are on it, the harder it gets. No matter what your score level, eventually you'll hit the limit of your vocabulary and see some words you don't know. This is not merely a possibility, it's a virtual certainty. (Sure, there are a few people each year who get every question right and score an 800, but if you're one of these rare logophiles you probably don't need this book.)

Since guessing is inevitable, it's important that you accept that fact, and learn to guess effectively. Just because we're forced to guess doesn't mean we have to guess blindly. One of the most important benefits of the Process of Elimination is that it sets us up to guess intelligently when we can't narrow down the answers to one choice. It's also important to keep an eye out for trap answers. Difficult questions are precisely the place where ETS is most likely to include some answer choices that lure you in with words that remind you of the question. Applying rigorous POE and making smart choices will raise your guessing odds and, thus, your score.

One last point about guessing is that you need to recognize when it's time to guess and move on. To some people, guessing feels like a failure and they will spend inordinate amounts of time staring at a question, turning it over in their minds, hoping desperately that some flash of insight is just around the corner. And the longer they look at it, the harder it is to let go. But guessing is not a defeat; it's an inescapable part of the GRE. Of course guessing on few questions is better than guessing on many questions, but when it's time to guess, don't hesitate. You can use that time more wisely on other questions.

PACING

And speaking of using time wisely, one of the most important things you need to do on the GRE is pace yourself properly. The most common pacing error people make is to move too quickly, rushing to reach the end of the test. It's understandable why this happens. Thirty minutes isn't a lot of time to answer 30 questions. You need to average one minute per question to work them all. The truth, however, is that most people need to slow down and focus more on the beginning of the test, rather than worry about the end. You need to work carefully and accurately on the early questions in order to achieve a high score on the GRE.

To understand why this is so important, we need to go back to the way the CAT determines your score. Remember, the computer starts you off with a question of medium difficulty. If you get it right, the computer raises its estimate of your ability and gives you a harder question. If you get it wrong, the computer lowers its estimate of your ability and gives you an easier question. The computer keeps doing this until it zeroes in on your score at the end of the section. Now let's consider the difference between the beginning of the section and the end. At the beginning of the section, the computer knows nothing about you. At the end of the section, the computer knows a great deal about you—it has your responses to all the previous questions you've answered. So in which part of the section are your responses going to affect your score most? If you said, "The beginning," you are starting to think like a GRE test taker.

At the beginning, the CAT is trying to figure out what your general score level is, so your score changes in larger intervals from question to question than at the end when the computer is merely fine-tuning your score, trying to decide whether to give you, say, a 620 or a 630. So you want to be as accurate as possible on the first 10 to 15 questions, even if this leaves you less time to work on the questions at the end. It's all right if you have to work quickly on the final third of the section and take some guesses at the very end. The extra time you spend increasing your accuracy in the early portion of the section will more than make up for some errors in the later portion. Think of the CAT as a judgmental person on whom you want to make a good early impression.

The last important thing to know about pacing is that you must leave yourself enough time to answer every question on the test. You should not leave any questions blank. The reason is that ETS assigns a harsh penalty for failure to complete the test. This penalty for questions left blank is greater than the penalty for wrong answers. If you find yourself running out of time at the end of the test, it's better for you to guess on the remaining questions (even if you're unlucky and get them all wrong) than it is to let time run out with questions left unanswered. Obviously, it's best if you don't have to guess blindly on any questions, but if you need to, pick a letter of the day and click through the rest of questions. It's all part of being a savvy test taker.

A Final Note on the Computer

One final feature of the computer-based GRE is that you'll get your Math and Verbal scores immediately at the end of the test (the essays still need to be read, so you'll receive your Analytical Writing score in about two weeks along with your official score report). Once you've completed the multiple-choice sections, the computer will give you the option to accept or cancel your scores. Of course you have to make that decision before learning what they are. If you choose to cancel, you will never find out how you did. If you accept, you can't cancel them later. Unless you were ill or there was a major distraction during the test (e.g., the person seated next to you had a seizure and was hauled away by paramedics), you should accept your scores. There's no reliable way to know how you did except by seeing the scores. Remember, the test is supposed to be hard for everyone.

Sentence Completions

THE GOAL: FILL IN THE BLANK

Your job on any given sentence completion question is to pick the answer choice that best completes the sentence by filling in the blank or blanks. Not too hard, right? Well, not too hard if you know what *not* to do.

What not to do is "plug and chug," which (unfortunately) is probably the most common thing people do when they hit a sentence completion. Here's a typical question:

> In celestial mechanics, scientists are required to make _____ calculations because the astronomical bodies are moving _____ and many different forces are acting at once.
>
> ○ precise . . obdurately
> ○ detailed . . auspiciously
> ○ comprehensible . . excessively
> ○ complicated . . concurrently
> ○ facile . . nominally

And here's what plugging and chugging entails.

(A) In celestial mechanics, scientists are required to make *precise* calculations because the astronomical bodies are moving *obdurately* and many different forces are acting at once.

(B) In celestial mechanics, scientists are required to make *detailed* calculations because the astronomical bodies are moving *auspiciously* and many different forces are acting at once.

(C) In celestial mechanics, scientists are required to make *comprehensible* calculations because the astronomical bodies are moving *excessively* and many different forces are acting at once.

(D) In celestial mechanics, scientists are required to make *complicated* calculations because the astronomical bodies are moving *concurrently* and many different forces are acting at once.

(E) In celestial mechanics, scientists are required to make *facile* calculations because the astronomical bodies are moving *nominally* and many different forces are acting at once.

In other words, when you plug and chug, you just take an answer choice and pop it back into the blank or blanks. How effective is this? Not very. People tend to plug and chug because they think it's the fastest way to answer a sentence completion, but guess what? It's not. In fact, it's the slowest way, because when you plug and chug, too many answer choices *sound* good. That is, more than one answer choice may seem as if it could work.

It's Your Word

Instead of plugging and chugging, the first thing you should do (and this goes for every single sentence completion) is ignore the answer choices. Ignore the answer choices so your mind is a complete blank as you start to read the sentence. The key to beating a sentence completion is not to get distracted by the answer choices. Rather, it's to focus on the sentence itself.

Let's take a look at an example. Remember, the first thing to do is to ignore the answer choices.

> The actress, though portrayed by the
> media as an arrogant prima donna, was, in
> fact, both charming and _____.
>
> ○ improvident
> ○ gracious
> ○ enthusiastic
> ○ exceptional
> ○ lithesome

In reading the sentence, did you fill in your own word when you got to the blank? If so, you took control of the sentence. You should always do this: Ignore the answer choices, read the sentence, and come up with your own word(s).

What word might fit into the blank? *Nice, modest, delightful.* Anything in that vein. Now that you have your own word, go to the answer choices and pick the one that most closely matches your word. The best match doesn't have to be your word exactly—it doesn't even have to be a synonym of your word. It just needs to get across the same idea or feeling.

Before you do that, however, let's go over a very important point. On many questions, you may come across answer choices that contain words you don't know. What should you do? Well, you have to leave those answer choices in. You can't cross them out because they might be right. *Never* eliminate an answer choice if you don't know what a word means.

To go back to the above example: You want to find a word that matches *nice.* Don't cross out (A) if you don't know what *improvident* means. What about (B)? Does it work? Yes—*gracious* is a good match for *nice.* How about (C) and (D)? *Enthusiastic* and *exceptional* don't really match your word. And (E)? If you don't know what *lithesome* means, then you can't cross it out. So you're left with (A), (B), and (E). When you're down to a few answer choices and one works while the others contain words you just don't know, go with the answer choice that works. (B) is the best answer.

Note that in working through this example, we went through each and every answer choice. On any sentence completion—on any verbal question—you *have* to do this. You must. Why? Because Verbal is about finding the *best* answer, not the right answer. That means you may come across an answer choice that seems to work, but another answer choice further down the road works even better. The lesson: Always, always look at every single answer choice. Let's try another sentence completion.

> Although perfumes were first created
> from the natural oils of plants, chemists
> have, since the early nineteenth century,
> produced thousands that contain _____
> ingredients.
>
> ○ uncultivated
> ○ piquant
> ○ synthetic
> ○ aromatic
> ○ variable

Did you remember to ignore the answer choices? What word did you fill in for the blank? Probably something along the lines of *man-made*. (A) doesn't match your word, so eliminate it. (B) is a slightly hard word. If you don't know what *piquant* means, then you have to leave it in. (C) looks good—*synthetic* is a good match for *man-made*—still, don't forget to check out (D) and (E). *Aromatic* and *variable* aren't close to *man-made* at all. So you're left with (B) and (C). Which do you think is right? You know (C) is a good match and (B) contains a word you don't know. Pick the answer choice that works. The best answer is (C), *synthetic*.

QUICK QUIZ #1

In the following questions, come up with your own word for the blank. The answers are on page 39.

1. The kidnapping of the son of Charles A. Lindbergh in 1932 so _____ the public that laws were soon adopted with severe penalties for the _____.

2. Though, in his lifetime, Mark Twain received much _____, today's critics esteem him to such a degree that they _____ him.

3. By mapping all of the genes on the human chromosomes, the Human Genome Project, established in 1990, hopes to gain _____ into human evolution and study the genetic similarities _____ by all species.

4. Even with the _____ of the battering ram and catapult, which reduced the effectiveness of large-scale fortifications, castles during the Middle Ages still remained _____.

5. Mosses, though limited to _____ habitats because they require water for fertilization and lack a vascular system for absorbing water, are considered _____ plants due to their resilience.

6. Wilson's reputation for being irresolute was _____ by her ability to make snap decisions whenever a crisis arose.

7. The judge did not wish to _____ the tensions between the feuding parties by seeming to favor one side over the other.

A CLUE, A CLUE, A CLUE

Let's take a look at a sentence completion that you'll never see on the real GRE.

> ETS is _____ company.
>
> ◯ a nonprofit
> ◯ a wealthy
> ◯ a devious
> ◯ a cautious
> ◯ an enormous

How should you always approach a sentence completion? By ignoring the answer choices and coming up with your own word for the blank. But if you do that for this particular question, guess what? Anything could go in the blank. (A) through (E) could all be right.

This particular question would never show up on the real GRE because there is no right answer—any of the five answer choices could work. But what if we changed the question a little so that it looked like the following:

> ETS, which earns over four million dollars
> each year, is _____ company.
>
> ◯ a nonprofit
> ◯ a wealthy
> ◯ a devious
> ◯ a cautious
> ◯ an enormous

What's the answer now? (B), right? How do you know (B) is correct? You know the answer is (B) because of the clause "which earns over four million dollars each year." That clause gave you a clue as to what belonged in the blank. Let's change the question again.

> ETS, which likes to trick test takers on
> hard questions, is _____ company.
>
> ◯ a nonprofit
> ◯ a wealthy
> ◯ a devious
> ◯ a cautious
> ◯ an enormous

The answer now is (C). What tells you the answer is (C)? The clue "which likes to trick test takers on hard questions."

On every single sentence completion, there must be a clue that tells you what belongs in the blank. Without a clue, there would be no right answer. So, anytime you're coming up with your own word for the blank, look for the clue to help you out. In fact, often you can repeat the clue itself in the blank. For example, in the last question, you might have said, "ETS . . . is a *tricky* company." *Tricky* is the word you came up with based on the clue.

Keep in mind that clues can show up anywhere in the sentence: at the beginning, in the middle, or at the end. If you're having trouble finding the clue, look for the most descriptive part of the sentence. That's usually where the clue is. Try to identify the clue in the following example:

> Though some of her peers _____ the theoretical approach she had taken, no one could find fault with her conclusions: not only _____ but also profound.
>
> ○ disregarded . . original
> ○ applauded . . seminal
> ○ exhausted . . penetrating
> ○ criticized . . insightful
> ○ ridiculed . . mundane

Let's start with the first blank. What word comes to mind after reading the sentence? The clue is "no one could find fault with her conclusions." Everybody liked her conclusions, but did everybody feel that way about her theoretical approach? Nope. Let's repeat the clue in the blank. Some of her peers *found fault with* her theoretical approach. Does (A) work? Not really. They had problems with her approach; they didn't ignore it. (B) definitely doesn't work, and (C) just doesn't make sense. What about (D) and (E)? They both could be matches for *found fault with*, so leave them both in.

Let's look at the second blank now. Her conclusions were something and profound. The clue for this blank is "profound." Well, for your own word, let's just repeat the clue again. Her conclusions were *profound* and profound. Is it okay to do this? Sure. The word won't be *profound* exactly, but it'll be something pretty close to it. You already eliminated (A), (B), and (C), so let's move on to (D). Does *insightful* match *profound*? Yes—it could work. What about (E)? Does *mundane* match *profound*? No—*mundane* means boring. So the best answer is (D).

TRIGGERS

Besides the clue, there are other parts of the sentence that tell you what should go in the blank. These other parts of the sentence are what we call triggers.

Triggers are, for the most part, small words. They're important, though, because they usually give structure to the sentence: They either keep the sentence going in the same direction, or they change the direction of the sentence.

Let's take a look at two classic triggers: *and* and *but*. Fill in the blank for each of the sentences below.

- I don't want to go to the party, and _____.
- I don't want to go to the party, but _____.

For the first sentence, you might have come up with something like: "I don't want to go to the party, and you can't make me go." For the second sentence, you might have had something along the lines of "I don't want to go to the party, but I'll go anyway."

Notice the function of *and* in the first sentence. It continues the flow of the sentence. In contrast, *but* in the second sentence changes the flow—it takes the sentence in the opposite direction.

Let's take a look at a question you've already seen to get an idea of how triggers work.

> The actress, though portrayed by the
> media as an arrogant prima donna, was, in
> fact, both charming and _____.
>
> ○ improvident
> ○ gracious
> ○ enthusiastic
> ○ exceptional
> ○ lithesome

First, let's stop and look for the clue. The most descriptive part of the sentence is "portrayed by the media as an arrogant prima donna." Now, let's look for triggers. Do you see any?

There are not one, but two, triggers in this sentence. The first is the word "though" and the second is the word "and." The "though" tells you the sentence is going to change in direction. Therefore, what goes in the blank should be the opposite of "an arrogant prima donna." What about the second trigger? The "and" tells you the sentence is going to continue in the same direction. So what goes in the blank should be similar to "charming."

More Triggers

Not all sentences have triggers, but many do. The chart below shows some of the most common triggers.

Same-Direction Triggers	Changing-Direction Triggers
and	but, yet
since	though, although, even though
because	however
so	despite, in spite of
not only . . . but also	rather, instead
thus	whereas
therefore	while
consequently	notwithstanding
hence	ironically
:	however
;	

Triggers aren't always words. Note that the last two triggers in the same-direction column are punctuation marks. ETS loves to use the colon (:) and semicolon (;), so always be on the watch for them. Take a look at an example:

> Born of the blood of Uranus, the mythic
> Furies are _____ creatures: they punish
> those who have wronged blood relatives,
> regardless of the perpetrators' motiva-
> tions.
>
> ○ vehement
> ○ unforgiving
> ○ gloomy
> ○ quarrelsome
> ○ caustic

The clue is everything that comes after the colon; the trigger is the colon itself. Therefore, you know that whatever goes in the blank should continue the direction of "they punish those who have wronged blood relatives, regardless of the perpetrators' motivations."

Given the clue and the trigger, a good word for the blank is *vengeful*. You can eliminate (A) since *vehement* isn't a good match. (B) looks okay, but let's go through the rest of the answer choices just to make sure. (C) definitely isn't right, and neither is (D). (E) doesn't fit since *caustic* means sarcastic, so you're left with (B). It's the best answer.

QUICK QUIZ #2

In the following questions, underline the clue and circle any triggers. Then, use the clue and triggers to help you determine what word should go in the blank. Remember, the clue is typically the most descriptive part of the sentence. Also, don't forget you can often repeat a part of the clue as the word that goes in the blank. The answers are on page 39.

1. In the Bible, handwriting appeared on the wall at the feast of Belshazzar, a _____ of doom according to Daniel; that night, Babylon fell to Cypress.

2. Because the reclogging of an artery often occurs after balloon angioplasty, some physicians have turned to the use of such _____ techniques as laser angioplasty.

3. Even though the evidence produced did not _____ his guilt, the jury still believed in his _____.

4. Jane's naiveté was often charming, but her _____ all too easily led her to be deceived and therefore _____.

5. The jealousy of the goddess Hera has been _____ in Greek mythology: numerous stories tell of her _____ Zeus and his philandering.

6. Early ethologists classified animal behavior as either _____ or learned; current ethologists, however, believe there is an _____ genetically determined and environmental responses.

7. It remains a mystery as to how the _____ of the early universe evolved into its present-day diversity.

NO WORD OF YOUR OWN?

Together the clue and the triggers help you come up with your own word for the blank. There are times, however, when you won't be able to come up with your own word—even though you've found the clue and the triggers. What do you do then?

You can still use the clue and the triggers to help you. Even though you may not be able to come up with your own word, you can often tell if what goes in that blank is positive or negative. If you know the word is positive, then you can eliminate any answer choice that contains a negative word. If you know the word is negative, then you can eliminate any answer choice that contains a positive word.

This technique—Positive/Negative—is very powerful, but a word of caution: Don't use it as a crutch. It's going to be very tempting to use this technique instead of coming up with your own word, but you shouldn't. Your first goal is always to come up with your own word. Only if you can't do that should you move on to Positive/Negative. For those times when you do use Positive/Negative, remember that you still need to find the clue and triggers. Otherwise you won't know what should go in the blank. Let's try applying Positive/Negative to a question.

> Because he did not want to appear _____, the junior executive refused to dispute the board's decision, in spite of his belief that the decision would impair employee morale.
>
> ○ –
> ○ –
> ○ +
> ○ –
> ○ +

Let's say that you can't come up with your own word, which means you need to rely on Positive/Negative. What's the clue in the sentence? The most descriptive part is "refused to dispute." There's also the trigger "Because." Together, the clue and trigger tell you that a negative word belongs in the blank. So what can you eliminate? (C) and (E).

This is a good example why Positive/Negative can be a very powerful technique. You can't figure out exactly what should go in the blank, but you can still manage to eliminate two answer choices. If you were stuck after that, who cares? You now have a one-in-three chance of getting the question right.

Here's what the complete question looks like:

> Because he did not want to appear _____,
> the junior executive refused to dispute
> the board's decision, in spite of his belief
> that the decision would impair employee
> morale.
>
> ○ contentious
> ○ indecisive
> ○ solicitous
> ○ overzealous
> ○ steadfast

(C) and (E) are gone because they're positive words. You can't eliminate (A) if you don't know what *contentious* means. (B) doesn't work because the clue is "refused to dispute." That doesn't work with *indecisive*. For the same reason, (D) doesn't work either. So the best answer is (A). Even though you might not know *contentious,* you can still get to the right answer.

QUICK QUIZ #3

Find the clue and triggers in the following questions and determine whether the word in the blank should be positive or negative. The answers are on page 40.

1. Though Californians claim to be _____ to earthquakes, the smallest of tremors are _____ to most people.

2. Even when injured, Jane has always been a _____ opponent; indeed, a problematic back and foot did not _____ her from winning several championships during the 2002 season.

3. The nouveau riche often strive for the same social standing as the established wealthy, but they usually find themselves left with only the _____ of affluence.

4. Joseph's _____ was misleading: his appearance suggested innocence and artlessness, but he was, in fact, quite _____.

5. Though it is important to stand by one's beliefs, it is also important not to cling _____ to them.

6. It is not necessary for a scientific theory to be proved in order to be _____; rather, it need only be _____ —the best explanation offered for a phenomenon at the time.

7. A pioneer in modern population study, Thomas Malthus was the first to suggest that _____ and distress are _____ because population increases more quickly than the means of subsistence.

TWO BLANKS

So far the majority of sentence completions we've looked at have been one-blank questions. However, not all sentence completions have only one blank. Some have two.

For those of you who hate sentence completions, you should thank your lucky stars that at least some have two blanks. Two-blank sentence completions are often easier than one-blank sentence completions because two-blank sentence completions tend to have more clues. After all, each blank in a sentence completion has to have a clue. (It is possible, however, for two blanks to share a clue.)

The key to two-blank sentence completions is to focus on one blank at a time. Two-blank questions are only hard when you try to do too much at once—i.e., try to work on both blanks at the same time. To make two-blank questions easy, focus on one blank and then focus on the other.

Which blank should you do first? It doesn't matter. Whichever one is easier. We will say, however, that you shouldn't always tackle the first blank first. The second blank can be easier at times because by the time you get to the second blank, you've got more information about the sentence. Let's try one:

> Though the statement released by the press secretary was deliberately _____ in neutral language, many people were _____ by its implications.
>
> ○ framed . . bemused
> ○ discounted . . enervated
> ○ couched . . perturbed
> ○ phrased . . nonplussed
> ○ confounded . . incensed

Let's start with the second blank. The clue for the second blank is "neutral language" and the trigger is "Though." The statement had neutral language, but how did people respond? Not in a positive way, so a good word for the blank might be *angry*. (A) doesn't make sense if you know that *bemused* means confused. (B) doesn't make sense either if you know that *enervated* means weakened. (C) might work since *perturbed* could match *angry*, but (D) doesn't work because *nonplussed* means perplexed. *Incensed* means very angry, so (E) might work, too. You're left, then, with (C) and (E).

Now you can move on to the first blank. Remember, there's no need to look at (A), (B), and (D) because once one part of an answer choice is wrong, the entire answer choice is wrong. A good word for the first blank is *expressed*. (C) can still work, but (E) can't because *confounded* means baffled. The best answer, then, is (C).

It's really important that, for every two-blank sentence completion, you focus on one blank at a time. Don't get confused by trying to do too much at once. Once you figure out what should go in one blank, use POE *right away*. If you know one word in an answer choice is wrong, you know the entire answer choice is wrong. Don't even look at that answer choice when you come around to look at what should go in the second blank.

RELATIONSHIP BETWEEN THE BLANKS

There are a few two-blank questions where you won't know *exactly* what should go in the blanks. Why not? Because what you put in one blank has an effect on what you put in the other blank. On questions like these, determine the relationship between the blanks. For example, both blanks could contain positive words, or both blanks could hold negative words. It could go either way.

So what should you do? Go to each answer choice and look at the relationship between the two words. If you know the blanks could be both positive or both negative, then the right answer choice can never have one positive word along with one negative word. Similarly, if you know the relationship is such that one blank is positive and the other negative (or vice versa), the right answer choice can never have two positive words or two negative words. Let's take a look at the following example. What is the relationship between the two blanks?

> In spite of the numerous articles and
> books devoted to the works of William
> Shakespeare, there is no criticism so
> _____ that his plays and sonnets no longer
> _____ the academia of English literature.

Both blanks should have the same type of word—most likely, the words are both positive. So eliminate any answer choice that contains a positive word coupled with a negative word. Here are the answer choices:

- ◯ severe . . interest
- ◯ exhaustive . . engage
- ◯ demanding . . engross
- ◯ comprehensive . . effect
- ◯ astute . . tax

You can eliminate (A), (C), and (E) because each contains one positive word and one negative word. At this point, if you're stuck, just guess. You have a 50 percent chance of getting the question right. The best answer turns out to be (B). Notice that the clue for the second blank is actually the word for the first blank. Anytime you come across a question where the clue for one blank is the other blank, focus on what the relationship between the two blanks is.

LAST RESORT

As a last resort—and we mean it when we say this is the *last* resort—pick the answer choice that contains the most difficult words. Why? Because chances are, if you're having a really hard time with a sentence completion, it's probably a hard question and hard questions tend to have hard answers. For example, let's say that you come across a question and that you're able to get it down to two answer choices.

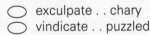

- ◯ exculpate . . chary
- ◯ vindicate . . puzzled

If, after checking the clue and triggers one more time, you have no idea which one is better, then pick the one with the hardest (or the weirdest) words. (A), in this case, should be your choice.

This isn't to say that the answer choice with the hardest word or words is always right. It's just a good guessing technique when you're absolutely stuck.

IN SUMMARY...

A sentence completion is hard only when you get distracted by the answer choices and forget about the sentence itself. Focus on the sentence—that's where the clue and triggers are.

1. Ignore the answer choices. Remember, it's the sentence that's important.

2. Come up with your own word for the blank. If you're having trouble coming up with your own word, look for the clue and triggers.

3. If you can't come up with your own word, use the clue and triggers to determine if what goes in the blank is positive or negative.

4. If it's a two-blank sentence completion, focus on one blank at a time.

5. If the clue for one blank is actually the other blank, determine what the relationship between the blanks is.

6. As a last resort, pick the answer choice that contains the hardest (or weirdest) words.

PRACTICE QUESTIONS #1

<u>Directions:</u> Each sentence below has one or two blanks, each blank indicating that something has been omitted. Beneath the sentence are five lettered words or sets of words. Choose the word or set of words for each blank that <u>best</u> fits the meaning of the sentence as a whole. The answers are on page 41.

1. In science, _____ is only conjecture until it is proven or disproved by _____ experimentation.

○ a hypothesis . . rigorous
○ a prediction . . controversial
○ an abstraction . . cursory
○ a theory . . public
○ a deliberation . . thorough

2. An experienced film critic is one who not only calls attention to the _____ of a particular feature, but also puts forth legitimate _____ that, if employed, would create a more satisfying product.

○ interpretations . . observations
○ construction . . synopses
○ allusions . . complaints
○ inadequacies . . recommendations
○ influences . . modifications

3. Louis was so painfully shy that his friends had to cajole him not to _____ even the smallest social gathering.

○ confront
○ subdue
○ flout
○ shun
○ attend

4. The salmon was prepared with such care that even those who did not have _____ seafood found the meal to be delicious.

○ a contention with
○ an assurance of
○ a penchant for
○ a preconception of
○ an endorsement of

5. The movement in literature known as realism was so labeled because of its attempt to describe life without idealization or romantic subjectivity; similarly, the realist movement in art had as its intent the _____ of natural forms without _____.

○ portrayal . . adulation
○ subjection . . sentimentality
○ depiction . . vulgarity
○ abstraction . . refinement
○ rendering . . embellishment

6. The field of science known as nonlinear dynamics may appear, at first, to be paradoxical: it attempts to reveal _____ in systems that are seemingly random and therefore _____.

○ imperfection . . chaotic
○ structure . . unpredictable
○ unity . . unfathomable
○ definition . . frenetic
○ organization . . inimitable

7. It would be both unwise and unfair to criticize bell hooks's writings on the intersection of race and gender as either obscure or _____; though she often does discuss abstract ideas, in no way does she express them in _____ fashion.

○ contemplative . . a practical
○ incomprehensible . . a seminal
○ harried . . an ingenuous
○ opprobrious . . a theoretical
○ inaccessible . . an abstruse

PRACTICE QUESTIONS #2

Directions: Each sentence below has one or two blanks, each blank indicating that something has been omitted. Beneath the sentence are five lettered words or sets of words. Choose the word or set of words for each blank that best fits the meaning of the sentence as a whole. The answers are on page 43.

1. In conducting field research, one must observe every detail, no matter how small, for it is often the seemingly unimportant that actually leads to scientific _____.

   ○ recessions
   ○ obstructions
   ○ incapacities
   ○ breakthroughs
   ○ dissolutions

2. Isaac Asimov's Foundation trilogy explores the idea of psychohistory, a science that disregards the _____ and focuses instead on the tendencies of masses to act in particular ways.

   ○ nonconformist
   ○ individual
   ○ revolutionary
   ○ trifling
   ○ legislator

3. Whereas the flexing of a muscle is viewed as a motion that requires _____ effort, breathing is considered an involuntary act.

   ○ careful
   ○ conscious
   ○ minimal
   ○ thoughtful
   ○ intensive

4. Thompson _____ the integrity of his paper by failing to cite the authors whose ideas he employed to reach his conclusions, thus making charges of _____ possible.

   ○ enhanced . . imposture
   ○ debased . . recidivism
   ○ moderated . . audacity
   ○ compromised . . plagiarism
   ○ expunged . . deception

5. Although the formation of a union was not _____ by the management of the company, it was _____ that any effort on the part of employees to unionize would not be welcomed.

   ○ prevented . . imperceptible
   ○ facilitated . . infamous
   ○ barred . . implicit
   ○ sundered . . manifest
   ○ commandeered . . calculated

6. The issue of capital punishment draws a highly charged response, each side refusing to see the merits of the other's position, unwilling to _____ or engage in _____ of any kind.

   ○ evaluate . . imputations
   ○ demur . . conversation
   ○ compromise . . reprisals
   ○ advance . . formulations
   ○ yield . . discourse

7. Christopher Columbus Langdell was _____ in legal studies: as dean of Harvard's law school, he _____ the approach to law, introducing the case method to the curriculum and instituting the Socratic method in the classroom.

   ○ an innovator . . extirpated
   ○ a patriarch . . simplified
   ○ a pundit . . facilitated
   ○ a pedagogue . . invigorated
   ○ a pioneer . . reconstructed

PRACTICE QUESTIONS #3

Directions: Each sentence below has one or two blanks, each blank indicating that something has been omitted. Beneath the sentence are five lettered words or sets of words. Choose the word or set of words for each blank that best fits the meaning of the sentence as a whole. The answers are on page 46.

1. It is _____ to argue that, because a superconductor permits a current to flow more easily, _____ electrical resistance, scientists should devote more time and effort to its study.

   ○ faulty . . connected to
   ○ reasonable . . unchecked by
   ○ singular . . common to
   ○ hasty . . hampered by
   ○ interesting . . resigned to

2. Unless David decides to _____ himself from the rest of humanity and live as a hermit, he must learn how to compromise and _____.

   ○ distance . . suppress
   ○ delude . . initiate
   ○ seclude . . cooperate
   ○ conceal . . command
   ○ protect . . collaborate

3. May's tendency to worry excessively over even the _____ of problems so confused her colleagues that they never knew whether her so-called plights were of a calamitous or _____ nature.

   ○ slightest . . a trifling
   ○ most trivial . . a hapless
   ○ most relevant . . a deplorable
   ○ most unfeasible . . a grievous
   ○ profanest . . an inconsequential

4. Although Jonathan himself admitted that he had yet to master the piano, his _____ could not be doubted with the _____ with which he performed the concerto.

   ○ rectitude . . ardor
   ○ competence . . ineptitude
   ○ ungainliness . . expression
   ○ proficiency . . facility
   ○ virtuosity . . simplicity

5. Although she conveyed the message calmly and without to-do, Lin's expression betrayed the message's _____ nature.

   ○ facetious
   ○ impartial
   ○ puerile
   ○ uncommunicative
   ○ dire

6. Shi-yu's art is to be admired not for its realism, but rather for its distortion of reality: he creates _____ of the world, exaggerating not only its beauty but also its meanness and pettiness.

   ○ a mockery
   ○ a personification
   ○ a caricature
   ○ a sublimation
   ○ an allegory

7. Though law is often perceived to be _____, it is not, in fact, expressive of objective truths: law is a contract created by society to regulate the interactions among its members, and as such, law is _____.

   ○ even-handed . . a statute
   ○ expedient . . an invention
   ○ universal . . a construct
   ○ politic . . an execution
   ○ logical . . ratiocination

PRACTICE QUESTIONS #4

Directions: Each sentence below has one or two blanks, each blank indicating that something has been omitted. Beneath the sentence are five lettered words or sets of words. Choose the word or set of words for each blank that best fits the meaning of the sentence as a whole. The answers are on page 48.

1. It is common practice for a scientific journal to have several experts _____ an article's findings before publication in order to discourage scientists from reporting _____ assertions.

   ○ revise . . conceptual
   ○ critique . . unsubstantiated
   ○ expand . . . false
   ○ verify . . extreme
   ○ employ . . unwarranted

2. Some scientists believe that certain human beings may be more _____ than others because the former possess a gene that predisposes them toward aggressive behavior.

   ○ reserved
   ○ timorous
   ○ self-possessed
   ○ uncouth
   ○ quarrelsome

3. During her lectures, Professor Hsing speaks as eloquently and effectively as she writes, thus earning from her students the moniker "queen of _____."

   ○ debate
   ○ logic
   ○ metaphor
   ○ bombast
   ○ rhetoric

4. Political parties must find a way to deal with the _____ a structure that permits no _____ and one that is inclusive, allowing for different mind-sets and appreciative of diversity.

   ○ appeal of . . submission
   ○ hostility to . . might
   ○ deliberation between . . neutrality
   ○ inconsistency between . . dissent
   ○ discreteness of . . tradition

5. Professor Xavier was so well known for his radical experimentation with form and language, that his devotees responded to his most recent short story, characterized by a linear plot and traditional characters, with _____.

   ○ stupefaction
   ○ abashment
   ○ diffidence
   ○ aplomb
   ○ criticism

6. The class was purportedly an exhaustive study of Jane Austen's works, yet since it failed to include either *Emma* or *Pride and Prejudice* in its analysis, it was, by no means, _____.

   ○ prudent
   ○ acceptable
   ○ comprehensive
   ○ adequate
   ○ authoritative

7. After _____ for months without resolution, the parties agreed to defer to _____, a third party to evaluate each side and then settle the dispute.

   ○ engaging . . a magistrate
   ○ recessing . . an adjudicator
   ○ wrangling . . an arbiter
   ○ feuding . . a diplomat
   ○ haggling . . a reprobate

PRACTICE QUESTIONS #5

__Directions:__ Each sentence below has one or two blanks, each blank indicating that something has been omitted. Beneath the sentence are five lettered words or sets of words. Choose the word or set of words for each blank that __best__ fits the meaning of the sentence as a whole. The answers are on page 50.

1. Some historians have portrayed the reformers of the Progressive era as people _____ seeking to improve the lives of the lower class; other historians, however, have interpreted the reformers' efforts at betterment as an attempt to control and

   _____.

   ○ intentionally . . convert
   ○ consciously . . amend
   ○ earnestly . . confirm
   ○ surreptitiously . . civilize
   ○ honestly . . constrain

2. Although honesty is a trait to be valued, it is not always appropriate because when one is too forthright, one can often be

   _____.

   ○ objective
   ○ equitable
   ○ deluded
   ○ tactless
   ○ corrupt

3. Newspapers often lose money when their customers, who purchase two or three papers, discover articles being _____, and, not wanting to purchase the same item twice, _____ the number of papers to which they subscribe.

   ○ reproduced . . reduce
   ○ repeated . . appraise
   ○ censored . . cut back on
   ○ abridged . . settle on
   ○ copied . . augment

4. Sexual harassment lawsuits often question whether the defendant _____ acted to discriminate against the plaintiff; however, this line of reasoning fails to _____ the fact that one can cause offense without having intended it.

   ○ rationally . . challenge
   ○ precisely . . discuss
   ○ conscientiously . . uphold
   ○ hesitantly . . disregard
   ○ purposefully . . address

5. The scientific interest with which impressionist artists studied nature proved to be limiting; however, their movement produced an aesthetic revolution, successfully _____ the academic standards of the time.

   ○ promulgating
   ○ eschewing
   ○ repudiating
   ○ objectifying
   ○ plundering

6. Unfortunately, Jeannie's shy demeanor was often misinterpreted by those who did not know her: indeed, strangers typically construed her _____ behavior as coyness.

   ○ unresponsive
   ○ supercilious
   ○ amenable
   ○ acquiescent
   ○ demure

7. The Reformation was, in large part,
responsible for the _____ of life, because it
rejected the hold of the church on society
and _____ instead the import of personal
responsibility and individual freedom.

- ◯ sublimation . . emphasized
- ◯ appreciation . . highlighted
- ◯ revitalization . . imbued
- ◯ abnegation . . imparted
- ◯ secularization . . cited

ANSWERS AND EXPLANATIONS

Quick Quiz #1

1. outraged . . offense

2. acclaim . . deify

3. insight . . shared

4. advent . . defensible

5. moist . . hardy

6. belied

7. exacerbate

Quick Quiz #2

1. In the Bible, handwriting appeared on the wall at the feast of Belshazzar, a _____ of doom according to Daniel; that night, Babylon fell to Cypress.

   portent

2. Because the reclogging of an artery often occurs after balloon angioplasty, some physicians have turned to the use of such _____ techniques as laser angioplasty.

   alternative

3. Even though the evidence produced did not _____ his guilt, the jury still believed in his _____.

   prove . . culpability

4. Jane's naiveté was often charming, but her _____ all too easily led her to be deceived and therefore _____.

   credulousness . . duped

5. The jealousy of the goddess Hera has been _____ in Greek mythology: numerous stories tell of her _____ Zeus and his philandering.

   well documented . . resentment toward

6. Early ethologists classified animal behavior as either _____ or learned; current ethologists, however, believe there is an _____ genetically determined and environmental responses.

   instinctual . . interaction between

7. It remains a mystery as to how the _____ of the early universe evolved into its present-day diversity.

   homogeneity

QUICK QUIZ #3

1. (Though) Californians claim to be
   _____ to earthquakes, the smallest of
   tremors are _____ to most people.

   + . . −

   inured . . disconcerting

2. Even when injured, Jane has always
   been a _____ opponent; indeed, a
   problematic back and foot did not
   _____ her from winning several
   championships during the 2002
   season.

   + . . −

   formidable . . keep

3. The nouveau riche often strive for
   the same social standing as the
   established wealthy, (but) they usually
   find themselves left with only the
   _____ of affluence.

   −

   trappings

4. Joseph's _____ was misleading; his
   appearance suggested innocence and
   artlessness, (but) he was, in fact, quite
   _____.

   neither + nor − . . −

   mien . . cunning

5. (Though) it is important to stand by
   one's beliefs, it is also important not
   to cling _____ to them.

   −

   dogmatically

6. It is not necessary for a scientific
   theory to be proved in order to be
   _____; (rather), it need only be _____
   —the best explanation offered for a
   phenomenon at the time.

   + . . +

   adopted . . plausible

7. A pioneer in modern population
   study, Thomas Malthus was the first
   to suggest that _____ (and) distress are
   _____ because population increases
   more quickly than the means of
   subsistence.

   − . . −

   privation . . ineluctable

PRACTICE QUESTIONS #1

1. **A** For a two-blank sentence completion, focus on one blank at a time. Start with the first blank since it has an easier clue. The clue for this blank is "only conjecture." If something is "only conjecture," then a good word for the blank is *guess*. *Hypothesis* in (A), *prediction* in (B), and *theory* in (D) could mean *guess*, so leave them in. However, *abstraction* in (C) doesn't match *guess*, nor does *deliberation* in (E). So cross them out.

    Now move on to the second blank. The clue for this blank is "until it is proven or disproved by." If a *guess* is to be "proven or disproved," then it has to be subject to a lot of experimentation. So a good word for the blank is *a lot of*. Since (C) and (E) have already been eliminated, don't look at them a second time. Focus on (A), (B), and (D). *Rigorous* in (A) could mean *a lot*. *Controversial* in (B) and *public* in (C) are not good matches for *a lot*. Therefore, the best answer is (A).

2. **D** For a two-blank sentence completion, focus on one blank at a time. Start with the second blank because it has an easier clue. The clues for this blank are "legitimate" and "if employed, would create a more satisfying product." If the critic puts forth something legitimate that would improve the product, then she is making a *suggestion*. *Observations* in (A) and *synopses* in (B) don't mean *suggestion*, so cross them out. *Complaints* in (C) doesn't work either, so eliminate it. *Recommendations* in (D) and *modifications* in (E) could both mean *suggestion*, so leave them in.

    Now move on to the first blank. The clue for this blank is "not only calls attention . . . but also puts forth legitimate." Therefore, what goes in the first blank should be along the lines of *problems*—the critic is pointing out flaws *and* suggesting ways to make the film better. (Note the same-direction trigger "not only . . . but also.") *Inadequacies* in (D) is a good match for *problems*; *influences* in (E) isn't. Therefore, the best answer is (D).

3. **D** The clue for this blank is very straightforward: "so painfully shy." If Louis is "painfully shy," is he going to want to attend social gatherings? Probably not. Therefore, what goes in the blank is a negative word—probably something like *avoid*. (A) and (B) are both negative, but they don't mean *avoid*, so eliminate them. Don't cross out (C) if you don't know what *flout* means. (D) looks good, but don't forget to check out (E) just in case. *Attend* in (E) clearly doesn't work, so it's gone. You're left with a word you don't know in (C) and a word that works in (D). Go with what works. The best answer is (D).

4.   **C**   A good word for the blank is *a liking of* because of the clue "the salmon was prepared with such care that even those . . found the meal to be delicious." Don't cross out (A) if you don't know what *contention* means. (B) doesn't really match *liking*, so cross it out. (C) does mean *liking*, so leave it in. (D) definitely doesn't match *liking*, so cross it out. (E) doesn't match *liking* quite as well as (C). You're left with (A) and (C). Go with what you know. The best answer is (C).

5.   **E**   For a two-blank sentence completion, focus on one blank at a time. Start with the second blank because the clue is easier to work with. The clue for this blank is "without idealization or romantic subjectivity." The triggers are the semicolon and "similarly." If you know that the realist movement in art was similar to the realist movement in literature, then a good word for the blank is *idealization*. *Adulation* in (A) isn't quite what you're looking for, so cross it out. *Sentimentality* in (B) could work, so leave it in. *Vulgarity* in (C) definitely doesn't work, so eliminate it. Both *refinement* in (D) and *embellishment* in (E) are okay, so leave them in.

Move on to the first blank. The clue for this blank is "the attempt to describe life." The triggers are, once again, the semicolon and "similarly." Again, because the movements are similar, a good word for the blank is *describing*. The only answer choices remaining are (B), (D), and (E). *Subjection* in (B) doesn't match *describing*, nor does *abstraction* in (D). Since (E) is the only answer choice left, it's got to be right. *Rendering* does match *describing*, so the best answer is (E).

6.   **B**   Start with the second blank because it's easier. The clue for the second blank is "seemingly random." The trigger "and" tells you that what goes in the second blank has to continue the direction of "seemingly random." Therefore, a good word for the blank is *random*. *Chaotic* in (A) could mean *random*, as could *unpredictable* in (B), so leave them in. *Unfathomable* in (C) isn't quite what you're looking for, so cross it out. *Frenetic* in (D) could mean *random*, so keep it. If you don't know what *inimitable* in (E) means, you can't eliminate it.

Move on to the first blank. The clue for this blank is "paradoxical." If you know that nonlinear dynamics is paradoxical, then what goes in the blank has to be the opposite of "random." A good word might be *order*. *Imperfection* in (A) doesn't mean *order*, so cross it out. *Structure* in (B) could work, so leave it in. *Definition* in (D) isn't quite right, so cross it out. *Organization* in (E) could work, so keep it. You're down to (B) and (E). As always, go with what works. The best answer is (B).

7. **E** For a two-blank sentence completion, focus on one blank at a time. Start with the first blank because it's got a very strong clue. The clue for this blank is "obscure." Just repeat the clue as a good word for the blank—her writings shouldn't be criticized as "either obscure or" *obscure. Contemplative* in (A) doesn't match *obscure*, so cross it out. *Incomprehensible* in (B) could work, so leave it in. *Harried* in (C) doesn't work, so eliminate it. Don't cross out (D) if you don't know what *opprobrious* means. *Inaccessible* in (E) is a pretty good match, so leave it in. You're down to (B), (D), and (E).

Move on to the second blank. The clue for this blank is the same as the clue for the first blank: "obscure." There is another clue as well: "she often does discuss abstract ideas." Therefore, what goes in the second blank is something like *obscure* and *abstract*. If you don't know what *seminal* means, you can't cross out (B). *Theoretical* in (D) matches *abstract*, but it's not really negative—which is what you want in the blank because of *obscure*. Cross it out. Don't cross out (E) if you don't know what *abstruse* means.

You're left with (B) and (E). What should you do now? You could go with the hardest word or words, but *seminal* and *abstruse* are both pretty tough. At this point, just guess. You've got a 50 percent chance of getting the question right. As it turns out, the best answer is (E). *Seminal* means creative or original; *abstruse* means difficult to comprehend.

PRACTICE QUESTIONS #2

1. **D** Coming up with your own word should be fairly easy for this sentence completion because the clue is very direct. The clue is "the seemingly unimportant." Well, if the detail only seems unimportant, what is it actually? Very important. Therefore, a good word for the blank might be *wonders*. Does (A) match? No. (B) and (C) definitely don't match. (D) looks good—it's a very positive word—but don't forget about (E). (E) doesn't make any sense, so the best answer is (D).

2. **B** For this sentence completion, it's pretty easy to come up with your own word. The clue is "focuses instead on the tendencies of masses." If psychohistory is focusing on the masses, then what is it probably ignoring? The individual. A good word for the blank, then, is *individual*. (A) doesn't give you the sense of *individual*, so eliminate it. (B) is a perfect match, so definitely leave it in. (C) could look attractive only if you're moving too fast. If you remember the clue, you should know (C) can't be right. (D) isn't a good match, nor is (E). Therefore, the best answer is (B). (Keep in mind that even though (B) was a perfect match for your own word, you should still examine each and every answer choice.)

3. **B** It may be hard to come up with your own word at first, but if you find the clue, it shouldn't be a problem. The clue is "an involuntary act." There's also the changing-direction trigger "whereas." Together, the clue and trigger tell you that what goes in the blank is the opposite of "involuntary." So a good word for the blank is *voluntary*. (A) doesn't give you *voluntary*, so cross it out. (B) could mean *voluntary*, so leave it in. (C) doesn't match, and (D) isn't quite as good as (B)—eliminate both. Finally, (E) is no good. The best answer, then, is (B). This is a great example of why you should never plug and chug. If you go the route of plugging and chugging, guess what? Every answer choice *sounds* as if it could work.

4. **D** For a two-blank sentence completion, focus on one blank at a time. Start with the second blank because it's got a more direct clue. The clue for this blank is "failing to cite the authors whose ideas he employed." If Thompson did this, then he was basically stealing, right? A good word for the blank, then, is *stealing*. Is *imposture* in (A) along the lines of *stealing*? Sort of. Leave (A) in for now. What about *recidivism* in (B)? You can't cross out (B) if you don't know what *recidivism* means. *Audacity* in (C) doesn't work, so eliminate it. *Plagiarism* in (D) looks good, so leave it in. *Deception* in (E) also looks good, so leave it in, too. You're down to (A), (B), (D), and (E).

Move on to the first blank. The clue for this blank is the same as the clue for the second blank: "failing to cite the authors whose ideas he employed." If Thompson did this, then what did he do to the integrity of his paper? He hurt it. A good word for the blank, then, is *hurt*. *Enhanced* in (A) doesn't work, so cross it out. *Debased* in (B) could work, so leave it in. *Compromised* in (D) looks okay, so leave it in. If you don't know what *expunged* in (E) means, you have to leave it in.

(B), (D), and (E) are the remaining choices. You have one answer choice that works and two that contain words you don't know. Go with what works. The best answer is (D).

5. **C** This sentence completion is a little tricky, but as long as you work methodically, you should be okay. Start off with the first blank. The clue for this blank is "any effort . . to unionize would not be welcomed." There is also the changing-direction trigger "although." What do you know about the management of the company, then? That even though it wouldn't welcome unionization, it wouldn't ban employees from forming one. A good word for the blank is *ban*. *Prevented* in (A) looks good, so leave it in. *Facilitated* in (B) only looks good if you didn't find the right clue. It doesn't match *ban*, so cross (B) out. *Barred* in

(C) could work, so leave it in. If you don't know what *sundered* means, you can't eliminate (D). *Commandeered* in (E) definitely doesn't work, so cross it out. You're down to (A), (C), and (D).

Move on to the second blank. The clue for this blank is the same as the clue for the first blank. Also, the clue for this blank is, in part, the first blank itself. Given the clue, a good word for the second blank might be *clear*. *Imperceptible* in (A) doesn't give you *clear*, so cross it out. *Implicit* in (C) is okay, so leave it in. *Manifest* in (D) is also okay, so leave it in.

Only (C) and (D) are left. Again, go with what you know when you're left with an answer choice that works and one that contains words you don't know. (C) works, so pick (C). It's the best answer.

6. **E** For a two-blank sentence completion, focus on one blank at a time. Start with the first blank because it's a little more manageable. The clue for this blank is "each side refusing to see the merits of the other's position." If each side is so stubborn that it can't acknowledge anything good about the other side, then you know that the word in the first blank has to be positive. *Evaluate* in (A) isn't positive or negative, so cross it out. Don't cross out (B) if you don't know what *demur* means. *Compromise* in (C) and *advance* in (D) are both positive, so leave them in. *Yield* in (E) can be positive, so it's okay. You're down to (B), (C), (D), and (E).

Move on to the second blank. The clue for this blank is also "each side refusing to see the merits of the other's position." Because of the clue, you can tell that the word in the second blank is also positive. *Conversation* in (B) is slightly positive, so leave it in. *Reprisals* in (C) is negative, so cross it out. *Formulations* in (D) isn't really positive or negative, so eliminate it. *Discourse* in (E) is slightly positive, so leave it in.

(B) and (E) are the remaining answer choices. (B) contains a word you don't know; (E) works. Go with what works. The best answer is (E).

7. **E** For this sentence completion, the clue for the second blank is the other blank. This tells you that there is a relationship between the blanks. Are the words in the blanks going to be similar or dissimilar? Similar, in this case. So the correct answer choice has to have words that are similar to each other.

You may not know what *extirpated* in (A) means exactly, but you probably know that it's a negative word. That means (A) contains dissimilar words. Cross it out. (B) has words that aren't really similar. Eliminate it. (C) has similar words, so you can leave it in. (D) has similar words, so leave it in, too. (E) also has similar words, so leave it in.

You're down to (C), (D), and (E). What now? Take a look at the second blank. There's an additional clue for it: "introducing the case method . . and instituting the Socratic method." A good word for the blank, then, is *changed*. Does *facilitated* in (C) mean *changed*? No. Does *invigorated* in (D)? No. Does *reconstructed* in (E)? Yes. Therefore, the best answer is (E).

PRACTICE QUESTIONS #3

1.   **B**   For a two-blank sentence completion, focus on one blank at a time. Start with the second blank first because it's a little easier. The clue for this blank is "permits a current to flow more easily." If a superconductor makes it easier for the current to flow, what does it do to the resistance? It probably lessens the resistance. So a good word for the blank is *lessening*. Does *connected to* in (A) mean *lessening*? No. Eliminate (A). What about *unchecked by* in (B)? It could work. *Common to* in (C)? No. *Hampered by* in (D)? No. *Resigned to* in (E)? Definitely not. Therefore, the best answer is (B).

2.   **C**   For a two-blank sentence completion, focus on one blank at a time. Start with the first blank because it's easier. The clue for this blank is "live as a hermit." If David is going to "live as a hermit," then he's going to isolate himself from humanity. A good word for the blank, then, is *isolate*. Does *distance* in (A) match *isolate*? Sure. What about *delude* in (B)? No. *Seclude* in (C) works, as does *conceal* in (D). *Protect* in (E) doesn't quite work, so cross it out.

The remaining answer choices are (A), (C), and (D). Move on to the next blank. The clue for this blank is "compromise." There is also the same-direction trigger "and." "And" tells you that what goes in the blank is similar to "compromise." For the purpose of convenience, just repeat the clue as the word for the blank: David has to compromise and *compromise*. Does *suppress* in (A) match *compromise*? No. *Cooperate* in (C) looks okay. *Command* in (D) doesn't work, so the best answer is (C).

3.   **A**   It's a two-blank sentence completion, so focus on one blank at a time. Start with the second blank since it's more direct. The clue for this blank is "so confused her colleagues that they never knew whether her so-called plights were . . . calamitous." From the clue, you know that May's colleagues are confused. If they're confused, they don't know if one of her problems is "calamitous" or unimportant. A good word for the blank, then, is *unimportant*. Does *trifling* in (A) mean *unimportant*? Yes. What about *hapless* in (B)? No. *Deplorable* in (C) doesn't work, nor does *grievous* in (D). *Inconsequential* in (E) is a good match.

You're left with (A) and (E). Move on to the first blank. The clue for this blank is "worry excessively over even" and "so-called plights." If something isn't a plight, then it's something unimportant. So a good word for the blank is *least important*. Does *slightest* in (A) work? Yes. What about *profanest* in (E)? No. The best answer, then, is (A).

4.   **D**   For this two-blank sentence completion, focus on the first blank first—it's a little easier to work with. The clue for the first blank is "he had yet to master." There is also the changing-direction trigger "although." From the clue and trigger you know that Jonathan isn't a master but . . . But what? But he's still pretty good. Therefore, what goes in the first blank has to be a positive word—something like *talent*. *Rectitude* in (A) doesn't match *talent*, so eliminate it. *Competence* in (B) is okay. *Ungainliness* in (C) definitely doesn't work, but *proficiency* in (D) could. *Virtuosity* is a positive word, but it's too positive—it implies that David is a master. So get rid of (E).

You're left with (B) and (D). Go on to the second blank. The clue for this blank is really the first blank. You know Jonathan has *talent*, so he played the concerto well. A good word for the blank, then, is *talent*. *Ineptitude* in (B) doesn't match *talent*, but (D) could. The best answer, then, is (D).

5.   **E**   The clue for the blank is "conveyed the message calmly and without to-do." There is also the changing-direction trigger "although." Together the clue and trigger tell you that what goes in the blank is the opposite of calmness. A good word for the blank might be *serious*. (A) doesn't match, nor does (B). You can't cross out (C) if you don't know what *puerile* means. (D) doesn't work, but (E) does.

You're down to (C) and (E). When one answer choice has a word you don't know and the other works, go with what works. Pick (E). The best answer is, indeed, (E).

6.   **C**   The clue for this blank is really everything before the colon—which, don't forget, is a same-direction trigger. That means what goes in the blank should agree with "not for its realism, but rather for its distortion of reality." A good word for the blank, then, is *distortion*. Does (A) match *distortion*? No. What about (B)? No. (C) works, but (D) and (E) don't. The best answer is (C).

This question is a great example of why *not* to rush. If you don't stop to find the clue, then (A) becomes an attractive answer choice.

7. **C** For this two-blank sentence completion, focus on the first blank first—it's easier to deal with. The clue for this blank is "expressive of objective truths." If law has a claim to "objective truths," then a good word for the blank is *objective*. *Even-handed* in (A) could mean *objective*. *Expedient* in (B) doesn't work. *Universal* in (C) is okay, but *politic* in (D) isn't. Finally, *logical* in (E) isn't a good match.

You're left with (A) and (C). Look at the second blank. The clue for this blank is "created by society." There is also a trigger, the colon, which keeps the sentence moving in the same direction. If law is a creation, then a good word for the blank is *creation*. Does *statute* in (A) mean *creation*? No. Does *construct* in (C)? Yes. The best answer is (C).

PRACTICE QUESTIONS #4

1. **B** For two-blank sentence completions, focus on one blank at a time. Start with the second blank because it's a little easier. The clue for this blank is "to discourage scientists." Therefore, what goes in the second blank is something like *false*. *Conceptual* in (A) doesn't mean *false*, so eliminate it. *Unsubstantiated* in (B) is okay, so keep it. *False* in (C) is a perfect match, but you should still look at (D) and (E). *Extreme* in (D) isn't quite right, but *unwarranted* in (E) works.

You're left with (B), (C), and (E). Move on to the first blank. The clue for this blank is "several experts." The experts are somehow discouraging scientists from making false assertions, so the experts must be reviewing the articles. A good word for the blank, then, is *review*. *Critique* in (B) works, so leave it in. *Expand* in (C) doesn't, nor does *employ* in (E). The best answer is (B).

2. **E** The clue for the blank is "predisposes them toward aggressive behavior." Since some people have a gene that makes them aggressive, a good word for the blank is *aggressive*. (A) doesn't match *aggressive*, so cross it out. If you don't know what *timorous* means, you have to leave (B) in. (C) isn't a good match, nor is (D). (E), however, works.

You're down to (B) and (E). When you're left with one answer choice that contains a word you don't know and one that works, go with what works. (E) is the best answer.

3. **E** The clue for the blank is "speaks as eloquently and effectively as she writes." Just repeat the clue for the word in the blank. Professor Hsing is a queen of *eloquence*. Does (A) match *eloquence*? No. (B) and (C) don't work either. If you don't know what *bombast* means, then you can't eliminate (D). Finally, (E) works.

You're down to an answer choice that contains a word you don't know and one that works. Go with what works. The best answer is (E).

4. **D** For a two-blank sentence completion, focus on one blank at a time. Start with the first blank because it's easier. The clue for the first blank is "find a way to deal with." If political parties have to "find a way to deal with," then you can expect the word in the blank to be negative. *Appeal of* in (A) is positive, so eliminate it. *Hostility to* in (B) is negative, so it's okay. *Deliberation between* in (C) is either slightly positive or neither positive nor negative—either way, it needs to go. *Inconsistency between* in (D) is negative, as is *discreteness of* in (E), so leave them in.

   You're left with (B), (D), and (E). Go on to the second blank. What goes in this blank largely depends on what belongs in the first blank. In (B), the word for the first blank is *hostility*. This suggests that what goes in the second blank should be something like *arguing*—one structure doesn't allow for *arguing* and the other structure, because it is "inclusive," does. *Might* in (B) doesn't mean *arguing*, so get rid of it. In (D), the word for the first blank is *inconsistency between*. This also suggests that what goes in the second blank should be something like *arguing*. *Dissent* in (D) could mean *arguing*, so leave it in. In (E), the word for the first blank is *discreteness of*. As with (B) and (D), this suggests *arguing* should go in the second blank. Does *tradition* in (E) mean *arguing*? No. Therefore, the best answer is (D).

5. **A** The clue for this blank is "so well known for his radical experimentation." If Professor Xavier is typically radical, how would his fans react to something conventional? With surprise, naturally. A good word for the blank is *surprise*. Does (A) match? If you don't know what *stupefaction* means, you can't cross it out. Does (B) match? No—*abashment* means embarrassment. Does (C) match? No—*diffidence* means shyness. What about (D)? If you don't know what *aplomb* means, you can't eliminate it. What about (E)? No—be careful. Don't jump to any conclusions. The clue doesn't suggest anything about his fans being unhappy.

   So you're down to (A) and (D), each of which contains a word you don't know. At this point, just guess. You have a 50 percent chance of getting the question right. As a last resort technique, pick the one with the hardest word. That would probably be (A), and (A) is indeed the best answer. *Stupefaction* is just another form of the word *stupefied*.

6. **C** This sentence completion is actually very easy as long as you take the time to find the clue. The clue for the blank is "purportedly an exhaustive study." The class was supposedly "exhaustive" but if it didn't talk about two of her major books, then what was it? Not exhaustive. Therefore, a good word for the blank is *exhaustive*. (Take note of the two triggers: "yet" and "since.")

   Does (A) mean *exhaustive*? No. What about (B)? Not quite. (C)? It could. (D)? No—be careful. The clue doesn't mention anything about the class being bad—just not complete. And finally, what about (E)? It's not a good match. The best answer, then, is (C).

7. **C** For two-blank sentence completions, focus on one blank at a time. The second blank has a better clue, so start there first. The clue for the blank is "a third party to evaluate each side." A good word for the blank then is something like *mediator*. Does *magistrate* in (A) match *mediator*? No—a *magistrate* is just an official with authority of some sort. *Adjudicator* in (B) looks good, so leave it in. If you don't know what *arbiter* in (C) means, you have to leave it in. *Diplomat* in (D) isn't quite the right fit, so eliminate it. And finally (E)—you can't cross it out if you don't know what *reprobate* means.

   The remaining answer choices are (B), (C), and (E). The clue for the first blank is "settle the dispute." You know the parties were fighting; therefore, a good word for the blank is *fighting*. *Recessing* in (B) doesn't match, so throw it out. *Wrangling* in (C) could work, so leave it in. *Haggling* in (E) could also work, so keep it.

   You're left with (C) and (E), each of which contains a word you don't know. If you really don't know anything about either *arbiter* or *reprobate*, just pick one and go. You have a 50 percent chance of getting the question right. However, if you know that *reprobate* is a negative word, then you know (E) can't be right. (C) is the best answer.

PRACTICE QUESTIONS #5

1. **E** For two-blank sentence completions, focus on one blank at a time. Start with the second blank because it has an easier clue. The clue for this blank is "attempt to control." There is also the same-direction trigger "and." Together, the clue and trigger tell you that what goes in the blank is something similar to control. So just repeat the clue in the blank—a good word for the blank is *control*. *Convert* in (A) doesn't match *control*, so eliminate it. *Amend* in (B) doesn't match, so cross it out, too. *Confirm* in (C) doesn't work, nor does *civilize*

in (D), so eliminate both. *Constrain* in (E) is the only answer choice that remains, and it's the only answer choice that works. Don't even worry about what should go in the first blank. The best answer has to be (E).

2. **D** The clue for this blank is "too forthright." One is "too forthright" when one takes honesty too far. Therefore, what goes in the blank has to be a negative word. (A) is either slightly positive or neither positive nor negative. In either case, throw it out. (B) is positive, so it can't be right. (C) is negative but it doesn't have anything to do with being honest or forthright. (D) is negative and certainly could explain what happens when one is "too forthright." (E) is negative, but it goes too far. (D) is the best answer.

3. **A** For two-blank sentence completions, focus on one blank at a time. Start with the second blank because it's a little easier to work with. The clue for this blank is "not wanting to purchase the same item twice." If customers don't want "to purchase the same item twice," then what would they do to the number of papers they subscribe to? They would cut them down. So a good word for the blank is *cut down*. *Reduce* in (A) could mean *cut down*, so leave it in. *Appraise* in (B) doesn't match *cut down*, so eliminate it. *Cut back on* in (C) could work, so keep it. *Settle on* in (D) doesn't match, so cross it out. *Augment* in (E) is the opposite of what you're looking for, so eliminate it.

You're left with (A) and (C). Go on to the first blank. The clue for this blank is also "not wanting to purchase the same item twice." If the customers don't want to buy the same item twice, then the item—the articles—are being repeated. A good word for the blank is *repeated*. *Reproduced* in (A) means *repeated*, so keep it. *Censored* in (C) doesn't match *repeated*, so it can't be right. The best answer is (A).

4. **E** For two-blank sentence completions, focus on one blank at a time. Start with the first blank since the clue is easier to work with. The clue for this blank is "one can cause offense without having intended it." So what goes in the blank might be a word like *intentionally*. *Rationally* in (A) doesn't work, so get rid of it. *Precisely* in (B) doesn't work either, so eliminate it. *Conscientiously* in (C) is a possible match, so leave it in. *Hesitantly* in (D) doesn't match, so eliminate it. *Purposefully* in (E) might work, so keep it.

You're down to (C) and (E). Move on to the second blank. The clue for this blank is "fails to." If the line of reasoning fails, then it doesn't look at "the fact that one can cause offense without having intended it." So a good word for the blank is *look at*. *Uphold* in (C) doesn't work, so get rid of it. *Address* in (E) does work, so it has to be right. (E) is the best answer.

5. **C** The clue for this blank is "produced an aesthetic revolution." If the impressionist movement "produced an aesthetic revolution," then what did it do to "the academic standards of the time"? It went against them. So a good word for the blank is *went against*. If you don't know what *promulgating* means, then you can't get rid of (A). If you don't know what *eschewing* means, then you can't eliminate (B). (C) is a good match, so keep it. (D) isn't, so throw it out. (E) isn't quite right, so cross it out. You're left with (A), (B), and (C)—two contain words you don't know while the last one works. Go with what works. The best answer is (C).

6. **E** The clue for this blank is "shy demeanor was often misinterpreted." So what goes in the blank has to be something like *shyness*. (A) doesn't match, nor does (B), so cross them out. (C) doesn't work, so get rid of it, too. (D) isn't quite right, so eliminate it. (E) does work, so it has to be right. (E) is the best answer.

7. **E** For two-blank sentence completions, focus on one blank at a time. Start with the first blank because its clue is easier to work with. The clue for this blank is "rejected the hold of the church on society." If the church is less important, then life is more worldly. A good word for the blank, then, is *worldliness*. *Sublimation* in (A) doesn't work, so cross it out. *Appreciation* in (B) doesn't work either, so it's gone. *Revitalization* in (C) isn't quite right, so eliminate it. Don't eliminate (D) if you don't know what *abnegation* means. *Secularization* in (E) could work, so keep it.

    You're down to (D) and (E). Take a look at the second blank. The clue for this blank is really "instead." Instead of having the church keep its hold on society, what did the Reformation do? It emphasized "the import of personal responsibility and individual freedom." A good word for the blank is *emphasized*. *Imparted* in (D) could work, as could *cited* in (E). So you're still left with (D) and (E). (D) contains a word you don't know, and (E) works. Go with what works. The best answer is (E).

3
Analogies

THE GOAL: HOW TO RELATE

First things first—here's what a typical analogy question looks like:

DEFILE : FILTHY ::
- ◯ hasten : quick
- ◯ detail : precise
- ◯ level : flat
- ◯ fume : angry
- ◯ scrutinize : probing

The capitalized words are what we call the **stem words**. The answer choices are, of course, the answer choices.

Now that that's out of the way, what's the point of an analogy? It's to find the answer-choice words that have the same relationship as do the stem words. In short, the point of an analogy is to figure out how words relate to each other.

WHEN YOU KNOW THE STEM WORDS

We can divide analogies into two groups:

- Analogies where you know both of the stem words

- Analogies where you don't know one or both of the stem words

Let's start off with the first group: You know both of the stem words. If you know both of the stem words, make a sentence.

Now, "make a sentence" may sound easy, but don't get too confident yet. When we say "make a sentence," we mean make a sentence that defines one of the stem words in terms of the other. For example, let's think about what might be a good sentence for this stem pair:

KENNEL : DOG ::

What do you think of the following sentence? When I go on vacation, a KENNEL is where I leave my DOG.

If you don't like this sentence, give yourself a pat on the back. This sentence does use both stem words, which is good, but it doesn't define one word in terms of the other, which is bad.

How about this sentence? A KENNEL is a house for a DOG.

Not bad, right? In fact, quite good. What's nice about this sentence is that it's concise and to the point. You don't want to write a novel when you make a sentence with a stem pair. Instead, "KISS."

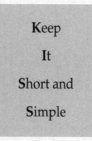

Keep

It

Short and

Simple

Let's try to make a sentence with another stem pair:

PEBBLE : BOULDER ::

If you thought of something like "a PEBBLE is a little BOULDER," you're on the right track. Again, this sentence is good because it's short and simple. Now, you may be thinking, "but a PEBBLE isn't exactly a little BOULDER." True. However, the point of an analogy is to convey the relationship between the words. Does "little" get across the relationship between PEBBLE and BOULDER? Yes.

APPLY YOUR SENTENCE

Once you've got a sentence for the stem pair, you want to apply that same sentence to each and every answer choice—then eliminate any that doesn't fit into your sentence. For example:

KENNEL : DOG ::
○ pond : alga
○ forest : mushroom
○ branch : bird
○ aquarium : fish
○ field : sheep

The sentence we had for the stem words was: A KENNEL is a house for a DOG. To apply the sentence to the answer choices, just pretend there are blanks where the stem words are. In other words:

A _____ is a house for a _____.

(A) A *pond* is a house for an *alga*. Is that true? No.

(B) A *forest* is a house for a *mushroom*. Nope.

(C) A *branch* is a house for a *bird*. This definitely doesn't work.

(D) An *aquarium* is a house for a *fish*. Sure.

(E) A *field* is a house for a *sheep*. Not really.

The only answer choice that fit your sentence was (D). Therefore, (D) is the best answer. Pretty easy, right? Yes—as long as you can make a good sentence.

Note that we went through every single answer choice in the example above. That's what you should do for every analogy. Always check out (A) through (E), even if you've found the answer choice that you think is right. Remember, verbal questions are all about the *best* answers. You may think an answer choice is correct, but you may find an even better one further down.

More Than One Answer Choice Left?

There may be times when you have a good sentence for the stem words and you apply your sentence to the answer choices, but guess what? You aren't able to eliminate all of the answer choices. If that's the case, then you need to make your sentence more specific. Take a look at the example below:

DISTANCE : KILOMETER ::
- ○ liquid : beaker
- ○ electricity : current
- ○ temperature : thermometer
- ○ length : perimeter
- ○ heat : calorie

A good sentence using the stem pair might be: "A KILOMETER measures DISTANCE." Notice that we flipped the order of the stem words. Is that OK? Sure. Just remember to flip the order of the words in the answer choices, too. Try applying the sentence to the answer choices.

(A)　A *beaker* measures *liquid*. Maybe.

(B)　A *current* measures *electricity*.　Nope—cross it out.

(C)　A *thermometer* measures *temperature*. Sure.

(D)　A *perimeter* measures *length*. Maybe.

(E)　A *calorie* measures *heat*. Yes.

With your sentence, you can only eliminate one answer choice. When you still have answer choices remaining after applying your sentence, you need to make your sentence more specific. How about: "A KILOMETER is a unit that measures DISTANCE"?

(A)　A *beaker* is a unit that measures *liquid*. No.

(B)　Already eliminated.

(C)　A *thermometer* is a unit that measures *temperature*. No.

(D)　A *perimeter* is a unit that measures *length*. No.

(E)　A *calorie* is a unit that measures *heat*. Yes.

The best answer is (E).

QUICK QUIZ #1

On the following questions, make a sentence with each stem pair. The answers are on page 78.

1. SHIRK : WORK ::

2. PENANCE : SORROW ::

3. SATIATE : SATISFY ::

4. TRICKLE : TORRENT ::

5. ELONGATE : LENGTH ::

6. AUTOMOBILE : GARAGE ::

7. IGNITE : FIRE ::

8. EXCESSIVE : MODERATION ::

9. INCONSPICUOUS : NOTICEABLE ::

10. MISER : FRUGAL ::

11. LURK : MOVEMENT ::

12. ANOMALY : NORM ::

13. MORTAL : DEATH ::

14. MUTE : SOUND ::

15. RESUMÉ : QUALIFICATION ::

16. SATIRE : SCORN ::

17. VORACIOUS : HUNGRY ::

18. DUBIOUS : CERTAINTY.

19. GUFFAW : LAUGH ::

20. SYLLABUS : COURSE ::

RECYCLED RELATIONSHIPS

There isn't a lot of positive stuff we can say about ETS, but here's something that we do like. On analogies, ETS has certain relationships that it likes to use again and again and again.

Below are ETS's top five recycled relationships. There's a good chance you may see some of them on the day of the GRE.

TYPE OF

SOFA : FURNITURE ::
A SOFA is a type of FURNITURE.

POODLE : DOG ::
A POODLE is a type of DOG.

IS USED TO

VEIL : COVER ::
A VEIL is used to COVER.

MEDAL : COMMEMORATE ::
A MEDAL is used to
    COMMEMORATE.

DEGREE

OBSEQUIOUS : ATTENTIVE ::
Someone OBSEQUIOUS is overly
    ATTENTIVE (ATTENTIVE to a
    great degree).

RECKLESS : BOLD
RECKLESS means very BOLD
    (BOLD to a great degree).

CHARACTERIZED BY/HAVING

ZEALOT : FERVOR ::
A ZEALOT is characterized by
    FERVOR.

PERSPICACIOUS : INSIGHT ::
PERSPICACIOUS means having
    INSIGHT.

WITHOUT/LACKS

AMORPHOUS : SHAPE ::
Something AMORPHOUS lacks
    SHAPE.

ACCURATE : ERROR ::
ACCURATE means without ERROR.

Two notes: First, whenever you think two stem words are synonyms, it's likely that the words have a degree relationship. Second, whenever, you think two stem words are antonyms, it's likely that the words have a without/lacks relationship. It's very important that you *never* make a sentence using one word as the synonym or the antonym of the other. That type of sentence does not define one word in terms of the other.

QUICK QUIZ #2

On the following questions, make a sentence with the stem pair and then apply the sentence to the answer choices. The answers are on page 78.

1. TRITE : ORIGINALITY ::

   ○ still : suppression
   ○ animated : interest
   ○ common : amazement
   ○ monotone : variation
   ○ notable : fame

2. WHISTLE : REFEREE ::

   ○ wood : lumberjack
   ○ needle : seamstress
   ○ gavel : judge
   ○ pulpit : preacher
   ○ stethoscope : physician

3. LUBRICATE : SLIPPERY ::

   ○ illuminate : radiant
   ○ humorous : funny
   ○ consecrate : sacred
   ○ desire : tempted
   ○ dilate : shut

4. BARTER : GOOD ::

   ○ conversation : idea
   ○ ration : provision
   ○ constitution : law
   ○ spoil : plunder
   ○ frugality : waste

5. HULL : COVERING ::

   ○ convention : discussion
   ○ spectacle : drama
   ○ freedom : liberty
   ○ compensation : payment
   ○ origin : beginning

6. ADROIT : SKILL ::

   ○ rueful : remorse
   ○ remarkable : memory
   ○ overstrung : temper
   ○ egotistical : impertinence
   ○ churlish : manners

7. IMPROVISED : REHEARSAL ::

   ○ lithe : inhibition
   ○ sloppy : care
   ○ preempted : appropriation
   ○ partial : favor
   ○ incurable : hope

8. INDECIPHERABLE : READ ::

   ○ unreal : envision
   ○ unstoppable : arrest
   ○ impolite : insult
   ○ untruthful : believe
   ○ incoherent : muddle

9. INTOXICANT: EXCITE ::

   ○ exercise : regroup
   ○ etiquette : behave
   ○ parody : ridicule
   ○ mirth : revel
   ○ contaminant : purify

WHEN YOU CAN'T MAKE A SENTENCE

So far, we've only looked at how to tackle analogies where you know both stem words. What about analogies where you know only one stem word? Or where you don't know either?

This is where a good vocabulary comes into play. The better your vocabulary, the more likely you are to know both stem words. And if you know both words in the stem, then you can make a sentence. In short, improve your vocabulary. It makes life on analogies much, much easier.

Still, there's no way you can learn every single word in the English language. The simple fact is that you're going to encounter words you don't know on the GRE. Luckily, we have a great technique to use on analogies when you don't know either one or both of the stem words.

When you don't know one or both of the stem words, you can't make a sentence, right? That much is clear. So what should you do? To answer this question, let's take a look at a stem pair that'll never show up on the real GRE:

DOG : COLD ::

Why won't this stem pair ever show up on the test? Well, let's think. We know both of the stem words, so let's try to make a sentence.

A DOG can be COLD.

A DOG can have a COLD nose.

Just about any DOG doesn't like the COLD.

Can you make a short and simple sentence that defines one word in terms of the other? No! Of course not. You can't because there is no relationship between the words.

Why did we show you this example, then? To point out that every single stem pair must have what we call a "defining" relationship. A defining relationship is simply one for which you can write a defining sentence, as we have been doing.

Now, if the stem pair has a defining relationship, then the correct answer must also have a defining relationship. In fact, it must have the same defining relationship as the stem pair—that's what makes it the correct answer in the first place. But what is so helpful about this fact is that many of the answer choices *don't* have defining relationships. If an answer choice doesn't have a defining relationship, it can't be the correct answer, and you should cross it off.

Therefore, your first step when you can't make a sentence with the stem pair is to turn to the answer choices and eliminate any that don't have defining relationships.

PROVING DEFINING RELATIONSHIPS

How do you determine whether an answer choice has a defining relationship? It's quite simple. We go back to our friend, the defining sentence. If you can make a defining sentence with the pair of words, then it has a defining relationship and you leave it in. If you can't make a defining sentence, then you get rid of it. Let's try some examples.

○ impartial : bias

Can you make a defining sentence with this pair? How about, "*Impartial* means without *bias*"? Looks pretty good. What about this one?

○ obvious : discover

Can you make a defining sentence? Maybe, "*Obvious* means easy to *discover.*" That works. Try another one.

○ riot : illegal

Can you make a defining sentence for this pair? Not really. You can't use either of these words to define the other. So you would eliminate this pair if you saw it as an answer choice. Here's another pair:

○ penchant : liking

Defining sentence? Yes. We could write, "*Penchant* means to have a strong *liking.*" One more:

○ monitor : verify

Well? *Monitor* means to watch, and *verify* means to prove the truth of. You can't use one of these words to define the other, so this pair doesn't have a defining relationship.

So checking for defining relationships in the answer choices allows us to eliminate answers even when we don't know what one of the stem words is.

Let's take a look at the following analogy. Eliminate those answer choices that don't have defining relationships.

PRECIPITATE : HASTE ::
○ meticulous : care
○ sagacious : competence
○ imminent : danger
○ reticent : silence
○ foreboding : quiet

Let's presume you didn't know what *precipitate* meant. You would turn to the answer choices.

Can you make a defining sentence with answer choice (A)? Yes. A good sentence would be, "*Meticulous* means marked by *care.*" Therefore, leave (A) in.

Can you make a defining sentence with answer choice (B)? No. *Sagacious* means discerning or wise. It has nothing to do with *competence*, so eliminate (B).

Can you make a defining sentence with answer choice (C)? No. Be careful here. *Imminent* means about to take place. You've probably heard the phrase "imminent danger" before, but that doesn't mean the definitions of the words are related. You can't make a sentence that uses one word to define the other, so get rid of (C).

Can you make a defining sentence with answer choice (D)? Sure. "*Reticent* means inclined to *silence*." Leave (D) in.

Can you make a defining sentence with answer choice (E)? No. *Foreboding* means ominous or menacing. Eliminate (E).

So, just by eliminating nondefining relationships, you can narrow the answers to (A) and (D). Not bad, considering we didn't even look at the stem pair to do it. The best answer turns out to be (A). PRECIPITATE means marked by HASTE.

No Wishy-Washy Sentences

One of the important things to watch out for when you're trying to make defining sentences with the answer choices is wishy-washy language. If you find that your sentence is using wishy-washy language to qualify the relationship between the words, then it's probably not a real defining sentence. For example, let's say we had the following pair:

◯ apple : red

Your first instinct might be to write something like, "*Red* is the color of an *apple*." But that's not necessarily true. There are green apples and yellow apples and others as well. It's important that your sentences be accurate. So the proper sentence would be something like, "*Red* is often the color of an *apple*." But that qualifier "often" is a problem. What it means is that *red* and *apple* don't really have a defining relationship.

A definition can't be something that is only true some of the time. It has to be true *all* of the time. If apples aren't always red, then *red* isn't really part of the definition of an apple.

If the insertion of wishy-washy language—such as *may, might, can, could, sometimes, often, probably*, and similar words—is necessary to make your sentence accurate, then it's not a real defining sentence and you should eliminate that answer choice. Let's look at one more.

◯ confident : successful

What kind of sentence can we make for this? "One who is *confident* will be *successful*." Is that necessarily true? Definitely not. To be accurate we would have to say something like, "One who is *confident* is more likely to be *successful*." Even this is a problematic sentence because it's based more on experience of life than on the definitions of the words themselves. But it doesn't matter because the wishy-washy language is enough reason to eliminate that pair.

We want our defining sentences to be strong and simple.

QUICK QUIZ #3

Determine whether each of the following answer choice pairs has a defining relationship. If you think an answer choice pair has a defining relationship, prove it with a sentence that defines one word in terms of the other. The answers are on page 79.

1. lassitude : energy

2. castigate : scold

3. nag : irritate

4. thought : logic

5. closet : shelves

6. castaway : discard

7. stockroom : supply

8. latent : manifest

9. charitable : amenable

10. ratify : approval

11. pilferage : deception

12. studious : sagacity

13. melee : confusion

14. terse : superfluous

15. inveterate : liar

16. charisma : charm

17. abrasive : irritation

18. entertain : enthrall

19. enchant : amuse

20. retain : lawyer

21. truncate : short

22. arduous : weaken

23. impertinent : forthright

24. inaugurate : beginning

25. satisfied : enjoyment

26. exert : muscle

27. wholesome : health

28. innocuous : harm

29. rationalize : reasonable

30. museum : art

QUICK QUIZ #4

On the following questions, use defining relationships to get rid of wrong answer choices. Remember, you can't cross out an answer choice if it contains a word you don't know. The answers are on page 79.

1. INCORRIGIBLE : REFORM ::
   - ⟳ inefficient : effectiveness
   - ⟳ ingenious : perfection
   - ⟳ intemperate : violence
   - ⟳ infallible : error
   - ⟳ incidental : chance

2. OPALESCENT : MONOCHROMATIC ::
   - ⟳ impervious : penetrable
   - ⟳ discursive : rambling
   - ⟳ complementary : mutual
   - ⟳ profitable : opulent
   - ⟳ infamous : shocking

3. TRANSMIGRATE : STATE ::
   - ⟳ invert : logic
   - ⟳ substitute : replacement
   - ⟳ metamorphose : form
   - ⟳ intimate : implication
   - ⟳ deduce : reasoning

4. INTOXICANT : EXCITE ::
   - ⟳ tonic : ameliorate
   - ⟳ antidote : sterilize
   - ⟳ sedative : cure
   - ⟳ stimulant : dull
   - ⟳ anesthetic : numb

5. INEXORABLE : AVOID ::
   - ⟳ gleeful : contain
   - ⟳ protean : versatile
   - ⟳ baseless : defend
   - ⟳ undeviating : swerve
   - ⟳ magnanimous : respect

6. SALACIOUS : LUST ::
   - ⟳ imperious : arrogance
   - ⟳ anemic : vitality
   - ⟳ pedantic : knowledge
   - ⟳ dolorous : simplicity
   - ⟳ capricious : resoluteness

7. OBFUSCATE : CONFUSE ::
   - ⟳ juxtapose : contrast
   - ⟳ decamp : depart
   - ⟳ proscribe : affirm
   - ⟳ routinize : steady
   - ⟳ pacify : diminish

8. TUMID : SWELLING ::
   - ⟳ lamentable : accusation
   - ⟳ dubious : proclamation
   - ⟳ oblique : clarity
   - ⟳ elastic : resilience
   - ⟳ insolent : provocation

9. GENUFLECT : RESPECT ::
   - ⟳ brook : intolerance
   - ⟳ coddle : complacency
   - ⟳ brood : deliberation
   - ⟳ sanction : acceptance
   - ⟳ enfranchise : privilege

WORKING BACKWARD

Let's take a step back and review before we go any further.

1. The first thing you do when you tackle an analogy is make a sentence.

2. If, after applying the sentence to the answer choices, you have more than one answer choice left, then you need to make the sentence more specific.

3. If you can't make any sentence whatsoever, then you go to the answer choices and eliminate those that do not have defining relationships.

After the third step, you may have more than one answer choice remaining. This is where the technique of Working Backward comes in.

Working Backward really works hand-in-hand with defining relationships. If an answer choice pair does not have a defining relationship, you can eliminate it. If an answer choice pair has a defining relationship, then you Work Backward.

What is Working Backward? You prove that an answer choice has a defining relationship by making a sentence with the two words. Working Backward entails applying that sentence to the stem words.

Let's look at the following answer choice pair. Does it have a defining relationship?

○ remiss : negligent

Yes. You know it has a defining relationship because you can make a sentence defining one of the words using the other. "*Remiss* means *negligent* in duty." Take this sentence and try to apply it to the following stem pair:

??? : DILIGENT ::

The question marks indicate that you don't know what the first word in the stem pair means. But that doesn't stop you from Working Backward. Ask yourself: "Could a word exist that means DILIGENT in duty?" Sure. You don't have to know what the exact word is. The point is that such a word could exist. Therefore, the answer choice pair (remiss : negligent) could be the right answer. Take a look at another answer choice pair.

○ lionize : extol

Does this pair have a defining relationship? Yes. The sentence proves it: "*Lionize* means to *extol* someone." Now that you've got a good sentence, apply it to the following stem pair:

??? : CHEAT ::

Again, the question marks indicate you don't know one of the words in the stem pair. Ask yourself: "Could a word exist that means to CHEAT someone?" Definitely. Therefore, this answer choice could be the right answer. Let's look at one more answer choice pair.

○ debatable : dispute

Does the pair have a defining relationship? Yes. A possible sentence is: "Something *debatable* is open to *dispute*." Apply the sentence to the following stem pair:

??? : LOYALTY ::

Ask yourself: "Could something that is something be open to LOYALTY?" No. It doesn't make a lot of sense. Therefore, what should you do? Eliminate this answer choice. It can't be the right answer.

To summarize: When you can't make a sentence with the stem words, go to the answer choices and look for defining relationships. Eliminate any answer choice that doesn't have a defining relationship. For those answer choices that do have defining relationships, Work Backward. Let's try an example:

DISABUSE : ERROR ::

- ⃝ quell : submission
- ⃝ liberate : domination
- ⃝ foil : expulsion
- ⃝ impair : health
- ⃝ sidle : movement

Let's say that you don't know the word DISABUSE. Since you can't make a sentence, go to the answer choices and use defining relationships along with Working Backward.

Does answer choice (A) have a defining relationship? Yes. You can make a sentence defining one word in terms of the other: *Quell* means to reduce to *submission*. Since (A) has a defining relationship, you now need to Work Backward. Could a word exist that means to reduce to ERROR? Doesn't make a lot of sense, does it? Therefore, eliminate this answer choice.

Does answer choice (B) have a defining relationship? Yes. A good sentence: *Liberate* means to free from *domination*. Since (B) has a defining relationship, you now need to Work Backward. Could a word exist that means to free from ERROR? Sure. Therefore, leave this answer choice in. It could be right.

Does answer choice (C) have a defining relationship? No. *Foil* means to *thwart*. If you look up *foil* in the dictionary, will you see *expulsion*? No. If you look up *expulsion* in the dictionary, will you see *foil*? No again. Therefore, (C) does not have a defining relationship. Because (C) does not have a defining relationship, you know it can't be the right answer. Eliminate it.

Does answer choice (D) have a defining relationship? No. Don't be deceived. If you look up *impair* in the dictionary, does it say *health*? No. If you look up *health* in the dictionary, does it say *impair*? Definitely not. Therefore, (D) does not have a defining relationship. Eliminate it.

Does answer choice (E) have a defining relationship? Yes. The sentence to prove it: *Sidle* is a type of *movement*. Since (E) has a defining relationship, you now need to Work Backward. Could a word exist that means a type of ERROR? Possibly. Leave (E) in because it could be the right answer.

So you're down to (B) and (E). By using defining relationships combined with Working Backward, you have a 50 percent chance of getting the question right—even though you don't know what DISABUSE means. At this point, what should you do? How about guess? After all, you have a 50 percent chance. As it turns out, the best answer is (B). DISABUSE means to free from ERROR.

QUICK QUIZ #5

For each of the following questions, determine whether the answer choice pair has a defining relationship. If it does have a defining relationship, then prove it by making a sentence. Finally, Work Backward with that sentence and see if it can be applied to the stem pair. If the sentence can be applied, then leave the answer choice in. If the sentence can't be applied (i.e., it doesn't make sense), then cross it out. The question marks indicate that you don't know the meaning of the stem word. The answers are on page 80.

1. ??? : TROOPS ::
   ◯ assemble : crowd

2. ??? : PROFIT ::
   ◯ arable : plowing

3. ??? : DISSOLUTE ::
   ◯ luminary : wealth

4. EXPEL : ??? ::
   ◯ touch : dab

5. ??? : CONDESCENSION ::
   ◯ kowtow : deference

6. ??? : DECLARE ::
   ◯ exhibit : display

7. ??? : FERMENTATION ::
   ◯ solvent : distillation

8. SADNESS : ??? ::
   ◯ word : laconic

9. ??? : TUMULTUOUS ::
   ◯ ruse : deceptive

QUICK QUIZ #6

On the following questions, use defining relationships combined with Working Backward to eliminate wrong answer choices. If an answer choice doesn't have a defining relationship, eliminate it. If an answer choice has a defining relationship, Work Backward. The answers are on page 81.

1. PECCADILLO : SIN ::

   ○ memorial : reminder
   ○ lapse : error
   ○ aptitude : intelligence
   ○ asperity : rigor
   ○ fortress : town

2. LAM : FLEE ::

   ○ bolt : swallow
   ○ suppress : revive
   ○ filch : deceive
   ○ ingratiate : dismiss
   ○ abstain : fulfill

3. LIBRETTO : OPERA ::

   ○ symphony : orchestra
   ○ prelude : event
   ○ buttress : stability
   ○ euphony : sound
   ○ script : play

4. CACHET : APPROBATION ::

   ○ discomfort : embarrassment
   ○ secret : disclosure
   ○ stockade : defense
   ○ malediction : dishonor
   ○ stigma : disgrace

5. NIP : NUMB ::

   ○ dally : playful
   ○ augment : greater
   ○ compel : pressing
   ○ tidy : proper
   ○ create : inventive

6. INDELIBLE : ERASE ::

   ○ irradicable : comprehend
   ○ incredible : doubt
   ○ indeterminate : fix
   ○ immobile : push
   ○ irredeemable : punish

7. HALE : VIGOR ::

   ○ hirsute : insight
   ○ craven : bravery
   ○ pitiless : vicious
   ○ circumspect : prudence
   ○ intransigent : concession

8. ODYSSEY : ADVENTURE ::

   ○ encyclopedia : book
   ○ condition : promise
   ○ chapter : unit
   ○ itinerary : trip
   ○ incivility : rudeness

9. DAUNTLESS : FEAR ::

   ○ licentious : freedom
   ○ stolid : emotion
   ○ fallible : liability
   ○ depraved : corruption
   ○ brazen : boldness

ABSOLUTELY STUCK

You should be picking up a lot of points by using defining relationships combined with Working Backward. However, if these techniques aren't getting you anywhere (and chances are they are), here are some last resorts.

SIDES OF THE FENCE

There may be times when you don't know the exact relationship between the stem words but you do know a little something about how they relate. That is, you can tell whether they're similar words or whether they're different words. Let's look at the following stem pair:

OVERWEENING : PRIDE ::

You may not know the exact relationship between OVERWEENING and PRIDE, but you may know that the two words are similar. In other words, they're on the same side of the fence. Take a look at the stem pair below. How is it different?

INGENUOUS : URBANE ::

These words are on different sides of the fence—that is, they don't share the same characteristics or qualities.

So how can Sides of the Fence help you? Well, if you know the stem words are on the same side of the fence, the correct answer must have words on the same side, too. Therefore, you can eliminate any answer choice that has words on different sides.

Similarly, if you know the stem words are on different sides, the correct answer must have words on different sides, too. Therefore, you can eliminate any answer choice that has words on the same side. Try the following example.

OBSTREPEROUS : CONTROL ::

- ◯ pugnacious : belligerence
- ◯ heterodox : convention
- ◯ euphoric : elation
- ◯ infallible : malfeasance
- ◯ precocious : maturity

OBSTREPEROUS and CONTROL are on different sides of the fence. Therefore, the right answer must be on different sides as well. Answer choice (A) has words on the same side, so it can't be correct. (B) has words on different sides, so leave it in. (C) has words on the same side, so eliminate it. (D) has words on different sides, so it's okay. (E) has words on the same side, so throw it out. (B) and (D) are the only possible choices, and if you look at (D) closely, you can see that the words don't have a defining relationship. The best answer is (B).

QUICK QUIZ #7

On the following answer choice pairs, determine whether the words are on the same side or different sides of the fence. The answers are on page 83.

1. nullify : invalid

2. prepossessing : unpleasant

3. litigious : lawsuit

4. altercation : dispute

5. nauseous : disgust

6. adversity : fortune

7. arbitrary : random

8. pacify : agitation

9. patent : obvious

10. penchant : disinclination

BREAD VS. MEAT

ETS likes to trick test takers by having them focus on the stem words themselves rather than on the relationship between the stem words. If you think of an analogy as a sandwich—the stem words are the pieces of bread and the relationship is the meat in between—ETS distracts test takers by using words in the answer choices that remind them of the bread. For example:

DEVOUT : PIETY ::

○ reverent : righteousness
○ prudent : discrimination
○ virtuous : grace
○ credulous : belief
○ dolorous : grief

The pieces of bread are DEVOUT and PIETY. If you look at the answer choices, what words remind you of DEVOUT and PIETY? In (A), *reverent*; in (C), *virtuous*; and in (D), *belief*. These words are all associated with religion—just like DEVOUT and PIETY. Don't let the bread distract you. It's the meat—that is, the relationship—that matters.

The point is: Don't rush. If your work is dominated by speed, guess what's going to happen. You're going to look at the bread, not the meat.

By the way, the meat in the above example is "a _____ person expresses _____." The best answer, then, is (E).

THE HARDEST (OR WEIRDEST) WORDS

The very last resort for analogies is the same as the very last resort for sentence completions: Pick the answer choice that has the hardest (or weirdest) word or words. Again, it's not a foolproof method of guessing, but when you're absolutely stuck, it can give you some guidance.

IN SUMMARY

It's a step-by-step process you need to take to tackle analogies. The more vocabulary you know, the easier analogies will be because you can make sentences with your stem words. But if you don't have the vocabulary, then defining relationships along with Working Backward are your salvation. The first three steps are the most important. By test time, these steps should be so ingrained in your mind that they're instinctive.

When you know both of the stem words . . .

1. Make a sentence. Then apply that sentence to the answer choices.

2. If you've applied your sentence and still have more than one answer choice left, make your sentence more specific.

When you know both of the stem words but can't make a sentence OR when you don't know one or both of the stem words . . .

3. Go to the answer choices and test for defining relationships. Remember, you prove something has a defining relationship by making a sentence.

    a. If the answer choice pair does not have a defining relationship, then eliminate it.

    b. If the answer choice pair has a defining relationship, Work Backward immediately.

When you're absolutely stuck . . .

4. Use Sides of the Fence.

5. Watch out for words in the answer choices that remind you of the stem words.

6. Pick the answer choice that has the hardest (or the weirdest) words.

PRACTICE QUESTIONS #1

Directions: In each of the following questions, a related pair of words or phrases is followed by five lettered pairs of words or phrases. Select the lettered pair that best expresses a relationship similar to that expressed in the original pair. The answers are on page 84.

1. AVIARY : BIRD ::
   - ◯ stable : horse
   - ◯ dam : beaver
   - ◯ field : cow
   - ◯ den : fox
   - ◯ nest : hamster

2. METHANE : FUEL ::
   - ◯ lathe : machine
   - ◯ ether : tool
   - ◯ drill : screw
   - ◯ benzene : ring
   - ◯ needle : sewing

3. RAMROD : RIGIDITY ::
   - ◯ heretical : orthodoxy
   - ◯ decorative : flamboyance
   - ◯ luminous : transparency
   - ◯ hectic : confusion
   - ◯ brackish : strength

4. SHELTER : PROTECTION ::
   - ◯ incentive : motivation
   - ◯ shield : injury
   - ◯ antiseptic : cure
   - ◯ inoculation : longevity
   - ◯ inundation : flood

5. IMPREGNABLE : ATTACK ::
   - ◯ phlegmatic : calm
   - ◯ salutary : health
   - ◯ immortal : death
   - ◯ ephemeral : brevity
   - ◯ iridescent : color

6. DOCILITY : INTRACTABLE ::
   - ◯ insurgency : oppressive
   - ◯ desolation : alone
   - ◯ anticipation : satisfied
   - ◯ victory : conquered
   - ◯ intrepidity : fearful

7. CORONATION : ROYAL ::
   - ◯ enlistment : soldier
   - ◯ excursion : adventurer
   - ◯ trial : mediator
   - ◯ commencement : student
   - ◯ frocking : cleric

8. SYLLOGISM : SPECIOUS ::
   - ◯ perversion : conventional
   - ◯ distillation : intense
   - ◯ conceit : fanciful
   - ◯ contingency : certain
   - ◯ truism : sincere

9. MAWKISH : SENTIMENT ::
   - ◯ overt : secrecy
   - ◯ rakish : codification
   - ◯ meretricious : simplicity
   - ◯ paramount : suspicion
   - ◯ carping : criticism

PRACTICE QUESTIONS #2

Directions: In each of the following questions, a related pair of words or phrases is followed by five lettered pairs of words or phrases. Select the lettered pair that best expresses a relationship similar to that expressed in the original pair. The answers are on page 87.

1. EYEGLASSES : VISION ::

   ○ anvil : metal
   ○ attraction : desire
   ○ heat : warmth
   ○ solution : beaker
   ○ spice : flavor

2. SMITH : METAL ::

   ○ jeweler : gold
   ○ meteorologist : weather
   ○ hunter : rifle
   ○ carpenter : wood
   ○ gymnast : vault

3. SUITCASE : CLOTHING ::

   ○ kitchen : pantry
   ○ parasol : fringe
   ○ attaché : contract
   ○ envelope : letter
   ○ encyclopedia : volume

4. HURL : PITCH ::

   ○ flag : tire
   ○ carp : fault
   ○ truckle : attend
   ○ pore : meditate
   ○ seize : take

5. RECONDITE : COMPREHEND ::

   ○ illegible : decipher
   ○ fastidious : care
   ○ treacherous : trick
   ○ credulous : believe
   ○ unforgiving : condone

6. UNEQUIVOCAL : QUESTION ::

   ○ officious : reprimand
   ○ staid : deride
   ○ insuperable : overcome
   ○ contiguous : abut
   ○ belated : delay

7. OXYMORON : INCONGRUOUS ::

   ○ polemic : conciliatory
   ○ alliteration : rhythmic
   ○ transport : pleasurable
   ○ phantasm : imaginative
   ○ subjunction : biased

8. TRANSMIT : SIGNAL ::

   ○ emend : correction
   ○ fulminate : invective
   ○ exaggerate : hyperbole
   ○ affront : humanity
   ○ trespass : property

9. DESCRY : DETECT ::

   ○ titter : grin
   ○ champ : chew
   ○ stutter : speak
   ○ slurp : sip
   ○ counterfeit : imitate

PRACTICE QUESTIONS #3

<u>Directions:</u> In each of the following questions, a related pair of words or phrases is followed by five lettered pairs of words or phrases. Select the lettered pair that best expresses a relationship similar to that expressed in the original pair. The answers are on page 91.

1. DRUM MAJOR : BAND ::

- ○ preacher : congregation
- ○ architect : designer
- ○ dancer : corps
- ○ adept : beginner
- ○ painter : viewer

2. SONATA : MOVEMENT ::

- ○ lampoon : ridicule
- ○ novel : prologue
- ○ tableau : stage
- ○ poem : stanza
- ○ fable : narrative

3. VIGILANCE : ALERT ::

- ○ flippancy : serious
- ○ garrulity : verbose
- ○ skepticism : doubting
- ○ judiciousness : merciful
- ○ sentience : attentive

4. WEALTH : INCOME ::

- ○ salary : performance
- ○ appetite : hunger
- ○ health : medicine
- ○ feeling : affection
- ○ wind : hurricane

5. EXTRINSIC : BELONG ::

- ○ submissive : resign
- ○ incontrovertible : challenge
- ○ evanescent : endure
- ○ protuberant : intrude
- ○ stigmatic : isolate

6. RECANT : BELIEF ::

- ○ reclaim : rescue
- ○ recoil : adoration
- ○ exact : requisition
- ○ repeal : law
- ○ calibrate : rectitude

7. PENURIOUS : FRUGALITY ::

- ○ philanthropic : grace
- ○ vainglorious : pettiness
- ○ priggish : integrity
- ○ lecherous : decency
- ○ perspicacious : insight

8. OBLOQUY : ABUSIVE ::

- ○ panegyric : laudatory
- ○ slander : inflammatory
- ○ diatribe : accusatory
- ○ calumny : criminal
- ○ travesty : contemptuous

9. LURID : MELODRAMA ::

- ○ redolent : fragrance
- ○ determinate : definition
- ○ alien : distinction
- ○ metaphysical : spirit
- ○ fortuitous : intention

PRACTICE QUESTIONS #4

Directions: In each of the following questions, a related pair of words or phrases is followed by five lettered pairs of words or phrases. Select the lettered pair that best expresses a relationship similar to that expressed in the original pair. The answers are on page 94.

1. LOSS : RECOUP ::
   - ○ tale : recount
   - ○ damage : recompense
   - ○ document : record
   - ○ health: recuperate
   - ○ generosity : reciprocate

2. APATHY : INDIFFERENT ::
   - ○ melancholy : sad
   - ○ enthusiasm : zealous
   - ○ stoicism : emotional
   - ○ talent : adequate
   - ○ discretion : secretive

3. SHEEP : FLEECE ::
   - ○ duck : bill
   - ○ insect : arthropod
   - ○ lion : courage
   - ○ kangaroo : pouch
   - ○ fish : scale

4. REBATE : FORCE ::
   - ○ tax : demand
   - ○ blunt : sharpness
   - ○ glean : information
   - ○ appease : calm
   - ○ cleave : division

5. TAMBOURINE : INSTRUMENT ::
   - ○ scene : tableau
   - ○ ship : yacht
   - ○ chaise : vehicle
   - ○ agenda : meeting
   - ○ solution : chemistry

6. ANODYNE : ASSUAGE ::
   - ○ diet : lighten
   - ○ antiseptic : promote
   - ○ vitamin : invigorate
   - ○ drug : prevent
   - ○ catalyst : hasten

7. APHORISM : CONCISE ::
   - ○ eulogy : cursory
   - ○ effigy : slanderous
   - ○ sophism : veracious
   - ○ provocation : irritating
   - ○ camp : theatrical

8. INCONTINENT : RESTRAINT ::
   - ○ impudent : suavity
   - ○ naive : deception
   - ○ impenitent : sin
   - ○ covetous : desire
   - ○ impolitic : tact

9. CHARY : TRUSTFUL ::
   - ○ munificent : stinting
   - ○ pragmatic : irrational
   - ○ mulish : forgiving
   - ○ treacherous : deceiving
   - ○ cynical : quibbling

PRACTICE QUESTIONS #5

Directions: In each of the following questions, a related pair of words or phrases is followed by five lettered pairs of words or phrases. Select the lettered pair that best expresses a relationship similar to that expressed in the original pair. The answers are on page 97.

1. WOLF : CANINE ::

○ alligator : crocodile
○ shrimp : crustacean
○ tadpole : frog
○ horse : hock
○ goose : gaggle

2. SENTRY : GUARD ::

○ judge : legislate
○ student : learn
○ producer : finance
○ fireman : save
○ conductor : direct

3. DANDY : FOPPISH ::

○ ingenue : naive
○ elocutionist : public
○ martyr : melancholy
○ recreant : disagreeable
○ mercenary : avaricious

4. MOVE : MEANDER ::

○ think : concentrate
○ talk : ramble
○ run : lope
○ stammer : mutter
○ work : labor

5. PAEAN : TRIBUTE ::

○ hymn : catholicism
○ elegy : grief
○ canticle : purity
○ psalm : gravity
○ eulogy : devotion

6. EPAULET : DECORATION ::

○ cameo : image
○ epée : rapier
○ cavalry : unit
○ lapel : jacket
○ medal : ornament

7 PERORATION : SPEECH ::

○ conference : discussion
○ itinerary : travel
○ epilogue : play
○ letter : alphabet
○ destruction : life

8. ABHOR : DISLIKE ::

○ venerate : esteem
○ procrastinate : delay
○ testify : affirm
○ condone : neglect
○ detract : dismiss

9. TOTTER : GAIT ::

○ furrow : brow
○ simper : smile
○ canter : gallop
○ stutter : speech
○ deduction : thought

ANSWERS AND EXPLANATIONS

QUICK QUIZ #1

1. SHIRK means to avoid WORK.

2. PENANCE is performed to show SORROW.

3. SATIATE means to SATISFY fully.

4. A TRICKLE is a little TORRENT.

5. ELONGATE means to increase in LENGTH.

6. A GARAGE is used to house an AUTOMOBILE.

7. IGNITE means to set on FIRE.

8. Something EXCESSIVE lacks MODERATION.

9. Something INCONSPICUOUS is not NOTICEABLE.

10. A MISER is a very FRUGAL person.

11. LURK is a type of MOVEMENT.

12. An ANOMALY goes against the NORM.

13. MORTAL means causing DEATH.

14. MUTE means to reduce the SOUND of.

15. A RESUMÉ shows one's QUALIFICATIONs.

16. A SATIRE's purpose is to SCORN.

17. Someone VORACIOUS is very HUNGRY.

18. Something DUBIOUS is without CERTAINTY.

19. A GUFFAW is a big LAUGH.

20. A SYLLABUS is a plan for a COURSE.

QUICK QUIZ #2

1. **D** Something TRITE lacks ORIGINALITY.

2. **C** A WHISTLE is used by a REFEREE to keep order.

3. **C** LUBRICATE means to make SLIPPERY.

4. **A** BARTER means an exchange of GOODs.

5. **D** A HULL is a type of COVERING.

6. **A** ADROIT means having SKILL.

7. **B** IMPROVISED means done without REHEARSAL.

8. **B** You cannot READ something that is INDECIPHERABLE.

9. **C** The purpose of an INTOXICANT is to EXCITE.

QUICK QUIZ #3

1. Defining relationship: *Lassitude* means a lack of *energy*.

2. Defining relationship: *Castigate* means *scold* a lot.

3. No defining relationship

4. No defining relationship

5. No defining relationship

6. Defining relationship: A *castaway* is something you *discard*.

7. Defining relationship: A *stockroom* contains *supplies*.

8. Defining relationship: Something *latent* does not *manifest* itself.

9. No defining relationship

10. Defining relationship: *Ratify* means to give *approval*.

11. No defining relationship

12. No defining relationship

13. Defining relationship: A *melee* is marked by *confusion*.

14. Defining relationship: Something *terse* is not *superfluous*.

15. No defining relationship

16. Defining relationship: Someone with *charisma* has a lot of *charm*.

17. Defining relationship: Something *abrasive* causes *irritation*.

18. No defining relationship

19. No defining relationship

20. No defining relationship

21. Defining relationship: *Truncate* means to cut *short*.

22. No defining relationship

23. No defining relationship

24. Defining relationship: *Inaugurate* means to bring about a *beginning*.

25. No defining relationship

26. No defining relationship

27. Defining relationship: Something *wholesome* promotes *health*.

28. Defining relationship: Something *innocuous* will not cause *harm*.

29. Defining relationship: *Rationalize* means try to make *reasonable*.

30. No defining relationship

QUICK QUIZ #4

1. **D** Someone INCORRIGIBLE is incapable of REFORM. Eliminate (B) and (C) because they do not have a defining relationship.

2. **A** Something OPALESCENT does not have the quality of being MONOCHROMATIC. Eliminate (C), (D), and (E) because they do not have a defining relationship.

3. **C** TRANSMIGRATE means to change STATE. Eliminate (A) and (E) because they do not have a defining relationship.

4. **E** The purpose of an INTOXICANT is to EXCITE. Eliminate (A), (B), and (C) because they do not have a defining relationship.

5. **C** Something INEXORABLE is not possible to AVOID. Eliminate (A) and (E) because they do not have a defining relationship.

6. **A** Someone SALACIOUS possesses LUST. Eliminate (C) and (D) because they do not have a defining relationship.

7. **B** OBFUSCATE means to CONFUSE. Eliminate (A), (C), (D), and (E) because they do not have a defining relationship.

8. **D** Something TUMID is marked by SWELLING. Eliminate (A), (B), and (E) because they do not have a defining relationship.

9. **C** GENUFLECT is an action that indicates RESPECT. Eliminate (B), (D), and (E) because they do not have a defining relationship.

QUICK QUIZ #5

1. ??? : TROOPS ::
assemble : crowd

This answer choice pair has a defining relationship. The sentence that proves it: *Assemble* means to gather together a *crowd*. Now Work Backward with that sentence. Could something mean to gather together TROOPS? Yes. A word like that could exist. Leave this answer choice in—it could be the right answer.

2. ??? : PROFIT ::
arable : plowing

This answer choice pair has a defining relationship. The sentence that proves it: *Arable* means suitable for *plowing*. Now Work Backward with that sentence. Could something mean suitable for PROFIT? The sentence doesn't make much sense. Therefore, this answer choice probably isn't right—cross it out.

3. ??? : DISSOLUTE ::
luminary : wealth

This answer choice pair doesn't have a defining relationship. A *luminary* is a famous person—not necessarily a rich one. Therefore, this can't be the right answer. Cross it out.

4. EXPEL : ??? ::
touch : dab

This answer choice pair has a defining relationship. The sentence that proves it: *Dab* means to *touch* gently or lightly. Now Work Backward with that sentence. Could something mean to EXPEL gently or lightly? The sentence doesn't make sense anymore. Therefore, this answer choice can't be right—cross it out.

5. ??? : CONDESCENSION ::
   kowtow : deference

   This answer choice pair has a defining relationship. The sentence that proves it: *Kowtow* means to show *deference*. Now Work Backward with that sentence. Could something mean to show CONDESCENSION? Sure. A word like that could exist. Leave this answer choice in—it could be the right answer.

6. ??? : DECLARE ::
   exhibit : display

   This answer choice pair has a defining relationship. The sentence that proves it: *Exhibit* means to *display* publicly. Now Work Backward with that sentence. Could something mean to DECLARE publicly? Sure. A word like that could exist. Leave this answer choice in—it could be right.

7. ??? : FERMENTATION ::
   solvent : distillation

   This answer choice pair doesn't have a defining relationship. Therefore, it can't be right—cross it out.

8. SADNESS : ??? ::
   word : laconic

   This answer choice pair has a defining relationship. The sentence that proves it: Someone *laconic* is sparing of *words*. Now Work Backward with that sentence. Could someone or something be sparing of SADNESS? The sentence doesn't make much sense. Therefore, this answer choice probably isn't right—cross it out.

9. ??? : TUMULTUOUS ::
   ruse : deceptive

   This answer choice pair has a defining relationship. The sentence that proves it: A *ruse* has the quality of being *deceptive*. Now Work Backward with that sentence. Could something have the quality of being TUMULTUOUS? Sure. A word like that could exist. Leave this answer choice in—it could be right.

Quick Quiz #6

1. **B**

(A) Defining relationship: A *memorial* serves as a *reminder*.
    Work Backward: Could a PECCADILLO serve as a SIN? Probably not.

(B) Defining relationship: A *lapse* is a small *error*.
    Work Backward: Could a PECCADILLO be a small SIN? Yes.

(C) No defining relationship

(D) Defining relationship: *Asperity* means *rigor*.
    Work Backward: Could a PECCADILLO mean a SIN? Yes.

(E) No defining relationship

2. **A**

(A) Defining relationship: *Bolt* means to *swallow* hastily.
    Work Backward: Could LAM mean to FLEE hastily? Yes.

(B) No defining relationship

(C) No defining relationship

(D) No defining relationship

(E) No defining relationship

3. **E**

(A) No defining relationship

(B) Defining relationship: A *prelude* is the beginning of an *event*.
Work Backward: Could a LIBRETTO be the beginning of an OPERA? Yes.

(C) Defining relationship: A *buttress* provides *stability*.
Work Backward: Could a LIBRETTO provide an OPERA? Probably not.

(D) Defining relationship: *Euphony* is a pleasing *sound*.
Work Backward: Could a LIBRETTO be a pleasing OPERA? Probably not.

(E) Defining relationship: A *script* is the text of a *play*.
Work Backward: Could a LIBRETTO be the text of an OPERA? Yes.

4. **E**

(A) No defining relationship

(B) No defining relationship

(C) Defining relationship: A *stockade* is a type of *defense*.
Work Backward: Could CACHET be a type of APPROBATION? Yes.

(D) No defining relationship

(E) Defining relationship: A *stigma* is a mark of *disgrace*.
Work Backward: Could CACHET mean a mark of APPROBATION? Yes.

5. **B**

(A) Defining relationship: *Dally* means to act in a *playful* manner.
Work Backward: Could NIP mean to act in a NUMB manner? Probably not.

(B) Defining relationship: *Augment* means to make *greater*.
Work Backward: Could NIP mean to make NUMB? Yes.

(C) No defining relationship

(D) No defining relationship

(E) No defining relationship

6. **C**

(A) No defining relationship

(B) No defining relationship

(C) Defining relationship: Something *indeterminate* is impossible to *fix*.
Work Backward: Could something INDELIBLE be impossible to ERASE? Yes.

(D) No defining relationship

(E) No defining relationship

7. **D**

(A) No defining relationship

(B) Defining relationship: Someone *craven* lacks *bravery*.
Work Backward: Could someone HALE lack VIGOR? No.

(C) No defining relationship

(D) Defining relationship: Someone *circumspect* possesses *prudence*.
Work Backward: Could someone HALE possess VIGOR? Yes.

(E) Defining relationship: Someone *intransigent* will not make a *concession*.
Work Backward: Could someone HALE not make a VIGOR? Probably not.

8. **A**

(A) Defining relationship: An *encyclopedia* is a series of *books*.
Work Backward: Could an ODYSSEY be a series of ADVENTURES? Yes.

(B) No defining relationship

(C) Defining relationship: A *chapter* is a type of *unit*.
Work Backward: Could an ODYSSEY be a type of ADVENTURE? Yes.

(D) Defining relationship: An *itinerary* is a plan for a *trip*.
Work Backward: Could an ODYSSEY be a plan for an ADVENTURE? Probably not.

(E) Defining relationship: An *incivility* is characterized by *rudeness*.
Work Backward: Could an ODYSSEY be characterized by an ADVENTURE? Yes.

9. **B**

(A) No defining relationship

(B) Defining relationship: Someone *stolid* shows no *emotion*.
Work Backward: Could someone DAUNTLESS show no FEAR? Yes.

(C) No defining relationship

(D) Defining relationship: Someone *depraved* is full of *corruption*.
Work Backward: Could someone DAUNTLESS be full of FEAR? Yes.

(E) Defining relationship: Someone *brazen* possesses *boldness*.
Work Backward: Could someone DAUNTLESS possess FEAR? No.

Quick Quiz #7

1. same side

2. different sides

3. same side

4. same side

5. same side

6. different sides

7. same side

8. different sides

9. same side

10. different sides

PRACTICE QUESTIONS #1

1. **A** Make a sentence with the stem words. An AVIARY is a house for a BIRD. Now apply the sentence to the answer choices. Is a *stable* a house for a *horse*? Yes. However, don't forget to check the remaining answer choices just to make sure. Is a *dam* a house for a *beaver*? Yes again. Is a *field* a house for a *cow*? No. Is a *den* a house for a *fox*? Sure. Is a *nest* a house for a *hamster*? No. You're left with (A), (B), and (D).

   When you have more than one answer choice remaining after you apply the sentence, what should you do? Make the sentence more specific. How about: An AVIARY is a man-made house for a BIRD. Is a *stable* a man-made house for a *horse*? Yes. Is a *dam* a man-made house for a *beaver*? No. Is a *den* a man-made house for a *fox*? No. The best answer, then, is (A).

2. **A** Make a sentence with the stem words. METHANE is a type of FUEL. Now apply the sentence to the answer choices. Is a *lathe* a type of *machine*? If you don't know what a *lathe* is, you have to leave (A) in. Is *ether* a type of *tool*? No—*ether* is a gas. Is a *drill* a type of *screw*? No. Is *benzene* a type of *ring*? Not in the way you're looking for. Is a *needle* a type of *sewing*? No. Even though you don't know what *lathe* means, (A) is the only answer choice remaining. (A) is the best answer.

3. **D** Most likely, you can tell that RAMROD and RIGIDITY are similar words, but if you're not absolutely positive what RAMROD means, you can't make a sentence. Go to the answer choices and check for defining relationships. Is (A) a defining relationship? Yes. The sentence that proves it: Something *heretical* goes against *orthodoxy*. Now Work Backward with that sentence. Could RAMROD mean going against RIGIDITY? Maybe. Leave (A) in for now. Is (B) a defining relationship? No. Just because something is *decorative* doesn't mean it possesses *flamboyance*. Similarly, just because something has *flamboyance* doesn't mean it's *decorative*. Cross out (B). Is (C) a defining relationship? No. If you look up *luminous* in the dictionary, it'll say something about giving off light—not *transparency*. Similarly, if you look up *transparency* in the dictionary, you won't see anything about *luminous*. Eliminate (C). Is (D) a defining relationship? Yes. The sentence that proves it: Something *hectic* is marked by *confusion*. Now Work Backward with that sentence. Could something RAMROD be marked by RIGIDITY? Sure. Leave (D) in. Is (E) a defining relationship? If you don't know what *brackish* means, you have to leave it in.

   You're left with (A), (D), and (E). Now, you sort of know that RAMROD and RIGIDITY are similar words. Therefore, (A) can't be right. (D) could still work.

(E) you still don't know anything about. At this point, guess. When you're left with something that works and something you don't know, go with what works. The best answer is (D).

4. **A** Make a sentence with the stem words. A SHELTER provides PROTECTION. Now apply that sentence to the answer choices. Does an *incentive* provide *motivation*? Yes. Does a *shield* provide *injury*? No. Does an *antiseptic* provide a *cure*? No—be careful. An *antiseptic* sterilizes; it doesn't necessarily *cure*. Does an *inoculation* provide *longevity*? If you don't know what *inoculation* means, you can't cross (D) out. Does an *inundation* provide a *flood*? No—an *inundation* is a *flood*. You're down to (A) and (D). As always, go with what works. (A) is the best answer.

5. **C** Make a sentence with the stem words. Something IMPREGNABLE is not susceptible to ATTACK. Is something *phlegmatic* not susceptible to *calm*? If you don't know what *phlegmatic* means, you have to leave (A) in. Is something *salutary* not susceptible to *health*? No—*salutary* has something to do with *health*. Is something *immortal* not susceptible to *death*? Looks good, but go through the remaining answer choices. Is something *ephemeral* not susceptible to *brevity*? No. Is something *iridescent* not susceptible to *color*. No—*iridescent* has something to do with *color*. You're left with (A) and (C). Go with what you know. The best answer is (C).

6. **E** If you can't make a sentence, go to the answer choices and test for defining relationships. Is (A) a defining relationship? No. If you look up *insurgency*, you won't see anything about *oppressive*, and if you look up *oppressive*, you won't see anything about *insurgency*. Cross out (A). Is (B) a defining relationship? Yes. The sentence that proves it: Someone in his *desolation* is all *alone*. Now Work Backward with the sentence. Could someone in his DOCILITY be all INTRACTABLE? Maybe. Leave (B) in. Is (C) a defining relationship? No. If you look up *anticipation*, you won't see anything about *satisfied*, and vice-versa. Eliminate (C). Is (D) a defining relationship? Yes. The sentence that proves it: You have a *victory* over something that is *conquered*. Now Work Backward with that sentence. Could you have DOCILITY over something that is INTRACTABLE? Not really. How can you have DOCILITY over something? Eliminate (D). Is (E) a defining relationship? If you don't know what *intrepidity* means, you can't cross out (E).

You're down to (B) and (E). Go with what works—pick (B). In this case, however, the best answer is actually (E). INTRACTABLE means stubborn, and *intrepidity* means fearlessness. Someone in his DOCILITY is not INTRACTABLE, and someone in his *intrepidity* is not *fearful*.

Note that even though you missed the question, you're doing the right thing. You followed the techniques and, at the end, had a 50 percent chance of getting the question right—even though you didn't know what INTRACTABLE means.

7.   **E**   You probably know both words, but if you can't make a good sentence, go to the answer choices and test for defining relationships. Is (A) a defining relationship? Yes. The sentence that proves it: *Enlistment* is the enrollment of a *soldier*. Now Work Backward with the sentence. Could CORONATION mean the enrollment of a ROYAL? No—you can't really enroll into royalty, can you? Eliminate (A). Is (B) a defining relationship? No. Be careful—if you look up *excursion*, do you see something about an *adventurer*? No. If you look up *adventurer*, do you see something about an *excursion*? No. Cross out (B). Is (C) a defining relationship? No. If you look up *trial*, you don't see *mediator*, and if you look up *mediator*, you don't see *trial*. Eliminate (C). Is (D) a defining relationship? Yes. The sentence that proves it: *Commencement* is the graduation of a *student*. Now Work Backward with that sentence. Could CORONATION mean the graduation of a ROYAL? Clearly not. Cross out (D). Is (E) a defining relationship? If you don't know what *frocking* means, you can't eliminate (E). In fact, you shouldn't eliminate (E) because it's the only answer choice remaining. (E) is the best answer—*frocking* is the making of a *cleric* just as CORONATION is the making of a ROYAL.

8.   **C**   Chances are you don't know what SYLLOGISM or SPECIOUS means, so go to the answer choices and look for defining relationships. Is (A) a defining relationship? Yes. The sentence that proves it: A *perversion* goes against what is *conventional*. At this point, you would usually Work Backward with the sentence. However, you can't in this case because you don't know what either stem word means. So go on to (B). Is (B) a defining relationship? Not quite. *Distillation* is the process of purifying. Is (C) a defining relationship? It may not seem so, because usually *conceit* means something like arrogance. But be careful. ETS often likes to test secondary definitions of words. Leave (C) in for now. Is (D) a defining relationship? No. A *contingency* is likely to happen—not *certain*. Is (E) a defining relationship? No. A *truism* doesn't have to be *sincere*.

So you're down to (A) and (C). Because you have no idea what the stem words mean, just guess. You have a 50 percent chance of getting the question right. Go with a last resort—pick the one that has the hardest word or words. In this case, that's (C). And guess what? (C) is the best answer. A SYLLOGISM has the quality of being SPECIOUS, and a *conceit* has the quality of being *fanciful*.

Always be on the watch for secondary meanings. It's clear that a secondary definition is being used in (C) because it would be too obvious that the words are not related if the primary definition were used.

9. **E** When you can't make a sentence, go to the answer choices and look for defining relationships. Is (A) a defining relationship? Yes. The sentence that proves it: Something *overt* lacks *secrecy*. Now Work Backward with the sentence. Could something MAWKISH lack SENTIMENT? Sure. Leave (A) in. Is (B) a defining relationship? If you don't know what *rakish* means, you have to leave (B) in. Is (C) a defining relationship? If you don't know what *meretricious* means, you have to leave (C) in. Is (D) a defining relationship? No. *Paramount* means superior to all others, so if you look up *paramount*, you won't see anything about *suspicion*. Similarly, if you look up *suspicion*, you won't see anything about *paramount*. Cross out (D). Is (E) a defining relationship? If you don't know what *carping* means, you have to leave (E) in.

You're left with (A), (B), (C), and (E). Go with what works—pick (A). As it turns out, however, the best answer is (E). MAWKISH means prone to excessive SENTIMENT, and *carping* means prone to excessive *criticism*.

As stated in a previous question, it's okay to miss a question. Ultimately, you want to get as many questions right as possible, but for now, as long as you're following the techniques, you're doing the right thing. Remember, you did some great POE for this question—you had a better chance of getting the question right even though you didn't know what MAWKISH means.

PRACTICE QUESTIONS #2

1. **E** You know both of the stem words, so make a sentence. EYEGLASSES enhance VISION. Now apply that sentence to the answer choices. Does an *anvil* enhance *metal*? No. Does *attraction* enhance *desire*? Not necessarily. Does *heat* enhance *warmth*? Not really—it provides *warmth*. Does a *solution* enhance a *beaker*? Definitely not. Does a *spice* enhance *flavor*? Yes. (E) is the best answer.

2. **D** When you know both of the stem words, make a sentence. A SMITH works with METAL. Now apply that sentence to the answer choices. Does a *jeweler* work with *gold*? Not necessarily. Does a *meteorologist* work with *weather*? Sort of. Does a *hunter* work with a *rifle*? Not necessarily. Does a *carpenter* work with *wood*? Yes. Does a *gymnast* work with a *vault*? Not necessarily.

You're down to (B) and (D). If you have more than one answer choice remaining, make the sentence more specific. A SMITH works with METAL with his hands. Does a *meteorologist* work with *weather* with his hands? No. Does a *carpenter* work with *wood* with his hands? Yes. The best answer is (D).

3. **D** You know both of the stem words, so make a sentence. A SUITCASE contains CLOTHING. Now apply that sentence to the answer choices. Does a *kitchen* contain a *pantry*? Not necessarily. Does a *parasol* contain a *fringe*? Not necessarily. Does an *attaché* contain a *contract*? It could, if it were a written contract, but that's not a good defining sentence. Does an *envelope* contain a *letter*? Yes. Does an *encyclopedia* contain a *volume*? No. The best answer is (D).

4. **E** You know both of the stem words, so make a sentence. HURL means to PITCH. Now apply that sentence to the answer choices. Does *flag* mean to *tire*? Yes. Does *carp* mean to *fault*? Yes. Does *truckle* mean to *attend*? If you don't know what *truckle* means, you can't eliminate (C). Does *pore* mean to *meditate*? No. Does *seize* mean to *take*? Yes.

    You're left with more than one answer choice—(A), (B), (C), and (E)—so make the sentence more specific. HURL means to PITCH with force. Does *flag* mean to *tire* with force? No. Does *carp* mean to *fault* with force? No. Does *truckle* mean to *attend* with force? You may not know what *truckle* means, but you do know that you can't *attend* with force. Does *seize* mean to *take* with force? Yes. The best answer is (E).

5. **A** Most likely, you don't know what RECONDITE means. When you can't make a sentence, go to the answer choices and test for defining relationships. Is (A) a defining relationship? Yes. The sentence that proves it: Something *illegible* is hard to *decipher*. Now Work Backward with that sentence. Could something RECONDITE be hard to COMPREHEND? Sure. Is (B) a defining relationship? Yes. The sentence that proves it: *Fastidious* means you *care* excessively. Could RECONDITE mean you COMPREHEND excessively? Doesn't make sense, so eliminate (B). Is (C) a defining relationship? No. If you look up *treacherous*, you won't necessarily see *trick*, and vice versa. Is (D) a defining relationship? Yes. The sentence that proves it: Someone who is *credulous* has a tendency to *believe*. Now Work Backward with that sentence. Could someone RECONDITE have a tendency to COMPREHEND? Maybe. Is (E) a defining relationship? No. If you look up *unforgiving*, you won't see *condone*, and if you look up *condone*, you won't see *unforgiving*.

    You're left with (A) and (D). Which sentence do you feel is stronger? Probably (A). It doesn't make complete sense to say that someone has a tendency to COMPREHEND. (A) is a good guess—it's the best answer.

6. **C** If you don't know what UNEQUIVOCAL means, you can't make a sentence. Therefore, go to the answer choices and look for defining relationships. Is (A) a defining relationship? No. Just because someone is *officious* doesn't mean he *reprimands*. Is (B) a defining relationship? No. If you look up *staid*, you don't see *deride*, and when you look up *deride*, you don't see *staid*. Is (C) a defining relationship? Yes. You cannot *overcome* something that is *insuperable*. Now Work Backward with that sentence. You cannot QUESTION something that is UNEQUIVOCAL. That could make sense. Is (D) a defining relationship? Don't eliminate it if you don't know what *abut* means. Is (E) a defining relationship? Yes. The sentence that proves it: Something *belated* has been *delayed*. Now Work Backward. Something UNEQUIVOCAL has been QUESTIONED. That makes sense.

You're left with (C), (D), and (E). What now? Do you know whether UNEQUIVOCAL and QUESTION are on the same side of the fence or different sides? UNEQUIVOCAL is a positive word, so the stem words are on different sides. The correct answer, then, must also be on different sides. Does (C) contain words on different sides? Yes. You don't know about (D) since it has a word you don't know. What about (E)? The words are on the same side, so cross it out.

The remaining answer choices are (C) and (D). Go with what works over what you don't know. The best answer is (C).

7. **C** If you can't make a sentence, go to the answer choices and look for defining relationships. Is (A) a defining relationship? You can't eliminate it if you don't know what *polemic* means. Is (B) a defining relationship? No. If you look up *alliteration*, you don't see *rhythmic*, and if you look up *rhythmic*, you don't see *alliteration*. Is (C) a defining relationship? Be careful—it looks as if *transport* has a secondary definition that you don't know. Leave it in. Is (D) a defining relationship? No. If you look up *phantasm*, it doesn't say *imaginative*, and vice versa. Is (E) a defining relationship? If you don't know what *subjunction* means, you can't cross it out.

You're down to (A), (C), and (E)—each answer choice contains a word you don't know. What now? You can't use Sides of the Fence since you don't know what some of the words in the answer choices mean. At this point, then, guess. You have a one-in-three chance of getting the question right, which isn't bad, especially if you aren't sure what OXYMORON means. How about picking the answer choice that has the hardest word or words? That would probably be (A) or (C). As it turns out, the answer is (C). An OXYMORON has the quality of being INCONGRUOUS, and a *transport* has the quality of being *pleasurable*.

Always be on the watch for secondary meanings. It's clear that a secondary definition is being used in (C) because *transport* is being used as a different part of speech than usual.

8. **B** If you can't make a good sentence, go to the answer choices and look for defining relationships. Is (A) a defining relationship? You can't eliminate (A) if you don't know what *emend* means. Is (B) a defining relationship? You can't eliminate (B) if you don't know what *fulminate* or *invective* means. Is (C) a defining relationship? Yes. *Hyperbole* means you *exaggerate* a lot. Now Work Backward with the sentence. Does SIGNAL mean you TRANSMIT a lot? Doesn't make a lot of sense, so eliminate (C). Is (D) a defining relationship? No. Don't get stuck on the phrase "an affront to humanity." *Affront* means offense. If you look it up, you won't see anything about *humanity*, or vice versa. Eliminate (D). Is (E) a defining relationship? Yes. The sentence that proves it: *Trespass* means to invade *property*. Now Work Backward with the sentence. Does TRANSMIT mean to invade SIGNAL? Doesn't make a lot of sense, so cross out (E).

    You're down to (A) and (B). As a last resort, go with the hardest word or words. Pick (B). As it turns out, (B) is the best answer. TRANSMIT means to send forth a SIGNAL, and *fulminate* means to send forth an *invective*.

9. **B** If you don't know what DESCRY means, you can't make a sentence. Therefore, go to the answer choices and look for defining relationships. Is (A) a defining relationship? No. *Titter* means laugh in a nervous way. Is (B) a defining relationship? If you don't know what *champ* means, you can't cross it out. Is (C) a defining relationship? Yes. *Stutter* means to *speak* in an indistinct way. Now Work Backward with that sentence. Could DESCRY mean to DETECT in an indistinct way? Doesn't make a lot of sense. Eliminate it. Is (D) a defining relationship? No. *Slurp* means to eat or drink in a noisy way. Is (E) a defining relationship? Yes. The sentence that proves it: *Counterfeit* means to *imitate* with the intent to deceive. Now Work Backward with that sentence. Could DESCRY mean to DETECT with the intent to deceive? Probably not. You're left with (B)—a choice that contains a word you don't know. But that's okay. It's fine to pick (B) if you're able to eliminate the other answer choices by using defining relationships along with Working Backward. (B) is the best answer. DESCRY means to DETECT, and *champ* means to *chew*.

PRACTICE QUESTIONS #3

1. **A** When you know both of the stem words, make a sentence. A DRUM MAJOR leads or guides a BAND. Now apply that sentence to the answer choices. Does a *preacher* lead or guide a *congregation*? Yes. Does an *architect* lead or guide a *designer*? No. Does a *dancer* lead or guide a *corps*? If you don't know what *corps* means, you can't cross it out. Does an *adept* lead or guide a *beginner*? Not necessarily. Does a *painter* lead or guide a *viewer*? No. You're left with (A) and (C)—an answer choice that works and an answer choice that contains a word you don't know. Go with what you know. The best answer is (A).

2. **D** You probably know both of the stem words, but if you're not sure how the stem words relate, don't make a sentence. Instead, go to the answer choices and test for defining relationships. Is (A) a defining relationship? Yes. The sentence that proves it: A *lampoon* is a work of *ridicule*. Now Work Backward with that sentence. Could a SONATA be a work of MOVEMENT? Doesn't make a lot of sense. Is (B) a defining relationship? Yes. The sentence that proves it: The beginning of a *novel* is the *prologue*. Now Work Backward with that sentence. Could the beginning of a SONATA be a MOVEMENT? Maybe. Is (C) a defining relationship? Yes. The sentence that proves it: A *tableau* is presented on a *stage*. Now Work Backward with that sentence. Could a SONATA be presented on a MOVEMENT? No. Is (D) a defining relationship? Yes. The sentence that proves it: A *poem* is made up of *stanzas*. Now Work Backward with that sentence. Could a SONATA be made up of MOVEMENTS? Yes. Is (E) a defining relationship? No. If you look up *fable*, you won't necessarily see *narrative*, and if you look up *narrative*, you won't necessarily see *fable*.

   You're left, then, with (B) and (D). Which one is better? Well, which is more likely: The beginning of a SONATA is a MOVEMENT, or a SONATA is made up of MOVEMENTS? Just pick one—you have a 50 percent chance of getting the question right. The best answer is (D).

3. **C** You know both of the stem words, so you can probably make a sentence. How about: VIGILANCE means being very ALERT? Now that you have a sentence, apply it to the answer choices. Does *flippancy* mean being very *serious*? No. Does *garrulity* mean being very *verbose*? No—be careful. Just because someone is talkative doesn't mean he's wordy. Does *skepticism* mean being very *doubting*? Yes. Does *judiciousness* mean being very *merciful*? Not necessarily. Does *sentience* mean being very *attentive*? No. The best answer, then, is (C).

4. **B** You know both of the words, so try to make a sentence. How about: INCOME determines WEALTH? Apply that sentence to the answer choices. Does *performance* determine *salary*? Not necessarily. Does *hunger* determine *appetite*? Yes. Does *medicine* determine *health*? Not always. Does *affection* determine *feeling*? No. Does *hurricane* determine *wind*? Not quite. The best answer is (B).

This analogy is a good example of why you shouldn't rush. Carefully applying the sentence gets you to (B). Speed makes both (A) and (C) attractive.

5. **C** When you can't make a sentence, go to the answer choices and look for defining relationships. Is (A) a defining relationship? No. If you look up *submissive*, you don't see *resign*, and if you look up *resign*, you don't see *submissive*. Is (B) a defining relationship? Yes. The sentence that proves it: You can't *challenge* something that is *incontrovertible*. Now Work Backward with that sentence. You can't BELONG to something that is EXTRINSIC. Huh? (B) can't be right. Is (C) a defining relationship? Yes. The sentence that proves it: Something *evanescent* does not *endure*. Now Work Backward with that sentence. Something EXTRINSIC does not BELONG. Makes sense, right? Is (D) a defining relationship? No—something that is *protuberant* doesn't have to *intrude*. Is (E) a defining relationship? Yes. The sentence that proves it: Something *stigmatic* *isolates* you. Now Work Backward with that sentence. Does something EXTRINSIC BELONG to you? Doesn't make sense. The best answer, then, is (C).

6. **D** When you're not sure about a sentence, go to the answer choices and look for defining relationships. Is (A) a defining relationship? Yes. The sentence that proves it: *Reclaim* means to carry out a *rescue*. Now Work Backward with that sentence. Could RECANT mean to carry out a BELIEF? Yes. Is (B) a defining relationship? No. *Recoil* means to shrink away or withdraw—not necessarily from *adoration*. Is (C) a defining relationship? No. If you look up *exact*, you won't see anything about *requisition*, and vice versa. Is (D) a defining relationship? Yes. The sentence that proves it: *Repeal* means to take back a *law*. Now Work Backward with that sentence. Could RECANT mean to take back a BELIEF? Yes. Is (E) a defining relationship? No. If you look up *calibrate*, you don't see *rectitude*, and if you look up *rectitude*, you don't see *calibrate*.

You're left with (A) and (D). What now? Well, try Sides of the Fence. (A) has words on the same side, while (D) has words on different sides. Are RECANT and BELIEF on the same side or different sides? Different. Since the stem words are different, the correct answer has to have different words, too. So the best answer is (D).

7.   **E**   When you can't make a sentence with the stem words, go to the answer choices and look for defining relationships. Is (A) a defining relationship? No. Someone *philanthropic* doesn't have to possess *grace*. Is (B) a defining relationship? You can't cross it out if you don't know what *vainglorious* means. Is (C) a defining relationship? No. If you look up *priggish*, you won't see *integrity*, and if you look up *integrity*, you won't see *priggish*. Is (D) a defining relationship? Yes. The sentence that proves it: Someone *lecherous* lacks *decency*. Now Work Backward with that sentence. Could someone PENURIOUS lack FRUGALITY? It's possible. Is (E) a defining relationship? If you don't know what *perspicacious* means, you can't cross it out.

You're down to (B), (D), and (E). As always, go with what works. Pick (D). As it turns out, however, (E) is the best answer. Someone PENURIOUS is characterized by a lot of FRUGALITY, and someone *perspicacious* is characterized by a lot of *insight*.

If you missed this problem, but got it down to (B), (D), and (E), you're on the right track. For now, you want to be concerned with whether you're applying techniques correctly. And remember—you had a one-in-three chance of getting the problem right even without knowing what PENURIOUS means.

8.   **A**   Chances are you don't know what OBLOQUY means, so you can't make a sentence. Since that's the case, go to the answer choices and look for defining relationships. Is (A) a defining relationship? You can't eliminate it if you don't know what *panegyric* means. Is (B) a defining relationship? No. *Slander* can be *inflammatory*, but it doesn't have to be. Is (C) a defining relationship? You can't eliminate it if you don't know what *diatribe* means. Is (D) a defining relationship? You can't eliminate it if you don't know what *calumny* means. Is (E) a defining relationship? No. If you look up *travesty*, you won't see *contemptuous*, and if you look up *contemptuous*, you won't see *travesty*.

You're left with (A), (C), and (D)—each of which contains a word you don't know. At this point, guess. A good last resort to use is to pick the choice that has the hardest words. That's (A), and indeed, (A) is the best answer.

9.   **A**   You may know what both stem words mean, but if you're not sure about the relationship, don't make a sentence. Use defining relationships instead. Is (A) a defining relationship? Yes. The sentence that proves it: Something *redolent* is full of *fragrance*. Now Work Backward with that sentence. Could something LURID be full of MELODRAMA? Yes. Is (B) a defining relationship? No. Something *determinate* is fixed; it doesn't have to have *definition*. Is (C) a defining relationship? No. If you look up *alien*, you won't see *distinction*, and if you look up *distinction*, you won't see *alien*. Is (D) a defining relationship? You

can't eliminate it if you don't know what *metaphysical* means. Is (E) a defining relationship? You can't eliminate it if you don't know what *fortuitous* means.

You're left with (A), (D), and (E). One answer choice works and the other two contain words you don't know. Go with what works. The best answer is (A).

PRACTICE QUESTIONS #4

1. **D** When you know both of the stem words, make a sentence. RECOUP means to regain a LOSS. Since you flipped the stem words in making the sentence, be sure to flip the words in the answer choices when you apply the sentence. Does *recount* mean to regain a *tale*? No. Does *recompense* mean to regain *damage*? No. Does *record* mean to regain a *document*? No. Does *recuperate* mean to regain *health*? Yes. Does *reciprocate* mean to regain *generosity*? Not quite. The best answer is (D).

2. **A** When you know both of the stem words, make a sentence. Someone with APATHY is INDIFFERENT. Now apply that sentence to the answer choices. Someone with *melancholy* is *sad*. That's true. Someone with *enthusiasm* is *zealous*. Not necessarily. Someone with *stoicism* is *emotional*. No. Someone with *talent* is *adequate*. Not quite. Someone with *discretion* is *secretive*. Not necessarily. The best answer is (A).

3. **E** When you know both of the stem words, make a sentence. If you're not sure what part of speech FLEECE is, check the second word in each of the answer choices—each is a noun. Therefore, FLEECE is a noun. So a good sentence using the stem words might be the following: A SHEEP is covered with FLEECE. Now apply the sentence to the answer choices. Is a *duck* covered with a *bill*? No. Is an *insect* covered with an *arthropod*? If you don't know what *arthropod* means, then you can't cross it out. Is a *lion* covered with *courage*? No. Is a *kangaroo* covered with a *pouch*? No. Is a *fish* covered with *scales*? Yes. (B) contains a word you don't know, and (E) works. Go with what works. The best answer is (E).

4. **B** If you're not sure what REBATE means, then you can't make a sentence. Go to the answer choices, then, and test for defining relationships. Is (A) a defining relationship? Yes. The sentence that proves it: *Tax* means to make a *demand* on. Now Work Backward with that sentence. Could REBATE mean to make a FORCE on? Probably not. Is (B) a defining relationship? Yes. The sentence that proves it: *Blunt* means to reduce the *sharpness* of. Now Work Backward with that sentence. Could REBATE mean to reduce the FORCE of? Sure. Is (C) a defining relationship? Yes. The sentence that proves it: *Glean* means

to gather *information*. Could REBATE mean to gather FORCE? Sure. Is (D) a defining relationship? Yes. The sentence that proves it: *Appease* means to make *calm*. Now Work Backward with that sentence. Could REBATE mean to make FORCE? Doesn't make sense. Is (E) a defining relationship? Yes. The sentence that proves it: *Cleave* means to make a *division*. Now Work Backward with that sentence. Could REBATE mean to make a FORCE? Not likely.

The remaining answer choices are (B) and (C). What can you do now? Try using Sides of the Fence. If you sort of know what REBATE means, then you might know REBATE and FORCE are on different sides. The right answer, then, has to be on different sides. *Blunt* and *sharpness* in (B) are on different sides, so leave it in. *Glean* and *information* are on the same side, so it can't work. The best answer is (B).

5. **C** When you know both of the stem words, make a sentence. A TAMBOURINE is a type of INSTRUMENT. Now apply that sentence to the stem words. Is a *scene* a type of *tableau*? Not necessarily. Is a *ship* a type of *yacht*? Again, not necessarily. Is a *chaise* a type of *vehicle*? If you don't know what *chaise* means, don't cross it out. Is an *agenda* a type of *meeting*? No. Is a *solution* a type of *chemistry*? No. The best answer has to be (C) because it's the only remaining answer choice.

6. **E** If you don't know what ANODYNE means, then you can't make a sentence. Go to the answer choices, then, and look for defining relationships. Is (A) a defining relationship? No. Be careful. You might think a *diet*'s purpose is to *lighten*, but it isn't. We often use *diet* in association with losing weight, but the definition of the word is actually food or drink that is regularly consumed. Eliminate (A). Is (B) a defining relationship? No. If you look up *antiseptic*, you won't see *promote*, and if you look up *promote*, you won't see *antiseptic*. Is (C) a defining relationship? No—a *vitamin* doesn't necessarily *invigorate*. Is (D) a defining relationship? No. A *drug* doesn't have to *prevent*. For example, a *drug* could ease. Is (E) a defining relationship? Yes. The sentence that proves it: The purpose of a *catalyst* is to *hasten*. Now Work Backward with that sentence. Could the purpose of an ANODYNE be to ASSUAGE? Yes. (E) is the only answer choice that is a defining relationship—and Work Backward-able—so it has to be the best answer.

7. **E** If you can't make a sentence, then go to the answer choices and look for defining relationships. Is (A) a defining relationship? If you're not sure what *cursory* means, then you can't eliminate it. Is (B) a defining relationship? No—an *effigy* is a crude representation of a person, usually one who is hated,

but an *effigy* doesn't have to be *slanderous*. Is (C) a defining relationship? If you don't know what *sophism* means, then you can't cross it out. Is (D) a defining relationship? No. A *provocation* incites—so it doesn't necessarily have anything to do with *irritating*. Is (E) a defining relationship? If you're not sure what *camp* means, then you can't cross it out.

You're left with (A), (C), and (E), each of which contains a word you don't know. At this point, just guess. Try picking the answer choice with the hardest word or words. It's really a toss-up as to which one contains the hardest word or words. So just pick a choice and go. As it turns out, the best answer is (E). An APHORISM has the quality of being CONCISE, and *camp* has the quality of being *theatrical*. Note the use of *camp*'s secondary definition.

8. **E** If you're not sure what INCONTINENT means, then go to the answer choices and look for defining relationships. Is (A) a defining relationship? No. If you look up *impudent*, you're not going to see *suavity*, and if you look up *suavity*, you're not going to see *impudent*. Is (B) a defining relationship? Yes. The sentence that proves it: Someone *naive* is an easy prey for *deception*. Now Work Backward with that sentence. Could someone INCONTINENT be an easy prey for RESTRAINT? Doesn't make a lot of sense. Is (C) a defining relationship? Yes. The sentence that proves it: Someone *impenitent* does not have regret for his *sins*. Now Work Backward with that sentence. Could someone INCONTINENT not have regret for his RESTRAINT? Again, doesn't make a lot of sense. Is (D) a defining relationship? Yes. The sentence that proves it: Someone *covetous* possesses *desire*. Now Work Backward with that sentence. Could someone INCONTINENT possess RESTRAINT? Sure. Is (E) a defining relationship? Yes. The sentence that proves it: Someone *impolitic* lacks *tact*. Now Work Backward with that sentence. Could someone INCONTINENT lack RESTRAINT? Yes.

You're down to (D) and (E). At this point, think about Sides of the Fence. (D) has words on the same side; (E) has words on different sides. So ask yourself: Are INCONTINENT and RESTRAINT on the same side or different sides? The answer: Different sides. Therefore, the answer is (E).

9. **A** If you don't know what CHARY means, then you can't make a sentence. Go to the answer choices, then, and test for defining relationships. Is (A) a defining relationship? Yes. The sentence that proves it: Someone *munificent* is not *stinting*. Now Work Backward with that sentence. Could someone CHARY be not TRUSTFUL? Yes. Is (B) a defining relationship? No. Be careful—if you look up *pragmatic*, you won't see *irrational*, and if you look up *irrational*, you won't see *pragmatic*. Is (C) a defining relationship? *Mulish* means stubborn—and just because you're stubborn, doesn't mean you can't be *forgiving*. Is (D) a defining

relationship? No. Just because someone is *treacherous* doesn't mean she is also *deceiving*. Is (E) a defining relationship? No. If you look up *cynical*, you won't see *quibbling*, and if you look up *quibbling*, you won't see *cynical*. The only answer choice that works is (A). (A) is the best answer.

PRACTICE QUESTIONS #5

1. **B** When you know both of the stem words, make a sentence. A good sentence might be: A WOLF is a type of CANINE. Now apply that sentence to the answer choices. Is an *alligator* a type of *crocodile*? No. Is a *shrimp* a type of *crustacean*? Yes. Is a *tadpole* a type of *frog*? No. Is a *horse* a type of *hock*? No. Is a *goose* a type of *gaggle*? No. The best answer is (B).

2. **E** When you know both of the words, make a sentence. A SENTRY's job is to GUARD. Now apply that sentence to the answer choices. Is it a *judge*'s job to *legislate*? No. Is it a *student*'s job to *learn*? Not quite. Is it a *producer*'s job to *finance*? It doesn't have to be. Is it a *fireman*'s job to *save*? Again, it doesn't have to be. Is it a *conductor*'s job to *direct*? Yes. The best answer is (E).

3. **A** If you're not quite sure what the relationship is between the stem words, don't make a sentence. Go to the answer choices and test for defining relationships. Is (A) a defining relationship? If you're not sure what *ingenue* means, then you can't eliminate it. Is (B) a defining relationship? If you don't know what *elocutionist* means, then you can't eliminate it. Is (C) a defining relationship? No. A *martyr* doesn't have to be *melancholy*. Is (D) a defining relationship? If you're not sure what *recreant* means, then you can't eliminate it. Is (E) a defining relationship? No—just because a *mercenary* works for money doesn't mean he's *avaricious*.

    You're left with (A), (B), and (D). What now? Try Sides of the Fence. DANDY and FOPPISH are on the same side of the fence. If you know a little something about *ingenue*, then you might know it's on the same side of the fence as *naive*. Leave (A) in. If you don't know what *elocutionist* means at all, then you can't do anything with (B). If you know a little something about *recreant*, you know it's on the same side of the fence as *disagreeable*. Leave (D) in.

    So you're still left with (A), (B), and (D). At this point, just guess. You've managed to eliminate two answer choices, so you've got a pretty good chance of getting the question right. Pick the one that has the hardest word or words. (A), (B), and (D) are all good choices—each has a tough word. As it turns out, the best answer is (A). A DANDY has the quality of being FOPPISH, and an *ingenue* has the quality of being *naive*.

4. **B** When you know both of the stem words, make a sentence. MEANDER means to MOVE aimlessly. Now apply that sentence to the answer choices. Does *concentrate* mean to *think*? Not quite. Does *ramble* mean to *talk*? Yes. Does *lope* mean to *run*? Yes. Does *mutter* mean to *stammer*? No. Does *labor* mean to *work*? Yes. You're left with more than one answer choice, so now what? Make the sentence more specific. MEANDER means to MOVE aimlessly. Does *ramble* mean to *talk* aimlessly? Yes. Does *lope* mean to *run* aimlessly? No. Does *labor* mean to *work* aimlessly? No. The best answer is (B).

5. **B** If you're not sure what PAEAN means, then don't make a sentence. Go to the answer choices instead and test for defining relationships. Is (A) a defining relationship? No. If you look up *hymn*, you don't see *catholicism*, and if you look up *catholicism*, you don't see *hymn*. Is (B) a defining relationship? Yes. The sentence that proves it: An *elegy* is a song of *grief*. Now Work Backward with that sentence. Could a PAEAN be a song of TRIBUTE? Sure. Is (C) a defining relationship? No. If you look up *canticle*, it doesn't say *purity*, and if you look up *purity*, it doesn't say *canticle*. Is (D) a defining relationship? No. If you look up *psalm*, you don't see *gravity*, and if you look up *gravity*, you don't see *psalm*. Is (E) a defining relationship? No. A *eulogy* is a speech of praise—not of *devotion*. The only answer choice that is a defining relationship is (B), so it has to be the right answer. And it is—(B) is the best answer.

6. **C** When you can't make a sentence, go to the answer choices and look for a defining relationship. Is (A) a defining relationship? Yes. The sentence that proves it: A *cameo* shows an *image*. Now Work Backward with that sentence. Could an EPAULET show a DECORATION? Probably not—it doesn't make a lot of sense. Is (B) a defining relationship? No. An *epée* is a sword, as is a *rapier*, but the words are not related. Is (C) a defining relationship? Yes. The sentence that proves it: A *cavalry* is a military *unit*. Now Work Backward with that sentence. Could an EPAULET be a military DECORATION. Possibly. Is (D) a defining relationship? Yes. The sentence that proves it: A *lapel* is a part of a *jacket*. Now Work Backward with that sentence. Could an EPAULET be a part of a DECORATION? It could. Is (E) a defining relationship? No. A *medal* is supposed to honor—it doesn't have to be an *ornament*.

    You're left, then, with (C) and (D). Both are defining relationships, and both are Work Backward-able. So what now? At this point, just guess. You've got a 50 percent chance of getting the right answer. Pick the one that has the hardest word or words. As it turns out, the answer is (C).

7. **C** If you don't know what PERORATION means, then don't make a sentence. Go to the answer choices instead and test for defining relationships. Is (A) a defining relationship? Yes. The sentence that proves it: A *conference* is a meeting for *discussion*. Now Work Backward with that sentence. Could a PERORATION be a meeting for SPEECH? Doesn't make a lot of sense. Is (B) a defining relationship? Yes. The sentence that proves it: An *itinerary* is a plan for *travel*. Now Word Backward with that sentence. Could a PERORATION be a plan for a SPEECH? Possibly. Is (C) a defining relationship? Yes. The sentence that proves it: An *epilogue* is the end of a *play*. Now Work Backward with that sentence. Could a PERORATION be the end of a SPEECH? Yes. Is (D) a defining relationship? Yes. The sentence that proves it: *Letters* make up the *alphabet*. Now Work Backward with that sentence. Could PERORATIONS make up a SPEECH? Sure. Is (E) a defining relationship? No. *Destruction* doesn't have to deal with the ruin of a *life*.

    The remaining answer choices are (B), (C), and (D). If you don't know anything else about PERORATION, then just guess—you have a one-in-three chance of getting the question right. Pick the answer choice that has the hardest word or words. That would be either (B) or (C). Either is a good guess. As it turns out, the best answer is (C). A PERORATION is the end of a SPEECH.

8. **A** When you know both of the stem words, make a sentence. ABHOR means to DISLIKE a lot. Now apply that sentence to the answer choices. Does *venerate* mean to *esteem* a lot? It could. Does *procrastinate* mean to *delay* a lot? No—it just means to *delay*. Does *testify* mean to *affirm*? No. Does *condone* mean to *neglect* a lot? No—it means to *neglect* or overlook purposefully. Does *detract* mean to *dismiss*? No. The best answer is (A).

9. **D** When you know both of the stem words, make a sentence. TOTTER is a type of GAIT. Now apply that sentence to the answer choices. Is a *furrow* a type of *brow*? No. Is a *simper* a type of *smile*? Yes. Is a *canter* a type of *gallop*? No. Is a *stutter* a type of *speech*? Yes. Is a *deduction* a type of *thought*? No. Be careful—a *deduction* is a type of reasoning, not *thought*.

    Since you're left with more than one answer choice, make the sentence more specific. TOTTER is an unsteady GAIT. Is a *simper* an unsteady *smile*? No. Is a *stutter* an unsteady *speech*? Yes. The best answer is (D).

Reading Comprehension

THE TERRAIN OF THE MUNDANE

Practically every test taker in the world hates reading comprehension, and for a very good reason: It's incredibly boring. Well, take heart. Though we can't make the passages any less dull, we can try to make the time spent here a little less painful.

How can we do that? Well, let's talk about how the typical person approaches reading comprehension. First, he reads the passage. That means he reads the *entire* passage—each and every word. He tries to digest this information as much as possible as he reads, and then he moves on to the questions. For each question, he reads the question, goes back to the passage to find the answer, rereads the part of the passage that contains the answer, and only then goes on to the answer choices. Finally, after reading all of the answer choices, he picks the one he thinks is best.

What's wrong with this approach? There's too much reading going on. Basically, the typical person reads the passage at least twice—a big waste of time. Why is reading and rereading passages a bad idea? In order to do well on reading comprehension, you don't need to read that much. It's not *how much* you read that's important; it's *what* you read.

TYPES OF PASSAGES

Subject matter for reading comprehension is going to vary from test to test, but you can expect to see three major categories represented:

- Science
- Humanities
- Social studies

You might see one science passage, one humanities passage, and one social studies passage. Or you might see two science passages and two social studies passages. We can't predict exactly what's going to show up because you can have anywhere from to two to four passages on the Verbal section of the test.

In the end, it doesn't really matter what the subject matter of a passage is. The important thing is not to let a particular category scare you. For example, if you hate science and haven't taken a science class since high school, don't think that a science passage is necessarily going to be a killer. Often, a science passage is relatively easy. Though the jargon may be hard to get past, all the information contained in the passage is factual. Therefore, there's no need for you to do any interpreting or analyzing. The passages ETS selects are pretty cut-and-dried.

POLITICALLY CORRECT

That said, there is one type of passage in which subject matter may count—and that's when ETS uses what we call a PC (or politically correct) passage. Most of the time a PC passage falls into either the humanities or social studies category. We call it a PC passage because it deals with a topic such as women, African Americans, Native Americans, or even the environment.

What can you expect about a PC passage? Everything in the passage is going to be either neutral or positive (sometimes even inspirational) in tone. In no way can a correct answer for a question be un-PC. For example: "Women should not work in the public sphere because they are not as rational as men." That sentence is *very* un-PC, and therefore could never be the right answer. So anytime you have a passage that has a subject matter such as women or minorities, you already know a little something. You know that every right answer must be PC and that any answer choice that is not PC must be wrong.

Keep in mind that ETS, for the most part, is always PC—obviously so on a PC passage, but also on other passages that aren't explicitly PC. Think of it this way: Does ETS want to say anything controversial? No. Why not? Lawsuit, lawsuit, lawsuit. ETS's whole goal is to make money. Lawsuits mean losing money. If anyone was in any way offended by anything, ETS could be subject to a lawsuit. Think of what the National Organization for Women might say if it read the sentence, "Women should not work in the public sphere…" on the GRE. ETS ain't stupid—so it's not going to do anything stupid.

WHAT'S THE BIG IDEA?

Okay, we've established that the typical person wastes time because she reads too much. Quite simply, there's no need to read so much. In fact, reading comprehension only becomes hard when you do read too much. Remember, it's not *how much* you read that counts. It's *what* you read.

So what should you do? Well, what's the primary goal the first time you see a passage? All you really want is a general idea of what the passage is about, right? You want the gist of the passage—that is, the main idea. You don't really care about the specifics, at least not yet. In order to get the main idea of a passage, do you really need to read the entire thing? No, of course not. To find the main idea of a passage, all you have to do is read a few sentences:

- The first two sentences of the first paragraph
- The first sentence of each following paragraph
- The final sentence of the entire passage

That's it. These sentences alone are sufficient to give you the main idea.

Why can these sentences alone tell you the main idea? You need to consider what good writing is—or rather, how good writing is organized. Good writing is well structured. That means for every paragraph there has to be a *topic sentence*. A topic sentence is a sentence that tells you what's going to happen in a particular paragraph. Technically, a topic sentence can be located anywhere in a paragraph, but usually, it's the first (sometimes the second) sentence of a paragraph.

So if a topic sentence tells you what's going to take place in a paragraph, then guess what? To get the main idea, all you really need to do is read the topic sentence of each paragraph in a passage. We make you read a little more at the beginning because it's the introductory paragraph, and a little at the very end because it often provides some sort of conclusion.

REALLY?

At this point, you're probably thinking, "There's no way that I can read so few sentences and actually get the main idea." You can. But you have to practice using this technique because you're not going to be comfortable with it at first—and therefore, you're not going to like it. But trust us, it works. After reading the first sentence in a paragraph, ask yourself: "Does what I've read give me enough information to *anticipate* what's going to be discussed?" If not, then it's okay to read one or two more sentences. But don't go hog-wild. The whole point is to save valuable time by not reading so much the first time around. Remember, the very first time you see a passage, you don't need to know specifics. All you want to do is find out what is the main idea.

COGITATE AND MASTICATE

In other words, think and chew. Once you've read the topic sentences, stop for a second. Don't leap ahead and start tackling the questions. Ask yourself: "What did I just read?" And then, in your own words, *state the main idea of the passage*. You don't have to articulate a beautiful sentence for the main idea. You just need to say what the main idea is in a short, simple sentence or phrase. It could be: "Macroeconomists good, microeconomists bad."

It is incredibly important that you state the main idea before you go on to the questions. By stating the main idea, you ensure that you understand the sentences that you read. If you aren't able to state the main idea, then you know something isn't right.

(Note: There is, on occasion, a passage that is made up of only one paragraph. In this case, you may need to do a little more reading than usual. However, don't lose sight of the fact that you should stop reading once you have enough information to anticipate what's going to happen in the rest of the paragraph.)

THE QUESTIONS

After you've got the main idea in your head, you can move on to the questions. For the purpose of simplicity, we break down all questions into three types:

- General
- Specific
- Weird

POE

To answer any of these question types, there's one thing you have to do: POE.

Finding the right answer is often hard to do on reading comprehension. Well, if you can't make it through the front door—that is, find the right answer—then try the back door: In short, find the wrong answers first and get rid of them. It's usually much easier to identify wrong answers than right ones because, after all, there are more wrong answers than there are right ones on any question. Also, don't forget that Verbal is really about the *best* answer, not the right one. Sometimes that means finding the least bad answer. And to find the least bad answer, you have to look for the ones that are *really* horrible first.

(Note that since reading comprehension is largely about POE, you must—as on all verbal questions—look at each and every single answer choice.)

EXTREME WORDING

The first thing to watch out for on reading comprehension is extreme wording. Typically, extreme wording in an answer choice will make that answer choice wrong. Take a look at the following sentence:

Everyone loves chocolate ice cream.

ETS would never have this sentence as part of the correct answer. Why? Because it's too easy to prove wrong. All you have to say is, "I hate chocolate ice cream."

The following provides a list of words that usually go "too far" in the land of ETS.

> everyone
>
> no one
>
> only
>
> never
>
> always
>
> must
>
> impossible

Keep in mind that, at first glance, some words may not look as if they are extreme. For example, the word *is*. Consider the following sentence:

It is the answer.

Does ETS know for sure that it is? How can ETS prove it without a doubt? Or think about the word *will*:

The United States will buy more imports in the next ten years.

Is ETS capable of predicting the future? This isn't to say that, if an answer choice contains *is* or *will*, it's wrong. Just remember that, in certain contexts, words can take on extreme meanings. Here's a list of words that ETS uses on the Reading Comprehension section that can often be extreme:

> resolve
>
> reconcile
>
> prove
>
> define
>
> trace

Well, if extreme wording is bad, then guess what? Wishy-washy wording is good—words like *can, may, most, some, sometimes, possible, seldom, few.*

So, the general rule of thumb: Answer choices that contain extreme wording are usually wrong. Answer choices that contain wishy-washy wording or are moderate in tone are usually right.

COMMON SENSE

The second POE tool to use on reading comprehension is common sense. Use it! Just because something's in print doesn't mean it's plausible. Indeed, ETS often includes ridiculous answer choices on reading comprehension. For example:

> According to the passage, the author believes the purpose of children's literature to be which of the following?
>
> ◯ Expose children to the cruelties of life
> ◯ Instruct children on the difference between right and wrong

Which is the better answer? Clearly (B). You don't have to read anything to know that (A) is wrong. All you have to do is exercise a little common sense.

PARAPHRASE, PARAPHRASE, PARAPHRASE

Finally, the most important POE tool on reading comprehension is to paraphrase. The right answer to a question is never going to be a direct quote from the passage. Rather, the right answer is going to be a paraphrase; that is, a restatement of what's in the passage. Which is why there's one thing you should always do for every question, no matter what type it falls into: Always state the answer to a question in your own words *before* you look at the answer choices. It's the same kind of thinking as coming up with your own word on sentence completions.

When you state the answer to a question in your own words, what you're doing is paraphrasing. And once you know what you're looking for, it's much easier to be discerning and figure out what's a bad answer choice. Rushing to the answer choices without taking the time to paraphrase is one of the worst mistakes people make on reading comprehension.

GENERAL QUESTIONS

Okay—let's go back and talk about the question types. Let's start off with general questions. These are questions that ask you to provide "big picture" information about the passage. Below are some examples of how general questions can be worded:

- Main Idea

  The primary purpose of the passage is to

  The main idea of the passage is

  The passage focuses primarily on which of the following?

  The passage is primarily concerned with

  Which of the following best states the central idea of the passage?

- Organization/Structure

  Which of the following best describes the organization of the passage as a whole?

  Which of the following is the most accurate description of the organization of the passage?

- Other

  Which of the following titles best describes the content of the passage?

  Which of the following is the best title for the passage?

  The passage would most likely be found in

  The passage would be most likely to appear as part of

- Tone

  The author's attitude toward . . . can best be described as

  The author's attitude toward . . . is best described as which of the following?

To answer any general question, focus on the main idea. Typically, an answer to a general question contains some sort of paraphrased version of the main idea. Also, don't forget about your tools for POE. As mentioned earlier, be wary of answer choices that:

1. Contain extreme wording

2. Don't make common sense

3. Don't match your paraphrase (i.e., the main idea you came up with)

Also, watch out for answer choices that:

1. *Mention something you haven't read about.* If it isn't mentioned at all in the topic sentences, there's no way it can be right.

2. *Are too detailed or specific.* People often miss general questions because they read the entire passage and get caught up in the specifics. That is, in reading the entire passage, they lose sight of the main idea. Therefore, they end up picking an answer choice that contains information from the passage, but that isn't the main idea.

3. *Are too general or beyond the scope of the passage.* Sometimes ETS is too vague. For example, if the main idea was about eighteenth-century *female poets*, an overly general answer choice would say something about eighteenth-century *writers*.

SPECIAL NOTE ON TONE QUESTIONS

Tone questions are a gift. Occasionally, they can be specific questions—that is, they ask about how the author feels about a particular paragraph rather than how he or she feels about the entire passage. But the approach to tone questions, whether general or specific, is basically the same. Take a look at the following answer choices:

○ overwhelming support
○ unabashed admiration
○ qualified appreciation
○ profound ambivalence
○ deep-rooted hostility

What's the right answer? Without reading the passage, you know it has to be (C). Why? Think of extremes. ETS doesn't like extremes, right? Therefore, the right answer to a tone question is never going to be extremely positive or extremely negative. It's going to be somewhere in between. An author can be neutral or objective. He or she can be appreciative or slightly critical. But the author is never going to love something to death or hate something completely. Again, extreme is bad; moderation is good.

(Note that *apathetic* or *indifferent* are always wrong answers on tone questions. If the author didn't care about something, why would he or she write about it?)

For each of the following passages, find the main idea. The answers are on page 133.

Passage #1

If my colleagues and I are right, we may soon be saying good-bye to the idea that our universe was a single fireball created in
Line the big bang. We are exploring a new theory
(5) based on a 15-year-old notion that the universe went through a stage of inflation. During that time, the theory holds, the cosmos became exponentially large within an infinitesimal fraction of a second. At the end of this period,
(10) the universe continued its evolution according to the big bang model. As workers refined this inflationary scenario, they uncovered some surprising consequences. One of them constitutes a fundamental change in
(15) how the cosmos is seen. Recent versions of inflationary theory assert that instead of being an expanding ball of fire the universe is a huge, growing fractal. It consists of many inflating balls that produce more balls, which in turn
(20) produce more balls, ad infinitum.

Cosmologists did not arbitrarily invent this rather peculiar vision of the universe. Several workers, first in Russia and later in the U.S., proposed the inflationary hypothesis that is
(25) the basis of its foundation. We did so to solve some of the complications left by the old big bang theory. In its standard form, the big bang theory maintains that the universe was born about 15 billion years ago from a cosmological
(30) singularity—a state in which the temperature and density are infinitely high. Of course, one cannot really speak in physical terms about these quantities as being infinite. One usually assumes that the current law of physics did not apply
(35) then. They took hold only after the density of the universe dropped below the so-called Planck density, which equals about 10^{94} grams per cubic centimeter.

As the universe expanded, it gradually
(40) cooled. Remnants of the primordial cosmic fire still surrounds us in the form of the microwave background radiation. This radiation indicates that the temperature of the universe has dropped to 2.7 kelvins. The 1965 discovery
(45) of this background radiation proved to be the crucial evidence in establishing the big bang theory as the preeminent theory of cosmology.

The big bang theory also explained the abundances of hydrogen, helium, and other
(50) elements in the universe.

As investigators developed the theory, they uncovered complications. For example, the standard big bang theory, coupled with the modern theory of elementary particles,
(55) predicts the existence of many super-heavy particles carrying magnetic charge—that is, objects that have only one magnetic pole. These magnetic monopoles would have a typical mass 10^{16} times that of the proton, or
(60) about 0.00001 milligram. According to the standard big bang theory, monopoles should have emerged very early in the evolution of the universe and should now be as abundant as protons. In that case, the mean density
(65) of matter in the universe would be about 15 orders of magnitude greater than its present value, which is about 10^{-29} grams per cubic centimeter.

1. Which of the following best expresses the main idea of the passage?

⃝ Scientists have proven the big bang theory to be inaccurate and replaced it with the concept that the universe inflated over time.

⃝ Because the big bang theory cannot account for the actual state of the universe, it is possible that the universe actually evolved through inflation.

⃝ The big bang theory cannot be discounted completely, but the inflationary theory is also plagued by inconsistencies.

⃝ The big bang theory is incorrect because of the absence of magnetic monopoles in the universe.

⃝ Cosmologists have combined the big bang theory with the inflationary theory to produce a new picture of the universe's evolution.

Passage #2

Over the last decade surrealism has returned with a vengeance, the subject of many exhibitions, symposia, books, and articles.
Line Lest I merely add another line to the list, I
(5) want to begin with a reflection on the past repression and present recovery of this movement. For not so long ago surrealism was played down in Anglo-American accounts of modernism (if not in French ones). In effect,
(10) it was lost twice to such art history: Repressed in abstractionist histories founded on cubism (where it appears, if at all, as a morbid interregnum before abstract expressionism), it was also displaced in neo–avant-garde
(15) accounts focused on dada and Russian constructivism (where it appears, if at all, as a decadent version of vanguardist attempts to integrate art and life).

In Anglo-American formalism, surrealism
(20) was considered a deviant art movement: improperly visual and impertinently literary, relatively inattentive to the imperatives of form, and mostly indifferent to the laws of genre, a paradoxical avant-garde concerned
(25) with infantile states and outmoded forms, not properly modernist at all. For neo–avant-garde artists who challenged this hegemonic three decades ago, its very deviance might have made surrealism an attractive object. But
(30) such was not the case. Since this formalist model of modernism was staked on the autonomy of modern art as separate from social practice and grounded in visual experience, its antagonist, the neo–avant-
(35) garde account of modernism, stressed the two movements, dada and constructivism, that appeared most opposed to this visualist autonomy—that sought to destroy the separate institution of art in an anarchic attack
(40) on its formal conventions, as did dada, or to transform it according to the materialist practices of a revolutionary society, as did constructivism. Again surrealism was lost in the shuffle. To the neo–avant-gardists who
(45) challenged the formalist account in the 1950s and 1960s, it too appeared corrupt: technically kitschy, philosophically subjective, hypocritically elitist. Hence when artists involved in pop and minimalism turned away from the likes
(50) of Picasso and Matisse, they turned to such figures as Duchamp and Rodchenko, not to precedents like Ernst and Giacometti.

Obviously times have changed. The formalist idea of optical purity has long since fallen,
(55) and the avant-gardist critique of categorical art is fatigued, at least in practices that limit "institution" to exhibition space and "art" to traditional media. A space for surrealism has opened up: an *impensé* within the old
(60) narrative; it has become a privileged point for the contemporary critique of this narrative. And yet for the most part art history has filled this new space with the same old stuff. Despite its redefining of the image, surrealism
(65) is still often reduced to painting; and despite its confounding of reference and intention, surrealism is still often folded into discourses of iconography and style. One reason for this art-historical failure is a neglect of the
(70) other principal precondition for the return of surrealism as an object of study: the dual demands of contemporary art and theory.

2. The author is primarily concerned with

   ◯ comparing surrealism with other movements in art such as dada and constructivism
   ◯ challenging the traditional view of surrealism as confined to the realm of art
   ◯ examining surrealism's place in the history of modern art movements
   ◯ exploring the reasons why surrealism has long been ignored as an object of study
   ◯ refuting the claim that surrealism focused on the literary over the visual

SPECIFIC QUESTIONS

These are questions that ask about particular details in the passage. Like general questions, specific questions can be phrased in several ways. For example:

> The author suggests that . . .
>
> According to the passage, . . .
>
> The author mentions . . .
>
> According to the author, . . .

Since specific questions ask you about details from the passage, there's one thing you must do for every specific question:

> Refer back to the passage.

No ifs, ands, or buts. You must do this. Never, never, never rely on your memory. Your memory is your worst enemy. That being said, let's talk about the two major groups of specific questions: line reference and lead word.

LINE REFERENCE

Line reference questions are easy to identify because they always contain a line reference. For example:

> The author mentions T. H. White (line 40)
> in order to . . .
>
> Which of the following situations is most
> analogous to the situation described by
> the author as . . . (lines 15–19)?

You get the idea. Line reference questions are great because they tell you where you should go in the passage to find the information. But they're also a little tricky because the information you're looking for typically isn't contained exactly in the line reference. Rather, it's usually a little bit before the line reference or a little bit after. Therefore, here's your approach to any line reference question:

1. Use the line reference to guide you to the right area of the passage.

2. Read roughly five lines above the line reference and roughly five lines below.

3. Answer the question, based on what you've read, in your own words (i.e., paraphrase) before moving on to the answer choices.

LEAD WORD

Lead word questions are basically line reference questions without the line reference. Well, if you don't have the line reference, how do you know where in the passage to look for the information? The answer is: the lead word.

The lead word is a word or phrase that's easy to skim for. Usually, the lead word stands out in the question because it's the most important or the most specific. What's the lead word in the following question?

> It can be inferred that, during the 1840s,
> the abolitionist movement did which of
> the following?

The lead word is *1840s*. *Abolitionist movement* could be a lead word(s), but only if the entire passage were not about the abolitionist movement. If the main idea were the abolitionist movement, would *abolitionist movement* be easy to skim for? Nope. *1840s* is a good lead word because it's specific and it's very easy to skim for. Numbers, words that have capital letters at the beginning, and italicized words are all good lead words because they're easy to skim for.

Once you've identified the lead word in a question, here's your approach:

1. Skim (not read) the passage for the lead word.

2. Once you find the line that contains the lead word, read roughly five lines before and five lines after.

3. Based on what you've read, answer the question in your own words (i.e., paraphrase). Do this before moving on to the answer choices.

Keep in mind that the lead word may appear more than once in the passage. So if you read the lines surrounding the lead word and don't find the answer to the question, skim the rest of the passage for another appearance of the lead word.

Also keep in mind that the lead word in the question won't necessarily be perfectly represented in the passage. For example, if the lead word in the question is "governmental intrusion," you may find the passage talking about "intrusive actions by the government."

POE FOR SPECIFIC QUESTIONS

Paraphrasing is the key to specific questions. However, you also have some POE tools to help you out as well. As always, watch out for answer choices that:

1. Contain extreme wording

2. Don't make common sense

3. Don't match your paraphrase

Also, watch out for answer choices that:

1. Contain information that's true according to the passage but that doesn't answer the question

2. Misrepresent information found in the same area of the passage as the correct answer

QUICK QUIZ #2

For each of the following questions, locate the answer in the passage by using either a line reference or a lead word. Make sure you paraphrase the answer to the question before looking at the answer choices. The answers are on page 134.

The feminists of revolutionary France were not the only persons hoping that the current paroxysm of social change would bring about
Line improvement of their state. A most singular
(5) category of men, the public executioners, had thought that the advent of a new regime would transform that peculiar disdain in which society held them. For hundreds of years, the post of Master of the High Works in France's
(10) major cities was held by men from ten or so dynastic families, members of an abominable elite that had developed as a consequence of social prejudice: Anyone who had ever been a *bourreau* could never hope to find another job,
(15) nor could he aspire to marry any woman not herself the daughter of a colleague. In this way the dreadful dynasties developed.
The best known recipients of this peculiar distinction were the Sanson family, who
(20) operated in Paris and Versailles from 1688 to 1847; the diary kept by Charles Henri Sanson, executioner of Paris during the Terror, provides details of the deaths of many illustrious victims.
(25) Several passages in the Sanson diary suggest that professional executioners did not particularly like having to kill women. This chivalrous repugnance later spread through the Court d'Assizes; while women were
(30) regularly condemned to death in the late nineteenth and early twentieth centuries, in fact they were almost always reprieved. A roughly contemporaneous reluctance to execute women in the United States has been
(35) explained by recent American feminists as evidence of women's almost nonexistent social status at that time; to compensate for legal inegality the men who were women's judges, prosecutors, and jurors adopted a "protective"
(40) stance, frequently acquitting women who, in modern retrospect, seem guilty. In France the egalitarian practices of earlier centuries were ultimately reinstated, which guillotined five women.

(45) This temporary preservation of execution as an exclusively male domain—a thing too necessary and revolting to be inflicted on or endured by half the population—apparently did not strike legislators as being intolerably
(50) illogical, or as being rather a back-handed sort of compliment to men. Proper equality would have involved either equal rights and equal punishment for men and women, or else abolition. However, arguments against
(55) the death penalty tend rather to develop from general humanitarian principles, and less from the putative equality of women.
Chivalry, indeed, would seem to have been the nineteenth century's solution to the
(60) problems posed to the authorities by "female" executions. But more importantly, chivalry enabled society to observe a version of that logic set forth in 1791 by Olympe de Gouges, a logic echoed later in the United States by
(65) Wendell Phillips, who bluntly declared, "You have granted that women may be hung; therefore you must grant that woman may vote." In not executing women, the judiciary body was able to sidestep these irritating
(70) formulations: If women did not receive equal punishment under law, perhaps they need not be assured of equal rights.

1. Which of the following best describes the author's attitude toward the formation of public executioner dynasties?

   ○ Qualified appreciation
   ○ Studied neutrality
   ○ Tempered disapproval
   ○ Vehement condemnation
   ○ Resigned acceptance

2. According to the passage, the unwillingness of men to condemn women to death in the United States during the late nineteenth century was

○ a reflection of the influence of the Court d'Assizes on the judicial system in the United States

○ in accordance with women's low standing in society and their lack of legal rights

○ a result of a popular movement promoting the chivalrous idea that women should be protected from harm

○ a misinterpretation on the part of modern historians, who believed many of the women to be guilty

○ a reaction to the excesses of the French Revolution and the large number of women who were guillotined

3. The passage suggests that, during the French Revolution, popular arguments against the death penalty did which of the following?

○ Emphasized the failure of the death penalty to suppress dissent

○ Asserted that the defense of the death penalty was based upon faulty logic

○ Supported indirectly the notion that men were equal to women

○ Addressed only the needs of men, at the expense of those of women

○ Failed to employ the reasoning that men and women should have equal rights

WEIRD QUESTIONS

Finally . . . weird questions. We call these questions weird because they have special formats. They're also weird because they tend to be more time-consuming than usual. The three types of weird questions are:

- Roman Numeral

    Which of the following can be inferred from the passage about the earliest observations of Mars?

    I. Though Aristotle correctly placed Mars farther from the earth than the moon, he drew this conclusion based upon a faulty assumption.

    II. Ptolemaeus's writings were based in large part on the work done by Hipparchus, though the two disagreed on the relationship of the earth to the universe.

    III. The recognition of Mars as a planet and not simply a star could not be confirmed until the development of the telescope.

    ○ I only
    ○ III only
    ○ I and III only
    ○ II and III only
    ○ I, II, and III

- Except/Least/Not

    All of the following are stated by the author as the advantages of hydroponics EXCEPT

    According to the passage, neutrinos are NOT

    It can be inferred from the passage that which of the following is LEAST compatible with Graham's approach to dance?

- Questions in the Answer Choices

    The passage supplies information to answer which of the following questions?

ROMAN NUMERAL

Roman numeral questions, as you can probably tell, all too easily eat up a lot of time. And that's because these questions actually have three questions for every one.

To save yourself a little time, here's the approach you should take.

1. Focus on one Roman numeral at a time.

2. If you discover that a certain Roman numeral is false, immediately go to the answer choices and cross out any that contain that Roman numeral. Similarly, if you discover that a certain Roman numeral is true, immediately go to the answer choices and cross out any one that doesn't contain that Roman numeral.

By using this process, you can often avoid looking at all three Roman numerals. Instead, you may only have to investigate two of them.

EXCEPT/LEAST/NOT

Often these questions are not that difficult, but they tend to consume a lot of time. Also, they can be a little tricky. What makes these questions easy to miss is the fact that you're trying to find information that's *incorrect* according to the passage—and usually, it's your job to find out the correct information. To sidestep this pitfall, here's how to approach EXCEPT/LEAST/NOT questions.

1. For each answer choice, ask yourself if it is true according to the passage or false.

2. If the answer choice is true, put a Y next to it; if the answer choice is false, put an N next to it.

3. After going through all the answer choices, you should have four Ys and one N. The answer is the one that doesn't belong—the N.

As long as you follow these steps, you should be okay. Just remember, you're looking for information that's *not* true.

QUESTIONS IN THE ANSWER CHOICES

These questions are also time-consuming, particularly because there's nothing like a line reference or a lead word to help you out. The approach you need to take on these questions is:

1. Look for a lead word in each answer choice.

2. Use that lead word to guide you to the right part of the passage.

3. Ask yourself if the question is answered by that part of the passage.

IN SUMMARY . . .

For reading comprehension, it's the approach that counts. Break bad habits. Don't rely on your memory. Always paraphrase. The bottom line is that reading comprehension is an open-book test. All of the answers are in the passage. It's your job to hunt them down, and you can do that most effectively through POE—that is, getting rid of bad answer choices first.

Finally, don't forget that reading a lot isn't necessarily a good thing. It's not how much you read, it's what you read. We hope that with our approach you're not reading as much as you were before. However, just because you're reading less doesn't mean you can afford to read quickly. You're not reading a lot anymore, so take the time to make sure you understand what you do read.

1. Before you answer any questions, always find the main idea. You can find the main idea by reading the first two sentences of the first paragraph, the first sentence of each succeeding paragraph, and the last sentence of the entire passage. Be sure to state the main idea in your own words.

2. Don't forget that POE is the best way to get the right answer on reading comprehension. Be wary of any answer choice that

   a) contains extreme wording,

   b) doesn't make common sense, or

   c) doesn't match your paraphrase.

3. General questions: These questions ask about "big picture" information such as "what's the main idea" or "how is the passage organized" or "what's the author's tone." To answer general questions, focus on the main idea. Watch out for answer choices that

   a) mention something you haven't read,

   b) are too detailed or specific, or

   c) are too general or go beyond the scope of the passage.

4. Specific questions: These questions ask about particular details in the passage. Use either line references or lead words to guide you to the part of the passage that contains the answer. Always remember to read five lines before and five lines after. Watch out for answer choices that

   a) contain information that's true according to the passage but that doesn't answer the question, or

   b) misrepresent information found in the same area of the passage as the correct answer.

5. Weird questions: These questions are the most time-consuming. For EXCEPT/LEAST/NOT questions, play the Y/N game. For Roman numeral questions, focus on one Roman numeral at a time. For questions in the answer choices questions, look for a lead word in each answer choice to take you to the right part of the passage.

6. Above all . . . never rely on your memory. Always refer back to the passage. And always, always paraphrase. Paraphrasing helps you see which answer choices are bad because it makes sure you understood what you just read.

PRACTICE QUESTIONS #1

Political parties today are consciously non-ideological, but in the 1840s and 1850s ideology made its way into the heart of the political system. Political sociologists have
(5) pointed out that the stable functioning of a political democracy requires a setting in which parties represent broad coalitions of varying interests, and that the peaceful resolution of social conflict takes place most easily
(10) when the major parties share fundamental values. Such a view implies that the peaceful operation of the political system is the highest social value, an implication which, under certain circumstances, may be justly
(15) questioned. But it does contain important insights about the normal functioning of the American polity. Government by majority rule, Carl Becker observed many years ago, works best when political issues involve superficial
(20) problems, rather than deep social divisions. The minority can accept the victory of the majority at the polls, because both share many basic values, and electoral defeat does not imply "a fatal surrender of . . . vital interests."
(25) Before the 1850s, the second American party system conformed to this pattern—largely because sectional ideologies and issues were consciously kept out of politics. In this sense, the party system had a certain artificial
(30) quality. Its divisions rarely corresponded to the basic sectional divisions which were daily becoming more and more pronounced. The two decades before the Civil War witnessed the development of conflicting sectional
(35) ideologies, each viewing its own society as fundamentally well-ordered, and the other as both a negation of its most cherished values and a threat to its existence.
The development of the two ideologies
(40) was in many ways interrelated; each grew in part as a response to the growth of the other. Thus, as southerners were coming more and more consciously to insist on slavery as the very basis of civilized life, and to reject the
(45) materialism and lack of cohesion in northern society, northerners came to view slavery as the antithesis of the good society, as well as a threat to their own fundamental values and interests. The existing political system
(50) could not contain these two irreconcilable ideologies, and in the 1850s each national party—Whigs, Know-Nothings, and finally Democrats—disintegrated. And in the end the South seceded from the Union rather than
(55) accept the victory of a political party whose ideology threatened everything Southerners most valued.
At the center of the Republican ideology was the notion of "free labor." This concept
(60) involved not merely an attitude toward work, but a justification of antebellum northern society, and it led northern Republicans to an extensive critique of southern society, which appeared both different from and inferior to
(65) their own. Republicans also believed in the existence of a conspiratorial "slave power" which had seized control of the federal government. Two profoundly different and antagonistic civilizations, Republicans thus
(70) believed, had developed within the nation, and were competing for control of the political system.

1. The primary purpose of the passage is to

 ◯ discuss the requirements for a stable political system, in particular, a democracy

 ◯ present a cause for the breakdown in relations between North and South that led, ultimately, to the Civil War

 ◯ explain the reason why political parties seek to avoid introducing ideology into their platforms

 ◯ analyze the effect of the Civil War on the political party system in the United States

 ◯ propose the theory that the Republican party was responsible for the South's secession from the Union

2. It can be inferred from the passage that political parties today

○ do not differ from each other markedly in terms of interests
○ consider freedom from conflict the most important social concern
○ keep their distance from ideology because of its potential to divide
○ look to the Civil War as a lesson on how to maintain national unity
○ address only problems of little weight and rarely dispute one another

3. The author mentions Carl Becker in order to

○ challenge the position popularly held by political sociologists regarding the power of ideology
○ argue that a democracy is characterized by the peaceful transition of power from one party to another
○ promote the notion that it is better for a democracy to address only issues that are not divisive
○ suggest that, in order for a democracy to flourish, the political system must represent diverse interests
○ lend credence to the assertion that political stability is founded upon the absence of ideological confrontation

4. The passage states the party system in the years preceding the Civil War did which of the following?

○ Did not accurately reflect the tensions existing between North and South
○ Was responsible for the conflicting northern and southern ideologies
○ Failed to acknowledge its inability to reconcile the North with the South
○ Exacerbated the differences among the Whigs, Know-Nothings, and Democrats
○ Could not suppress the dissent voiced by the Republicans

5. According to the passage, the antagonism of the North and South was, at heart, a result of

○ the South's insistence on an economy based on slave labor
○ the failure of the political parties to find common ground
○ the North's rejection of slavery as an immoral institution
○ the perception that "free labor" and slave labor were diametrically opposed
○ the Republican belief in a Southern plot to overthrow the federal government

6. The passage suggests that the concept of free labor

○ instigated immediately the secession of the South from the Union
○ was a creation of the North to define itself as distinct from the South
○ allowed the North to justify its condemnation of the South's secession
○ was an encapsulation of northern values and concerns
○ represented the materialist interests of the North

7. The author's attitude toward the Republican party of the mid-nineteenth century can best be described as

○ admiring
○ appreciative
○ sympathetic
○ objective
○ vehement

PRACTICE QUESTIONS #2

Directions: The passage below is followed by questions based on its content. After reading the passage, choose the best answer to each question. Answer all questions on the basis of what is <u>stated</u> or <u>implied</u> in that passage. The answers are on page 137.

How do we know what we believe we know? What we know is generally considered to be the result of our exploration and
Line understanding of the real world, of the way
(5) things really are. After all, common sense suggests that this objective reality can be discovered. How we know is a far more vexing problem. To solve it, the mind needs to step outside itself, so to speak, and observe itself at
(10) work; for at this point we are no longer faced with facts that apparently exist independently of us in the outside world, but with mental processes whose nature is not at all self-evident. If what we know depends on how we
(15) came to know it, then our view of reality is no longer a true image of what is the case outside ourselves, but is inevitably determined also by the processes through which we arrived at this view.

1. The author implies that an "objective reality" (line 6) is

○ a necessary part of life, even if it may not exist, because without it our existence would lack order and structure

○ accurate only if we take into account how we know and not what we know

○ not possible because knowledge is a result not only of concrete experience but also abstract thought processes

○ a false image that we construct so that we might come to some sort of understanding of the world outside us

○ a reflection of our inner reality, that is, the world inside us governed by mental processes

2. According to the passage, we tend to believe what we know is a product of our

○ imagination as well as our contact with other people

○ daily experiences with the outside world

○ analytical and logical reasoning

○ mental and physical activity combined

○ education, both formal and informal

3. The passage suggests that the author would be most likely to agree with which of the following statements?

○ We can only come "to know" through a rigorous examination of our customs and prejudices.

○ We can never determine with complete certainty whether something is true.

○ At the very best, our knowledge of the outside world is vague and incomplete.

○ So complex are our minds that we cannot, at times, discern the difference between the real and fantasy.

○ Our perception of reality can be inaccurate at times, but overall, we are rational beings.

PRACTICE QUESTIONS #3

E. M. Forster is an Edwardian in point of time, and he is equally so in spirit. His outlook on the world and his literary manner
Line were already thoroughly developed in
(5) that epoch and have passed through the subsequent years of turbulence and cataclysm with remarkably little modification. The various modern revolutions in physics, in psychology, in politics, even in literary style, have not
(10) escaped his intelligent notice, but they can scarcely be said to have influenced him deeply. His response to the explosion of the Victorian dream of benevolent progress has been a modest and orderly retreat to safer ground—
(15) to a tolerant individualism now unmixed with Utopian dreams, but nevertheless closer to Victorian ideals than to any of the popular creeds of today. Rather than conform to bad times, Forster prefers to remind us cheerfully
(20) that his views are atavistic.

The strength of Forster's resistance to the twentieth century is especially apparent when we place him beside some of his fellow writers. If Joyce, Lawrence, Pound, and the
(25) early Eliot represent the main current of the modern literary movement in English, we must admit that Forster's private stream runs in an older channel. These others were radical iconoclasts whose rejection of bourgeois-
(30) democratic life was violent and shattering. Equally shattering was their fragmentation of the polite cadences of Victorian literature. In seeing the falseness of the old psychology, they conceived a scorn for the *hypocrite*
(35) *lecteur*; their role as apocalyptic prophets, as naysayers to the boredom and specious rationality of modern life, demanded that they be obscure and idiosyncratic. Forster, in contrast, unashamedly calls himself a
(40) bourgeois and remains faithful to the tradition of calm intelligibility. He is anti-apocalyptic in both his politics and his literary sense. To some degree his novels return us to the congenial Victorian relationship between writer
(45) and reader, with its unspoken agreement over the usefulness of the sociable virtues and

its apotheosis of the happy family. Though Forster's heroes struggle against "society" as a body of inhibitions, their revolt is never truly
(50) radical. And Forster's ironical style, though it is unsparing in its probing at shams and half-truths, presupposes a confidence in the reader's sympathy and good judgment—a confidence that seemed quite archaic to the
(55) other writers named.

Forster's resistance to modernity may account for the fact that his novels, though they are almost universally esteemed, have never won him a cult of fanatical disciples.
(60) With a few exceptions, critics have tended to explicate and admire his works without becoming heated over the possible merit of his ideas. Yet Forster decidedly *is* a novelist of ideas, and didactic moral content is hardly less
(65) conspicuous in his work than in Lawrence's. Forster's persistent "moral" is that the life of affectionate personal relations, disengaged from political and religious zeal by means of a tolerant eclecticism, is supremely valuable.
(70) This is not a stirring creed; in fact, it is a warning against allowing oneself to be stirred by any creed.

1. The author's primary purpose in this passage is to

  ○ discuss E. M. Forster and his writing, particularly in the context of his reaction to modernity

  ○ compare E. M. Forster to other writers of the twentieth century such as Joyce and Lawrence

  ○ affirm that E. M. Forster is as much a novelist of ideas as other modern writers

  ○ suggest that E. M. Forster's writing is a reflection of not only Victorian ideals but also Edwardian

  ○ analyze E. M. Forster's response to the revolutions in science and art and how it affected his work

2. According to the passage, Forster's relationship to Victorianism is which of the following?

- ⭘ He believed Victorian ideals were preferable to those of modernity.
- ⭘ He did not believe in Victorian ideals but nevertheless clung to them.
- ⭘ He considered Victorian ideals to be not only oppressive but also false.
- ⭘ He rejected Victorian ideals, but not so completely as other modern writers.
- ⭘ He incorporated Victorian ideals into his own personal ideals.

3. The author most likely refers to Forster's "views as atavistic" (line 20) in order to

- ⭘ make a case for the importance of individualism to Forster and his work
- ⭘ isolate Forster as a writer unconnected to the revolutions of the modern world
- ⭘ emphasize that Forster was an atypical modern writer
- ⭘ suggest that Forster was an ardent supporter of the popular beliefs of his time
- ⭘ point out Forster's inherent belief in Victorianism

4. According to the passage, the literary style of modern writers

- ⭘ maintained the Victorian trust in the judgment of the reader
- ⭘ was revolutionary in its rejection of all beliefs and ideals
- ⭘ was ironical as well as difficult to decipher
- ⭘ was eccentric in nature and characterized by vagueness
- ⭘ lacked any structure and was riddled with ambiguity

5. It can be inferred from the passage that Lawrence's novels

- ⭘ condemn the life of the bourgeoisie, at the expense of destroying personal relations
- ⭘ are similar to Forster's as both men valued the relationship between reader and writer
- ⭘ are more conciliatory to Victorianism than Joyce's novels
- ⭘ have elicited much impassioned debate among critics
- ⭘ express ideas that are antithetical to those found in Forster's novels

6. The author's reaction to Forster's novels can best be described as one of

- ⭘ disparagement
- ⭘ skepticism
- ⭘ neutrality
- ⭘ appreciation
- ⭘ enthusiasm

7. The passage suggests that the author would be likely to agree with which of the following statements about Forster's works?

I. The characters in Forster's writings often rebel against a confining and restrictive society.

II. Forster's works ultimately fail to be radical and stand out as an aberration in the modern literary movement.

III. Literary critics, though respectful of Forster's writings, tend to believe his works lack moral tension.

- ⭘ I only
- ⭘ II and III only
- ⭘ II only
- ⭘ I and III only
- ⭘ I, II, and III

PRACTICE QUESTIONS #4

Directions: The passage below is followed by questions based on its content. After reading the passage, choose the best answer to each question. Answer all questions on the basis of what is stated or implied in that passage. The answers are on page 141.

Natural selection is an immensely powerful yet beautifully simple theory that has held up remarkably well, under intense and unrelenting
Line scrutiny and testing, for 135 years. In essence,
(5) natural selection locates the mechanism of evolutionary change in a "struggle" among organisms for reproductive success, leading to improved fit of populations to changing environments . . .
(10) Yet powerful though the principle may be . . . natural selection is not fully sufficient to explain evolutionary change. First, many other causes are powerful, particularly at levels of biological organization both above and below
(15) the traditional Darwinian focus on organisms and their struggle for reproductive success. At the lowest level of substitution in individual base pairs of DNA, change is often effectively neutral and therefore random. At higher levels,
(20) involving entire species or faunas, punctuated equilibrium can produce evolutionary trends by selection of species based on their rates of origin and extirpation, whereas mass extinctions wipe out substantial parts of biotas
(25) for reasons unrelated to adaptive struggles of constituent species in "normal" times between such events.
Second . . . no matter how adequate our general theory of evolutionary change, we also
(30) yearn to document and understand the actual pathway of life's history. Theory, of course, is relevant to explaining the pathway . . . But the actual pathway is strongly *underdetermined* by our general theory of life's evolution. This
(35) point needs some belaboring . . . Webs and chains of historical events are so intricate, so imbued with random and chaotic elements, so unrepeatable in encompassing such a multitude of unique (and uniquely interacting)
(40) objects, that standard models of simple prediction and replication do not apply.
History can be explained—with satisfying rigor if evidence be adequate—after a sequence of events unfolds, but it
(45) cannot be predicted with any precision beforehand . . . History includes too much chaos, or extremely sensitive dependence on minute and unmeasurable differences in initial conditions, leading to massively divergent

(50) outcomes based on tiny and unknowable disparities in starting points. And history includes too much contingency, or shaping of present results by long chains of unpredictable antecedent states, rather than immediate
(55) determination by timeless laws of nature.
Homo sapiens did not appear on the earth, just a geologic second ago, because evolutionary theory predicts such an outcome based on themes of progress and increasing
(60) neural complexity. Humans arose, rather, as a fortuitous and contingent outcome of thousands of linked events, any one of which could have occurred differently and sent history on an alternative pathway that would
(65) not have led to consciousness . . .
Therefore, to understand the events and generalities of life's pathway, we must go beyond principles of evolutionary theory to a paleontological examination of the contingent
(70) pattern of life's history on our planet—the single actualized version among millions of plausible alternatives that happened not to occur. Such a view of life's history is highly contrary both to conventional deterministic
(75) models of Western science and to the deepest social traditions and psychological hopes of Western culture for a history culminating in humans as life's highest expression and intended planetary steward.

1. The primary purpose of the passage is to

  ○ suggest that the natural selection theory is no longer applicable to today's world
  ○ point out the limitations of natural selection at the lower and higher levels
  ○ propose changes to the natural selection theory to improve its accuracy
  ○ discuss the reasons why natural selection is not a complete evolutionary theory
  ○ expose problems with the natural selection theory in light of recent historical studies

2. According to the passage, natural selection does not take into account the

○ tendency of certain species to evolve successfully due to isolation

○ dependence of some organisms on the successful evolution of other organisms

○ eradication of a species for reasons other than a failure to reproduce successfully

○ continuation of specific organisms and species due to human intervention

○ difficulty of successful reproduction for organisms at the lower and higher levels

3. It can be inferred that the author believes the study of history is

○ problematic
○ impossible
○ futile
○ not worthwhile
○ untenable

4. The author mentions *Homo sapiens* primarily in order to

○ highlight the short period during which humans have lived on the earth

○ suggest the notion that the pathway to consciousness was a long-term process

○ support the idea that the pathway of life is determined, in large part, by random events

○ explain evolution through natural selection by employing a specific species as an example

○ emphasize the intricacy of events that leads to the evolution of an organism or species

5. According to the passage, we might be reluctant to let go of traditional evolutionary theory because to do so would

○ refute the ideas of the long-venerated scientist Darwin

○ suggest that life cannot be ordered or structured

○ challenge the way we understand the world

○ throw other scientific theories into question as well

○ compel us to reexamine both biology and history

6. Which of the following statements is supported by information given in the passage?

○ The study of history will never be completely satisfactory.

○ The theory of natural selection addresses the possibility of random events.

○ The evolution of life does not follow a fixed or determined path.

○ It is possible to determine with a fair degree of accuracy historical events.

○ Theories will always be inadequate because they are at best predictions.

7. Which of the following best describes the organization of the passage?

○ A theory is rejected, and new theories are suggested to replace it.

○ A theory is considered, and conditions are stated under which the theory can apply.

○ A theory is explained, and observations are made that both support and contradict it.

○ A theory is described, and its limitations are noted and then further explored.

○ A theory is outlined, and its relevance questioned by employing it in a different field of study.

PRACTICE QUESTIONS #5

Directions: The passage below is followed by questions based on its content. After reading the passage, choose the best answer to each question. Answer all questions on the basis of what is <u>stated</u> or <u>implied</u> in that passage. The answers are on page 143.

Occupations foster gender differences among workers in a variety of ways, one of the most pervasive being "internal stratification."
Line That is, men and women in the same
(5) occupation often perform different tasks and functions. Even in those occupations that appear sexually integrated, the aggregate statistics often mask extreme internal segregation. Although the proportion of female
(10) bakers increased from 25 percent in 1970 to 41 percent in 1980, for example, the majority of female bakers are found in highly automated baking industries, while their male counterparts are located in less automated bakeries.
(15) The same phenomenon has been detected among pharmacists, financial managers, and bus drivers—all groups where the influx of women workers suggests a diminution of sex segregation.
(20) Another strategy used to maintain gender differences in supposedly integrated occupations is the use of sumptuary and etiquette rules. When women enter male-dominated occupations, certain rules are
(25) often introduced to govern their dress and demeanor. In office settings, for instance, dress codes—either formal or implicit—are not unusual; female employees may be required to wear dresses, nylons, and high-heeled shoes
(30) to enhance their femininity. So it is for female marines and male nurses, both of whom are required to dress differently from their male and female counterparts. Male nurses never wear the traditional nursing cap; female
(35) marines never sport the standard Marine Corps garrison cap.
Informal practices also play a role in constituting femininity in female marines and masculinity in male nurses. As members
(40) of visible minority groups, they stand out at work and receive far more than their fair share of attention. This phenomenon was first documented by Rosabeth Moss Kanter, who found that women in corporations,
(45) simply by virtue of their numerical rarity, were noticed and scrutinized more than their male

counterparts. This added pressure may actually result in different job performances from men and women in nontraditional occupations
(50) and exacerbate gender differences. Kanter's corporate women, for example, became more secretive, less independent, and less oppositional in response to their greater visibility—all traits that have traditionally been
(55) associated with femininity.
Another informal technique that enhances gender differences is practiced by supervisors who evaluate men and women differently. The very qualities that are highly praised in one sex
(60) are sometimes denigrated in the other. Thus, a man is "ambitious," a woman, "pushy"; a woman is "sensitive," a man, "wimpy."
But it would be a mistake to claim that all gender differences are forced on people. In
(65) addition to the external pressures I have just described, male nurses and female marines actively construct their own gender by redefining their activities in terms of traditional masculine and feminine traits. For example,
(70) women in the Marine Corps insist that their femininity is intact even as they march cadence in camouflage units. Likewise, male nurses contend that their masculinity is not at all threatened while they care for and nurture
(75) their patients.

1. The author is primarily concerned with

○ explaining how femininity and masculinity can be reconstructed for specific careers

○ examining jobs that, at first glance, seem to be nontraditional for men and women

○ proving that discrimination based on gender is pervasive in all workplaces

○ exploring the reasons why gender differences cannot be ignored in any occupation

○ discussing practices that serve to perpetuate gender differences in the workplace

2. Which of the following best describes the organization of the first paragraph?

○ A specific case is presented, its particulars are analyzed, and a conclusion is drawn from it.

○ A generalization is made, a clarification is put forth, and specific examples are offered in support.

○ An observation is made, specific situations that are applicable are cited, and a generalization is derived.

○ A hypothesis is presented, evidence to support it is given, and its implications are discussed.

○ A criticism is made, a specific problem is noted, and ways to rectify the problem are suggested.

3. The author suggests which of the following about internal stratification?

○ Although women now work in industries once dominated by men, they find it difficult, if not impossible, to be promoted to managerial positions.

○ As women enter the work force in greater numbers, men feel their jobs are threatened and their hostility results in increased tension on the job.

○ Because men and women rarely engage in the same activities on the job, certain specialties can be feminine-identified and others masculine-identified.

○ Since men and women are segregated in the workplace, men tend not to value the work carried out by women.

○ Even when men and women are given the same tasks to perform, women continue to receive less pay than do their male counterparts.

4. The primary purpose of the last paragraph is to

○ emphasize the importance of outside forces in establishing gender differences

○ point out that men and women act to enforce gender differences themselves

○ provide an example of men and women who defy the typical perceptions of masculinity and femininity

○ demonstrate that, even in a nontraditional context, conventional definitions of "masculine" and "feminine" are preserved

○ describe the tension that men and women feel when their sexuality is questioned

5. The passage supplies information to answer which of the following questions?

○ Do women favor rules that dictate how they should dress and behave?

○ Is internal stratification a worldwide phenomenon?

○ Why do corporate women feel undue pressure on the job?

○ Why do supervisors uphold gender differences in the work place?

○ How do male nurses cope with a job that challenges their masculinity?

6. The author specifically mentions all of the following as methods to maintain gender differences in the workplace EXCEPT

○ a manager's use of particular words for men and particular words for women although describing the same quality

○ the designation of dress codes so that the physical differences between men and women are highlighted

○ the internal pressure men and women feel to be traditionally masculine or feminine

○ pressure from coworkers to behave in a conventionally masculine or a feminine way

○ the assignation of different duties for men and women in the same occupation

7. Which of the following statements could most logically follow the last sentence of the passage?

○ Both groups redefine femininity and masculinity in their daily lives, which also reinforces gender differences.

○ However, both groups recognize their inability to change the mind-sets of those who see masculinity and femininity in rigid terms.

○ And so, each group internalizes the need to be masculine or feminine to such a degree that their lives are in a constant state of conflict.

○ In the end, internal pressures prove to be even greater than external pressures in maintaining gender differences.

○ This leads to the question: How can one defy gender differences when even these groups try to sustain them?

Although meningitis clone III-1 has caused hundreds of thousands of meningitis cases, it does not appear to be uniquely virulent. Now
Line that it is possible to perform clonal analysis
(5) of meningococcal strains, it is clear that other clones have caused similar epidemics in Africa and Asia. These findings do suggest, however, that the introduction of a potentially epidemic clone under the right circumstances can be
(10) devastating. Two explanations have been given for this process: Epidemic clones randomly expand as they progress through a population, or they survive by escaping herd immunity. As an analogy to influenza outbreaks, it has been
(15) proposed that epidemics might result from what are called antigenic shifts. Although all serogroup A meningococci share the same polysaccharide, individual clones differ in the other antigens exposed on the cell surface.
(20) Once immunity to the shared antigens wanes, a new clone with sufficiently different surface antigens might escape immune surveillance and start an epidemic. Epidemiologists following disease patterns will then see an
(25) "antigenic shift" as new clones supersede older clones.

1. Which of the following would be the best title for the passage?

   ○ Meningitis: What Are Its Causes?
   ○ How an Epidemic Can Result from a Meningitis Strain
   ○ A Scientific Overview of an Antigenic Shift
   ○ Problems Confronting an Outbreak of Meningitis
   ○ An Analysis of the Meningitis Clone III-1

2. The author uses each of the following devices in the passage EXCEPT

   ○ providing an explanation
   ○ making a comparison
   ○ suggesting a cause for an effect
   ○ providing a definition
   ○ making an inference

3. According to the passage, an antigenic shift takes place when

   ○ an epidemic causes specific clones to alter their surface antigens so that they are undetectable
   ○ shared antigens begin to be outnumbered by different antigens, thus allowing certain clones to pass through a population
   ○ certain clones are able to sidestep a weakened herd immunity and advance through a population
   ○ clones no longer randomly progress through a population but rather direct themselves toward the weakest elements
   ○ certain clones build resistance to herd immunity and share this ability with other clones through their antigens

PRACTICE QUESTIONS #7

New York stood at the center of the momentous processes that recast American society in the nineteenth century. Once
Line a modest seaport, the city early took the
(5) lead in developing new forms of commerce and mass production; by 1860 it was both the nation's premier port and its largest manufacturing city. The appearance of new social classes was both cause and result
(10) of industrial development and commercial expansion. Wealth from investments in trade and manufacturing ventures supported the emergence of an urban bourgeoisie; the expansion of capitalist labor arrangements
(15) brought into being a class of largely impoverished wageworkers. The resulting divisions fostered, on each side, new and antagonistic political ideas and social practices.
We know most about the male participants
(20) in these conflicts, workingmen and employers. Politically, bourgeois men upheld their right to protect, improve upon, and increase the private property on which rested, they believed, their country's welfare. In return, many workingmen
(25) affirmed a belief in the superior abilities of those who worked with their hands—as opposed to the idle, acquisitive, parasitical owners of property—to direct American society in accordance with republican values of social
(30) equality, civil virtue, and yeomanry that they inherited from the Revolution.
Class transformation was related to, but not synonymous with, the thorough-going transformation of the gender system in the
(35) first half of the nineteenth century: that is, the changes in all those arrangements of work, sexuality, parental responsibilities, psychological life, assigned social traits, and internalized emotions through which the sexes
(40) defined themselves respectively as men and women. Women of the emerging bourgeoisie articulated new ideas about many of these aspects of their lives. Designating themselves moral guardians of their husbands and
(45) children, women became the standard-bearers of piety, decorum, and virtue in northern society. They claimed the home as the sphere of society where they could most effectively exercise their power. In their consignment to
(50) the household as the sole domain of proper female activity, women suffered a constriction of their social engagements; at the same time, they gained power within their families that also vested them with greater moral authority
(55) in their own communities.
While the cult of domesticity spoke to female interests and emerged from altered relations between men and women, it also contained within it conflicts of class. As
(60) urban ladies increased their contacts with the working poor through Protestant missions and charity work, they developed domestic ideology as part of a vision of a reformed city, purged of the supposed perfidies of working-
(65) class life. Domesticity quickly became an element of bourgeois self-consciousness. In confronting the working poor, reformers created and refined their own sense of themselves as social and spiritual superiors
(70) capable of remolding the city in their own image. From the ideas and practices of domesticity they drew many of the materials for their ideal of a society that had put to rest the disturbing conflicts of class.

1. The author of the passage is primarily concerned with discussing

   ○ the authority possessed by middle-class women in New York both in public and in private

   ○ the transformation of New York into an industrial and commercial center of activity

   ○ social conflict in New York, in terms of class and gender, as a result of economic expansion

   ○ the social values of the middle class in New York, particularly the cult of domesticity

   ○ the attempt of the middle class in New York to reform the working class

2. The author states, "We know most about the male participants in these conflicts" (lines 19–20) primarily in order to

○ challenge past studies because they have largely ignored the female participants

○ preface a debate over the motivating factors for class conflict

○ propose possible reasons as to why only men's roles have been examined

○ emphasize the impact that class conflict had on industrial development

○ allude to a later discussion of the women who were active in such conflicts

3. According to the passage, middle-class men were similar to working-class men in that each group

○ perceived the other to be an obstruction to industrial and commercial expansion

○ placed a great deal of weight on private ownership and the entrepreneurial spirit

○ responded to the changing economy with both excitement and aversion

○ felt threatened by the activity of women who sought to lay claim to the home

○ considered itself responsible for the well-being and prosperity of the country

4. According to the passage, bourgeois women did which of the following by taking charge of the home?

○ Both enlarged the scope of their authority and circumscribed their power

○ Portrayed their challenge to male authority as an act necessary to preserve morality

○ Reconstructed the duties of parents as well as the role of children

○ Increased their missionary activity intended to assist the working class

○ Set out to reform the city, in particular the working class

5. According to the passage, the cult of domesticity did which of the following?

○ Oppressed women as their activities were now confined to the realm of the home

○ Represented values cherished by northerners, particularly working-class women

○ Drew from the tradition of republicanism in its promotion of reform

○ Engendered increased tensions between the middle class and working class

○ Encouraged women to speak out on behalf of female interests and issues

6. The passage suggests that middle-class reformers attempted to do which of the following?

○ Convert the poor of the working class to Protestantism

○ Promote domesticity as a means to gain power over the working class

○ Ameliorate class tensions by advocating citywide changes

○ Encourage women to participate in public activities such as missionary work

○ Compel the working class to adopt bourgeois values

7. According to the author, the changing economy in New York was

○ responsible for the increased reformist activity

○ both a cause and an effect of class divisions

○ able to temper somewhat conflict between the sexes

○ due primarily to the increase in trade at the port

○ a threat to the republican ideals of the Revolution

PRACTICE QUESTIONS #8

Directions: The passage below is followed by questions based on its content. After reading the passage, choose the best answer to each question. Answer all questions on the basis of what is <u>stated</u> or <u>implied</u> in that passage. The answers are on page 150.

The societies in which shamanism has flourished have been small, relatively self-sufficient social systems which see themselves
Line as coping directly with their natural worlds.
(5) Like all human beings, the members of such groups lived in a world of uncertainty. The presence of a person who could maintain contact with the cosmic forces of the universe directly, who could make sense of both the
(10) measured order of ordinary times and the catastrophes of drought, earthquake, or flood, was of incalculable value.

More complex social systems tend to have "institutionalized" specialists who transmit
(15) information without explicit recourse to the supernatural. Such societies have priests and prophets, not shamans, at the overt level. But the line between shaman and prophet is tenuous. The prophet usually does not
(20) enjoy the legitimacy within his society that is granted the shaman. His is a voice crying in the wilderness, not that of the legitimate curer and philosopher. Despite these differences, the prophet can be seen as a kind of shaman, and
(25) thus the study of shamanism illuminates some of the obscurities in religious traditions.

1. The primary purpose of the passage is to

○ explain the differences between shamans in small and large societies

○ describe the reasons why shamans are esteemed in certain societies

○ discuss the roles of shamans as well as prophets in social systems

○ compare religious leaders in small social systems to those in complex social systems

○ argue that the power of the shaman is derived from the supernatural

2. According to the passage, certain social systems rely on shamans in order to

○ empower them through a connection with the divine

○ mediate disputes and other conflicts between individuals

○ give structure and form to an unstable world full of mysteries

○ lead them in religious activities such as prayer and worship

○ protect them from hostile neighbors and unpredictable forces such as nature

3. The passage suggests that shamans and prophets differ because

○ shamans are more powerful because they have a mandate from their deity

○ shamans possess a higher social status, due to their ability to call upon the supernatural

○ shamans are revered as demigods while prophets are considered mortal

○ shamans are less likely to be challenged by members of their society

○ shamans maintain greater authority because they live in isolated social systems

4. According to the passage, shamans
   and prophets are similar in which of the
   following ways?

   I. The size and infrastructure of the
      societies in which they live resemble
      one another.

   II. Their roles in society are based, in part,
       on their ability to explain and provide
       information.

   III. They are accorded a special standing
        because of their ability to control nature.

   (A) II only
   (B) I and II only
   (C) I and III only
   (D) II and III only
   (E) I, II, and III

ANSWERS AND EXPLANATIONS

QUICK QUIZ #1

Passage #1

To find the main idea, here's all you need to read:

- "If my colleagues and I are right, we may soon be saying good-bye to the idea that our universe was a single fireball created in the big bang. We are exploring a new theory based on a 15-year-old notion that the universe went through a stage of inflation."

- "Cosmologists did not arbitrarily invent this rather peculiar vision of the universe."

- "As the universe expanded, it gradually cooled."

- "As investigators developed the theory, they uncovered complications."

- "In that case, the mean density of matter in the universe would be about 15 orders of magnitude greater than its present value, which is about 10^{-29} grams per cubic centimeter."

Given these sentences, how might you paraphrase the main idea? That the big bang theory may be wrong and that the inflationary theory may be right? Now you can go to the answer choices.

Eliminate (A) because it's too extreme. Scientists haven't *proven* the big bang theory wrong. Leave (B) in because it's a good match for your paraphrase. Also, note how moderate (B) is. Eliminate (C) because it says the inflationary theory is bad. Remember, it's the big bang theory that's problematic, not the inflationary theory. Eliminate (D) because it mentions stuff (magnetic monopoles) you didn't read about. Eliminate (E) because it suggests the big bang theory is okay. The best answer, then, is (B).

Passage #2

To find the main idea, here are the sentences you need to read:

- "Over the last decade surrealism has returned with a vengeance, the subject of many exhibitions, symposia, books, and articles. Lest I merely add another line to the list, I want to begin with a reflection on the past repression and present recovery of this movement."

- "In Anglo-American formalism, surrealism was considered a deviant art movement: improperly visual and impertinently literary, relatively inattentive to the imperatives of form and mostly indifferent to the laws of genre, a paradoxical avant-garde concerned with infantile states and outmoded forms, not properly modernist at all."

- "Obviously times have changed."

- "One reason for this art-historical failure is a neglect of the other principal precondition for the return of surrealism as an object of study: the dual demands of contemporary art and theory."

From these sentences alone, you can come up with the main idea. What is the main idea? To paraphrase: that surrealism is no longer being ignored as it once was.

Now that you've stated the main idea, go to the answer choices. Eliminate (A) because you didn't read anything about dada or constructivism. Eliminate (B) because you didn't read anything about surrealism being limited to art. Eliminate (C) because you didn't read anything about surrealism's place in history. Keep (D) for now because it says something about surrealism being ignored. Eliminate (E) because it's too specific— only the topic sentence of the second paragraph mentions the literary over the visual. The best answer, then, is (D).

QUICK QUIZ #2

1. **C** This tone question is specific, not general. Regardless, for any tone question, extreme answer choices are bad. What answer choices are too extreme here? Definitely (D), so cross it out. The other answer choices are fairly moderate, so leave them in for now. What now? Use "dynasties" as your lead word. That takes you to the first paragraph. How does the author feel about the formation of the dynasties? Not too good: She calls them an "abominable elite that had developed as a consequence of social prejudice." So what's the best answer? Something that's slightly negative. Eliminate (A) because it's positive. Eliminate (B) because it's not negative at all. Keep (C) for now because it's slightly negative. Finally, leave in (E) because it's slightly negative.

   The remaining answer choices are (C) and (E). Which one is better? Well, does the author dislike the formation of the dynasties or is she resigned to it? She dislikes it, right? So the best answer is (C).

2. **B** This is a specific question. Use "United States" as your lead words. Once you find the lead words, remember to read about five lines above and five lines below. So where is "United States"? In the second paragraph. What does the passage say about men in the United States? That they took a "'protective' stance" toward women to compensate them for their "nonexistent social status." Always make a paraphrase of the answer before moving on to the answer choices.

   Eliminate (A) because who cares about the Court d'Assizes. Keep (B) because it looks like a pretty good match for your paraphrase. Eliminate (C) because you didn't read anything about a popular movement. Eliminate (D) because who cares about the modern historians. Eliminate (E) because you didn't read anything about lots of French women being guillotined. The best answer is (B).

3. **E** This is a specific question. Use "death penalty" as your lead words. Once you find the lead word, don't forget to read about five lines above and five lines below. So where is "death penalty"? In the third paragraph. What does the passage say about popular arguments against the death penalty? That they focus on humanitarian principles and that they don't focus on equal rights. In other words, men and women are equal, so if women aren't subject to capital punishment, then men shouldn't be either. It's important that you paraphrase the answer to the question before moving on to the answer choices.

Eliminate (A) because it doesn't talk about humanitarian principles or equal rights. Eliminate (B) for the same reason. Eliminate (C) because it misinterprets information in the passage. Popular arguments *failed* to incorporate equal rights. Eliminate (D) because it also misrepresents information in the passage. It's the men that are getting killed, not the women. Keep (E) because it's a good match for your paraphrase. (E) is the best answer.

PRACTICE QUESTIONS #1

1. **B** To find the main idea, all you have to do is read the topic sentence for each paragraph and then the final sentence of the entire passage. Remember, always state the main idea in your own words (i.e., paraphrase) before moving on to the answer choices. So what's the main idea for this passage? You should have come up with something like the following: The Civil War was a result of conflicting political ideologies in the North and South.

(A) is too general. From the second paragraph, you know that the main idea has to have something to do with the Civil War. (B) is a possibility since it talks about the war. (C), like (A), is too broad because it doesn't mention the war. (D) does talk about the war, which is good, but it doesn't really talk about how the war affected the party system, which is bad. (E) is too specific. Though it does talk about the war, it doesn't take into account the topic sentence for the first paragraph. The best answer is (B).

2. **C** Use "political parties" as your lead word. It takes you to the very beginning of the passage. Remember, paraphrase what you read before you move on to the answer choices. What does the passage say about political parties today? That they purposefully avoid ideology.

(A) goes a little too far. The passage does say that parties should try to represent "broad coalitions of varying interests," but that doesn't mean that all parties are the same. (B) misrepresents information in the passage. Lines 11–13 ("Such a view implies . . . ") suggest that "the peaceful operation of the political system is the highest social value" in certain circumstances, but you don't know that to be true for political parties today. (C) is a good match for your paraphrase. (D) isn't mentioned at all in the passage. (E) goes a little too far. It's implied that political parties only address problems of little import because they don't want conflict, but you don't know that parties rarely have disputes. The best answer is (C).

3. **E**   "Carl Becker," clearly, should be the lead word you use, and you can find the lead word in the first paragraph. Well, why does the author mention Carl Becker? Paraphrase the answer before you look at the answer choices. The author mentions Carl Becker because he wants to cite someone who supports his main idea: Ideology can be very divisive—after all, it caused the Civil War.

(A) misrepresents information in the passage. The passage does talk about political sociologists, but it doesn't say they disagree with Becker. (B) may be true, but it's not the reason *why* the author mentions Becker. (C) goes too far. Becker thinks ideology is divisive, but he's not saying we should therefore avoid it. (D) is really the point the political sociologists are making, not Becker. (E) is the only answer left, and guess what? It matches your paraphrase. (E) is the best answer.

4. **A**   Use "party system . . . Civil War" as your lead words. This should take you to lines 25–30 ("Before the 1850s, the second American . . . "). What do the lines say about the party system? Basically, that it was artificial because it failed to reflect the tension between the North and South. Remember, always paraphrase before looking at the answer choices.

(A) looks as if it's a good match. (B) is the exact opposite of what you're looking for. (C) misrepresents information from the passage. (D) suggests the parties were responsible for conflict. From the passage, you know they wanted to avoid conflict. (E) mentions the Republicans, who are discussed in the passage, but not until much later. The best answer is (A).

5. **D**   This question can be answered using the main idea. What's the main idea? That ideology caused the Civil War. If you look at the last sentence of the passage, it confirms the main idea.

(A) talks about slavery, not ideology. (B) talks about political parties, not ideology. (C) talks about slavery again, not ideology. (D) does talk about ideology, so it looks good. (E) doesn't talk about ideology, so it's wrong. The best answer is (D).

6. **D** The lead words are clearly "free labor," which can be found at the beginning of the fourth paragraph. What does the passage say about free labor? That it was a "justification of . . . northern society." To paraphrase: Free labor was the ideology that motivated the North.

    (A) goes too far. The ideology of free labor was responsible for the Civil War, but it didn't cause the South to leave the Union immediately. (B) is tricky. Free labor did distinguish the North from the South, but the North didn't create the ideology just to make itself different from the South. (C) isn't quite right. The ideology allowed the North to condemn the South overall—not its secession. (D) looks like a good match. (E) goes too far. Free labor represented the interest of the North, period. The ideology was about more than just materialism.

7. **D** For a tone question, anything too extreme must be wrong. (E) is out, as a result, as is (A). So you're left with (B), (C), and (D)—each of which is pretty moderate. So use "Republican" as your lead word to find out how the author feels about the party.

    The fourth paragraph talks about the Republicans, and clearly, the author is pretty neutral in tone. So the best answer is (D).

PRACTICE QUESTIONS #2

1. **C** This specific question has a line reference, so the part of the passage that contains the answer isn't too hard to find. However, don't forget that you need to read about five lines before the line reference, as well as five lines after. Also, remember that once you locate the answer, paraphrase it before looking at the answer choices.

    The answer to the question is contained in the last few lines of the passage. It may seem that "objective reality can be discovered," but because "what we know depends on how we came to know it," maybe not. To paraphrase: It looks like the author is mentioning an objective reality because we think there is one but there really isn't.

    (A) is a bad answer choice because it mentions something you didn't read at all—a lack of order and structure. (B) misinterprets what you read—it's a combination of what we know and how we know that matters. (C) looks good since it says "not possible." (D) goes a little too far. An objective reality may not exist, but nothing in the passage says *why* we think there is one. (E) is incomplete. Our perception of reality is a combination of what we know and how we know—not just how we know. (C) is the best answer.

2. **B** This is a specific question. Use "what we know" in the question as lead words. Once you find the lead words, remember to read about five lines above and five lines below. So where do you find "what we know"? At the very beginning of the passage. Apparently, "What we know is generally considered to be the result of our exploration and understanding of the real world, of the way things really are." To paraphrase: It's our contact with the real world that determines what we know.

    (A) is a bad answer choice because it discusses the imagination. Imagination isn't mentioned at all in the passage. (B) is okay—it mentions interaction with the real world. (C) is talking about mental processes, so it can't be right. (D) mentions the physical, but since it also includes the mental, it's wrong. (E) is way out there—education isn't discussed at all in the passage. The best answer is (B).

3. **B** This is really a general question at heart—in other words, to answer this question, you need to focus on the main idea. What's the main idea of the passage? Well, if you read the first few sentences of the passage and then the last sentence, you should come up with something like this: What we know is a sticky process because it depends not only on the outside world but also on our mental activity.

    Given the main idea, which answer choice is best? (A) mentions customs and prejudices. From the passage, you really don't know what the author thinks about customs and prejudices. (B) is a possibility. The main idea, remember, talks about what we know and how it's a sticky process. (B) says something along the lines of truth being a sticky thing. (C) is a little tricky. The passage does discuss the outside world and our relation to it, but does it ever suggest that our knowledge is vague and incomplete? No—only that the process of knowing is very complicated. (D) goes a little too far. The author would certainly agree that the mind is complex—mental activity is an important factor in what we know. But use your common sense. Is the mind so complex that we can't determine what's real or not? No. (E) is half good and half bad. The author would probably agree that our perception of reality is sometimes skewed, but do you know anything about whether he thinks we're rational or not? No. The best answer, then, is (B).

PRACTICE QUESTIONS #3

1. **A** This is a main idea question. To find the main idea, all you have to do is read the first two sentences of the first paragraph, the topic sentence for each remaining paragraph, and then the last sentence of the entire passage. Remember to state the main idea in your own words before looking at the answer choices. So what's the main idea? To talk about Forster and how he really wasn't a very "modern" writer.

   (A) talks about Forster and modernity, so it looks okay. (B) is too specific. The passage does compare Forster to these writers, but it's not the main point. (C) is too specific as well. It's a summary of the last paragraph. (D) is off the mark entirely. Finally, (E) is too specific. Revolutions in science and art are mentioned in the first paragraph, but that's about it. The best answer is (A).

2. **D** This is a specific question. Use "Victorianism" as your lead word. Remember, once you find the lead word, read about five lines above and five lines below. So where can you find "Victorianism"? At the end of the first paragraph. What does the passage say about Forster and Victorianism? That Forster stepped away from Victorianism, but not entirely. Don't forget to paraphrase before you go to the answer choices.

   (A) goes too far. Forster did step away from Victorianism, just not completely. (B) goes too far as well. Forster didn't cling to Victorianism's ideals. (C) is too extreme. Forster moved away from Victorianism, but not that completely. (D) looks like a good match for your paraphrase. (E) goes off target. Again, Forster did reject Victorianism, at least to a certain extent. The best answer is (D).

3. **C** This specific question tells you exactly where in the passage to go because of the line reference. Remember, though, you need to read a little bit before the line reference as well as a little bit after. Well, why does the author say Forster is atavistic? To paraphrase: Even though he was a modern writer, and not a Victorian one, he was closer to Victorianism in some ways than he was to modernity. Don't forget to paraphrase before looking at the answer choices.

   Eliminate (A) because it discusses individualism, not Forster's tension with modernity. Eliminate (B) because it's a little off. The author doesn't say Forster was completely unconnected. (C) is okay for now; it suggests that Forster and modernity were somewhat in conflict. (D) is the opposite of what you're looking for. (E) goes too far. Forster didn't belief in Victorianism completely. So the best answer is (C).

4. **D** This is a specific question. Use "modern" and "literary" as the lead words. Remember, once you find the lead words, read about five lines before the lead words and five lines after. So where can you find "modern" combined with "literary"? In the second paragraph. How did most modern writers write? Well, they rejected Victorianism completely. Also, they wrote in an "obscure and idiosyncratic" fashion. Remember, always answer the question in your own words before going on to the answer choices.

    (A) is definitely out—don't forget modern writers hated Victorianism. (B) is too extreme. You don't know that modern writers rejected *all* beliefs and ideals. (C) is partly true—modern writers wrote obscurely. But were they ironic? Who knows. (D) is a good paraphrase for "obscure and idiosyncratic." (E) is too extreme. Did modern writers lack *any* structure? The best answer is (D).

5. **D** This is a specific question. Use "Lawrence" as your lead word. He's mentioned twice in the passage, once in the second paragraph and once in the third. From the second paragraph, you know that Lawrence rejected Victorianism and that he wrote in an "obscure and idiosyncratic" fashion. From the third, you know that Lawrence had a "didactic moral content." Now that you've got a paraphrase, go to the answer choices.

    (A) is half true. Lawrence probably did condemn the life of the bourgeoisie since he rejected Victorianism. But personal relations? The only thing mentioned in the passage about personal relations has to do with Forster. (B) isn't true at all. Remember, Lawrence writes obscurely. The congenial relationship between reader and writer is a characteristic of Victorianism. (C) is out because nowhere are Joyce and Lawrence compared. (D) is a possibility. Right before the passage talks about Lawrence's "didactic moral content," it says Forster never got critics in a big debate because they thought he lacked moral content. (E) goes a little too far. It's probably true that there are differences between Lawrence and Forster—Forster was a less typical modern writer than Lawrence. But you don't really know anything about the ideas in Lawrence's novels. Therefore, the best answer is (D).

6. **D** This tone question is general, and it's definitely a "gimme." How do you think the author feels? From the main idea alone, you can tell he likes Forster. That means (A), (B), and (C) aren't right. Between (D) and (E), which is better? The less extreme. So (D) is the best answer.

7. **D** This is a weird question. In other words, expect this question to be pretty time-consuming. What do you do for Roman numeral questions? Work with one Roman numeral at a time. For statement I, use "society" and "Forster's

writings" as the lead words. That should take you to the last few sentences in the second paragraph. What does the passage say about the characters in Forster's books and society? That they do rebel—although not completely—against a society that inhibits. So statement I is true. Eliminate (B) and (C) since they don't contain statement I.

Moving on to statement II . . . From the main idea, you know that Forster's works are not typical of the modern literary movement. But does that mean he failed to be radical? This statement goes too far. Eliminate (E) because it contains statement II.

Moving on to statement III . . . Use "moral" as a lead word. That takes you to the last paragraph. And it does say that critics don't get heated up over Forster's ideas. So statement III is true—which means the best answer is (D). (A) can't be right because it doesn't contain statement III.

PRACTICE QUESTIONS #4

1. **D** This is a general question. For any general question, focus on the main idea. The main idea of the passage can be found by reading the first two sentences of the first paragraph, the topic sentence of each remaining paragraph, and the last sentence of the entire passage. So what's the main idea? To paraphrase: that the natural selection theory doesn't explain all of evolution. Always state the main idea in your own words before looking at the answer choices.

    (A) goes too far. Natural selection isn't perfect at explaining all of evolution, but it's still very powerful according to the passage. (B) is true, but it's not the main point of the passage. (C) is a little off. The passage doesn't say anything about making changes to the theory—just that the theory doesn't cover everything. (D) looks like a good match for your paraphrase. (E) is way off target. The best answer is (D).

2. **C** This is a specific question. Use "natural selection" as your lead words. Once you find the lead words, don't forget to read about five lines before them and five lines after them. So where does the passage talk about "natural selection"? In the first and second paragraphs. The first paragraph defines natural selection; the second paragraph talks about the limitations of natural selection. Therefore, focus on the second paragraph. What does that paragraph say about natural selection? That it doesn't take into account other causes for evolution besides a struggle for reproductive success. Always paraphrase the answer to the question before looking at the answer choices.

(A) discusses isolation, which isn't mentioned anywhere in the lines you read. (B) also discusses something you didn't read. (C) is a good match for your paraphrase. (D) talks about human intervention, which you didn't read. (E) misinterprets what you read. Lower and higher levels are discussed, but not in terms of their having problems with reproducing. The best answer is (C).

3. **A** For this specific question, use "history" as your lead word. Don't forget, once you find the lead word, read about five lines above the lead word and five lines after it. History is mentioned in the third and fourth paragraphs. Both discuss the problems with history—that there's no way to predict what's going to happen. History is about events randomly coinciding. Therefore, the author probably sees the study of history as being very complex.

    (A) is okay for now. It sort of matches the idea of very complex. (B) is too extreme. (C) is also a bit on the extreme side. (D) goes too far. There are problems with the study of history but that doesn't mean the study of history isn't worthwhile. (E) goes too far. The study of history isn't insupportable. The best answer, then, is (A).

4. **C** This specific question has a very easy lead word to find: "*Homo sapiens.*" Still, don't forget that you need to read about five lines before the lead word and five lines after. So why does the passage talk about *Homo sapiens*? Look at the fifth paragraph: to give weight to the idea that life comes about through a random coinciding of events. Always paraphrase the answer before looking at the answer choices.

    (A) is mentioned in the paragraph, but it's not the reason why *Homo sapiens* are discussed. (B) focuses on length instead of randomness. (C) talks about randomness, so it should be kept. (D) discusses natural selection, which isn't the point. (E) is a little off. It's not the intricacy of events that matters—it's the randomness. The best answer is (C).

5. **C** This is a specific question. Use "evolutionary theory" as your lead words. Don't forget that once you find the lead words, you need to read about five lines before them and five lines after. So where is "evolutionary theory"? In the last paragraph. Why might we be reluctant to let go of traditional evolutionary theory? Because such an act would be "highly contrary both to conventional deterministic models of Western science and to the deepest social traditions and psychological hopes of Western culture." In other words, letting go of traditional evolutionary theory is a scary prospect because it would mean changing the way we look at the world. Always paraphrase before looking at the answer choices.

(A) talks about Darwin, so eliminate it. (B) is a little off. Giving up the theory doesn't mean we lose all order and structure. (C) is a good match for your paraphrase. (D) talks about other scientific theories, which isn't the point. (E) talks about history, which is off target. The best answer is (C).

6. **C** This is really a general question. What do we need to do for any general question? Think about the main idea. The main idea of this passage is the following: The natural selection theory is not a complete explanation of evolution. The best answer choice has to go with the flow of the main idea.

(A) misinterprets information from the passage. If you use "history" as a lead word, that takes you to the third and fourth paragraphs. Those paragraphs say that the study of history can be satisfactory, at least "if evidence be adequate." (B) isn't true. Natural selection is about the struggle for reproductive success— which doesn't take into account random events. The second paragraph says as much when it discusses lower levels of organisms. (C) goes with the flow of the main idea, especially since it conveys the idea of randomness. (D) goes back to history again. We found out from (A) that history can be satisfactory, but what else? That it's hard to predict, not easy. (E) is too extreme. Theories aren't *always* inadequate. So the best answer is (C).

7. **D** This is a general question. So focus on the main idea—in other words, the first two sentences of the first paragraph, the topic sentence of each remaining paragraph, and the final sentence of the entire passage. How is the passage organized? Well, natural selection is explained, and then problems with it are noted in a lot of detail. Always paraphrase the answer to a question before looking at the answer choices.

(A) is a bad answer choice because it says natural selection is rejected. The theory isn't rejected, just noted as incomplete. (B) is okay for the first half, but bad for the second half. Conditions are never stated. (C) is okay for the first half, but bad for the second half. Observations that support it aren't made. (D) is a good match for your paraphrase. (E) is okay for the first half, but bad for the second half. The passage does question natural selection but not by applying it to a different field of study. (Don't get thrown by the discussion of history.) The best answer is (D).

PRACTICE QUESTIONS #5

1. **E** This is a main-idea question. To find the main idea, all you have to do is read the first two sentences of the first paragraph, the topic sentence of each remaining paragraph, and then the last sentence of the entire passage. Don't forget to state the main idea in your own words before looking at the answer choices. So what's the main idea? How gender differences are preserved or enforced in the workplace.

(A) talks about the reconstruction of gender. Not what you're looking for. (B) discusses nontraditional jobs, not gender differences. (C) mentions pervasiveness, which isn't the point. (D) is a little off because of the word "why." The passage isn't about why we can't ignore gender differences. (E) is the only answer choice remaining, and it's a good match for your paraphrase. The best answer is (E).

2. **B** This is a specific question that tells you exactly where to go to find the answer: the first paragraph. So how is the first paragraph organized? Well, it starts out with a statement about gender differences. Then it makes a definition, and after that, it provides a specific example. Remember, it's important that you answer the question with your own words before looking at the answer choices.

    (A) is out because the paragraph doesn't start out with a specific. (B) is okay, as is (C), but (D) isn't because the paragraph doesn't start out with a hypothesis. Finally, (E) is out because there's no criticism made at the beginning of the paragraph.

    You're down to (B) and (C). Look at (B). A clarification (or definition) is made, and then specific examples are given. (B) is okay. What about (C)? Specific situations are cited, but there's no generalization at the end. (B) is the best answer.

3. **C** This is a specific question. "Internal stratification" is clearly the lead word, and you can find the lead word at the beginning of the very first paragraph. Don't forget to read about five lines before the lead word as well as five lines after. So what is internal stratification? When men and women have the same job, but in that job, they are given different tasks to perform. Remember, it's always important to paraphrase before looking at the answer choices.

    (A) isn't an inference you can make. Women and men have the same jobs is the point. (B) isn't an inference you can make. It might be true, but nothing about internal stratification suggests it. (C) looks good—especially because it agrees with the main idea about gender differences. (D) isn't quite as good as (C). It could be true, but nothing about internal stratification suggests it. (E), finally, is like (B) and (D). It could be true, but nothing about internal stratification suggests it. The best answer is (C).

4. **B** This is a specific question, and the question tells you exactly where to go in the passage: the last paragraph. What's the point of the last paragraph? That gender differences aren't always "forced on people." In other words, people sometimes enforce gender differences themselves. It's always important to paraphrase the answer to a question before looking at the answer choices.

(A) is the opposite of what you're looking for. It's the internal that's important, not the external. (B) looks like a good match for the paraphrase. (C) is a little off. Male nurses and female marines are nontraditional, but they actually enforce gender differences, too. (D) isn't quite right. The statement is true, but it's not the point of the last paragraph. (E) is way off target. The best answer is (B).

5.   **C**   This is a weird question. In other words, it's pretty time-consuming. What do you do for questions-in-the-answer-choices questions? Look for a lead word in each answer choice and then see if the question can be answered. A good lead word in (A) might be "dress" or "behave." That takes you to the second paragraph. Is the question answered? No. All you know is that rules are dictated, not how people feel about them. The lead words in (B) are "internal stratification." That takes you to the first paragraph. Is the question answered? No. How widespread internal stratification is is never discussed. Good lead words in (C) are "corporate women." That takes you to the third paragraph. In that paragraph, the author explains how corporate women are more visible and how this makes them more secretive and less independent. So can the question be answered? Yes. A lead word for (D) is "supervisors." That takes you to the fourth paragraph. Is the question answered? No. All you know is that supervisors uphold gender differences, not why. Finally, lead words for (E) are "male nurses." That takes you to the second paragraph and the last paragraph. Neither one discusses how male nurses cope, so the question is not answered. The best answer is (C).

6.   **D**   This is a weird question. What do we know about weird questions? That they're very time-consuming. Okay—what should you do for an EXCEPT question? Play the Yes/No game. Start by finding a lead word for each answer choice. The lead word in (A), "words," takes you to the fourth paragraph. Do managers use language to enforce gender differences? Yes. So put a Y next to (A). The lead word in (B), "dress," takes you to the second paragraph. Do dress codes enforce gender differences? Yes. So put a Y next to (B). The lead word in (C), "pressure," takes you to the last paragraph. Does internal pressure enforce gender differences? Yes. Put a Y next to (C). Use "coworkers" in (D) as a lead word. "Coworkers" doesn't take you anywhere in the passage, so put an N next to (D). The lead words in (E), "different duties," takes you to the first paragraph. Do different duties for men and women enforce gender differences? Yes. Put a Y next to (E).

Which answer choice is not like the others? (D). It's the only answer choice with an N next to it. So (D) is the best answer.

7. **A** This is a specific question. To find out what would logically follow the last sentence, read the last one or two sentences of the passage. What do the last two sentences discuss? How male nurses and female marines insist on their masculinity or femininity. So what would logically follow? Something about keeping gender differences intact.

(A) mentions gender differences and their reinforcement, so it looks good. (B) isn't right because the last few sentences don't mention changing the mind-sets of others. (C) goes too far. States of conflict aren't the issue. (D) misrepresents the information in the last paragraph. Internal pressures are discussed, but not as greater than the external. Finally, (E) goes off on a tangent. How to overcome gender differences isn't the point. The best answer is (A).

PRACTICE QUESTIONS #6

1. **B** To find the main idea of a passage, all you have to do is read the first two sentences of the first paragraph, the topic sentence for each remaining paragraph, and then the final sentence of the entire passage. Since this passage is only one paragraph long, you may want to read a little more than just the first two sentences at the beginning.

So what's the point of the passage? It's talking about epidemics caused by meningitis. Don't get caught up in the science. To say the main idea is epidemics and meningitis is fine.

(A) isn't right because there's no mention of epidemics. (B) looks good because it mentions both epidemic and meningitis. (C) is too specific—it says nothing about meningitis. (D) is a possibility since it talks about outbreak and meningitis. (E) is too specific—it doesn't say anything about epidemics.

You're down to (B) and (D). Which answer choice is better? Well, the first two sentences of the passage talk about the cause of the epidemics, not the problems. Therefore, the best answer is (B).

2. **D** This is a weird question—i.e., it's a very time-consuming question. On an EXCEPT question, what should you do? Play the Yes/No game. Start with answer choice (A). Does the author provide an explanation in the passage? Yes. He suggests what might cause a meningitis epidemic to occur. Put a Y next to (A). Move on to (B). Does the author make a comparison? Yes. He talks about making an analogy to an influenza outbreak. Put a Y next to (B). Go on to (C). Does the author suggest a cause for an effect? Yes. Once again, the author talks about what might cause a meningitis epidemic. Put a Y next to (C). On to (D). Does the author provide a definition? No. Nowhere in the passage is

a definition given. Put an N next to (D). Finally, (E). Does the author make an inference? Yes. He says in line 7, "These findings do suggest . . . ", which means he's making an inference. Put a Y next to (E).

Which answer choice is not like the others? (D)—it's the only N. Therefore, the best answer is (D).

3. **C** This is a specific question. Use "antigenic shift" as your lead words. They take you to the middle of the paragraph. Don't forget that you should read about five lines above the lead word as well as five lines after. So what does the passage say about antigenic shifts? That they take place when immunity wanes, which allows some clones to escape surveillance and start an epidemic. Make sure you make this paraphrase before moving on to the answer choices.

Does (A) match your paraphrase? No. Nowhere in the passage does it talk about clones *changing* their surface antigens. What about (B)? No. There's nothing in the passage about shared antigens outnumbering different antigens. (C)? It's a pretty good match. (D)? No. The passage doesn't say clones direct themselves at the weakest elements of the population. (E)? No. There's nothing about sharing a resistance to immunity. The best answer is (C).

Practice Questions #7

1. **C** To find the answer to this general question, determine what the main idea is. How do you find the main idea? By reading the first two sentences of the first paragraph, the topic sentence of each remaining paragraph, and then the last sentence of the entire passage. What is the main idea? That the evolving economy in New York produced class conflict and gender conflict. Always paraphrase the main idea before looking at the answer choices.

(A) is too specific. Middle-class women are discussed, but they're not the main point. (B) is too general. It talks about the economy, but not about class and gender. (C) looks like a good match for your paraphrase. (D) is too specific. The cult of domesticity is mentioned in the passage, but it's not the main point. (E) is too specific. It says nothing about the economy. The best answer is (C).

2. **E** This is a specific question that uses a line reference. Don't forget that you should read not just the line reference, but about five lines above the line reference and five lines below. So why does the author say, "We know most about the male participants"? As a way to discuss class conflict between men *and* as a way to preface class conflict between women. In other words, we don't know a lot about the female participants but here is what we do know. Always paraphrase the answer to a question before looking at the answer choices.

(A) isn't quite right. The author isn't *challenging* the studies about men.
(B) is a little off. Yes, class conflict is at issue, but debate is not. (C) is bad because the passage never talks about why only men have been looked at.
(D) contains a true statement—class conflict did have an impact on industrial development—but that's not the point of the author saying, "We know most about the male participants." (E) is the best match for your paraphrase and it is the best answer. This question is a great example of how much of reading comprehension is *not* about finding the best answer. It's about finding the answer that is *least bad*. In other words, get the right answer by eliminating the ones that have to be wrong.

3. **E** This is a specific question. Use "middle-class men" and "working-class men" as your lead words. That takes you to the second paragraph. What does the paragraph say about the similarities between the two groups? That they both believed the welfare of the country depended on them. Don't forget that you must paraphrase the answer to a question before looking at the answer choices.

   (A) misinterprets the information in the paragraph. It's suggested that the groups didn't particularly like each other, but you don't know whether they saw each other as obstructions. (B) is true of middle-class men, but not working-class men. (C) is not good because the passage does not address feelings that men had about the economic changes. (D) misinterprets information from the passage. You don't know that men felt threatened by the changing roles of women. (E) is a good match for your paraphrase. It's the best answer.

4. **A** This is a specific question. Use "home" as your lead word. That should take you to the third paragraph. What does the passage say about women and the home? That "In their consignment to the household as the sole domain of proper female activity, women suffered a constriction of their social engagements; at the same time, they gained power within their families that also vested them with greater moral authority in their own communities" (lines 49–55). In other words, women lost power by being restricted to the home, but also gained power at the same time. Always paraphrase before looking at the answer choices.

   (A) is a great match for your paraphrase. (B) misinterprets what you read. You don't know if taking charge of the home was a challenge to male authority. (C) misinterprets information from the passage. You don't know that women were responsible for reconstructing the duties of parents and the role of children. It could have been men. (D) is a little tricky. Women did participate in missionary activity, but you don't know they increased that participation after taking charge of the home. (E) is also tricky because women did try to reform the city, but was this a result of taking charge of the home? You don't know. The best answer is (A).

5. **D** This is a specific question. Use "cult of domesticity" as your lead words. That takes you to the fourth paragraph. The very first sentence in that paragraph sums up what the cult of domesticity did. It produced class conflict. Middle-class women went out and tried to get rid of the "perfidies of working-class life" in the name of domesticity. Always paraphrase the answer before looking at the answer choices.

   (A) is wrong because women weren't completely confined to the home. They were working in the public eye in their efforts to reform the city. (B) is off because middle-class women cherished the cult of domesticity—not lower-class women. (C) mentions republicanism, which you didn't read in the sentences surrounding the lead words. (D) talks about class conflict, so it looks good. (E) says something you just don't know to be true. The best answer is (D).

6. **E** This is a specific question. Use "middle-class reformers" as your lead words. That should take you to the last paragraph. What do you learn about reformers? That "In confronting the working poor, reformers created and refined their own sense of themselves as social and spiritual superiors capable of remolding the city in their own image" (lines 67–71). In other words, reformers were trying to make the working class just like them. Always paraphrase the answer to a question before going to the answer choices.

   (A) mentions Protestantism, which is discussed in the paragraph, but also mentions converting, which isn't discussed. (B) is almost right, but not quite. You don't know that the reformers were consciously trying to gain power. For all you know, their efforts were a sincere attempt to help. (C) suggests that reformers were actively seeking to end class tensions. That's something you just don't know. (D) contains information that is true—women did do missionary work—but you don't know if reformers *encouraged* women to do so. Finally, (E) is a good match for your paraphrase. It's the best answer.

7. **B** This is a specific question. Use "economy" as your lead word. That takes you to the first paragraph. According to the first paragraph, "The appearance of new social classes was both cause and result of industrial development and commercial expansion." In other words, class conflict was responsible for and a product of the changing economy. Always paraphrase before you go to the answer choices.

(A) mentions reform, which you didn't read about in the paragraph. (B) is a good match for your paraphrase. (C) says something that's not true. The economy caused gender conflict; it didn't temper gender conflict. (D) says something you don't know for sure to be true. (E) mentions the Revolution, which you didn't read about in the paragraph. The best answer is (B).

Practice Questions #8

1. **C** To find the main idea, just read the first two sentences of the first paragraph, the topic sentence of each remaining paragraph, and then the final sentence of the entire passage. What's the main idea, then? To talk about shamans and prophets.

    (A) is a little too general. It doesn't mention prophets at all. (B) is discussed in the passage, but it's not the main point. (C) looks good because it talks about both shamans and prophets. (D) is too general. Religious leaders is vague—you want an answer choice that mentions shamans and prophets explicitly. (E) is too specific. Shamans and the supernatural are mentioned in the passage, but that's not the main point. The best answer is (C).

2. **C** This is a specific question. "Shamans" isn't a great lead word since it's mentioned throughout the passage, but that's the best you can do. You could look for "shamans" along with "social systems" to guide you a little bit better. "Shamans" and "social systems" are both mentioned in the first paragraph, so try reading there first. Why do societies rely on shamans? Because they "could maintain contact with the cosmic forces of the universe directly . . . make sense of both the measured order of ordinary times and the catastrophes of drought, earthquake, or flood." In other words, shamans are good because they make the world make sense.

    (A) isn't quite right. Empowering isn't the point. (B) talks about mediation, which you didn't read about. (C) talks about structure and form, so it could match your paraphrase. (D) is never stated outright, so you don't know it to be true. (E) is half good, half bad. Shamans did explain unpredictable forces in nature, but hostile neighbors? You just don't know. The best answer is (C).

3. **D** This is a specific question. Use "shamans" and "prophets" as the lead words. That takes you to the second paragraph. What does the passage say about how they differ? "The prophet usually does not enjoy the legitimacy within his society that is granted the shaman. His is a voice crying in the wilderness, not that of the legitimate curer and philosopher." So the prophet doesn't have quite the standing or the power of the shaman. Always paraphrase the answer to a question before going to the answer choices.

(A) mentions a mandate from a god. You didn't read that, so it can't be right. (B) is half true. Shamans do have more standing, but is that based upon their communication with the supernatural? You don't know. (C) goes too far. Shamans are respected, clearly, but are they demigods? Who knows. (D) has to be true since shamans have more standing and power than do prophets. (Note the moderate language—"less likely.") Finally, (E) is half true. Shamans do have greater authority—but is it because they live in isolated social systems? You don't know. The best answer is (D).

4. **A** This is a weird question. In other words, it's very time-consuming. How do you deal with Roman numeral questions? By working on one Roman numeral at a time. Focus on statement I first. Use "size" as a lead word. In the first paragraph, the passage says shamans live in small societies. In the second paragraph, the passage says prophets live in more complex societies. Therefore, statement I isn't true. Eliminate (B), (C), and (E) because each contains statement I.

At this point, only (A) and (D) are left. They both contain statement II, so you know statement II has to be true. All you need to look at, then, is statement III. Statement III talks about controlling nature. This may be true for shamans, but what about prophets? You just don't know. The best answer is (A).

Antonyms

THE GOAL: FIND THE OPPOSITE

At heart, antonyms are a vocabulary test. The only difference is instead of finding a word with the same meaning as a particular word, you're looking for a word that's opposite in meaning. For example:

INCENSED:

- mollified
- ecstatic
- entertained
- peeved
- satisfied

As with analogies, we call the word in capitalized letters the stem. The answer choices are, of course, the answer choices.

Cover It Up

There are basically three groups into which we can divide words that show up on antonyms:

1. Words you know

2. Words you sort of know

3. Words you don't know at all

A word you know is one for which you can provide a definition. A word you sort of know is one that you can use in a sentence. Or maybe you can tell if it's a positive word or a negative word. However, you can't define it. A word you don't know at all is one that you've never heard or seen before.

A WORD YOU KNOW

Let's start with how to tackle a word that you know. The first thing you should do is focus on the word. In other words, don't get distracted by the answer choices. As in the sentence completions, you should ignore them. Now that your attention is on the stem word, make a simple opposite for it. Let's go back to the example above. The stem word is INCENSED. INCENSED means very angry. A simple opposite for INCENSED, then, is *very happy*.

Once you've made a simple opposite for the stem word, you can look at the answer choices. Go through each and every answer choice (as you always do in Verbal), and pick the one that's the best match for your simple opposite. As with sentence completions, the best match for your simple opposite doesn't have to be an exact match. In other words, you don't have to look for *very happy* in the answer choices. You just need to look for something very close to it.

- mollified
- ecstatic
- entertained
- peeved
- satisfied

In this case, the best answer is (B) because *ecstatic* does mean *very happy*. Notice that it's very important to look at all the answer choices because (A) and (E) are attractive, especially if you're working too quickly. Try another one:

DECAY:

- ○ adorn
- ○ arise
- ○ flower
- ○ beatify
- ○ bedaub

A simple opposite for DECAY is *grow*. Clearly, (A) and (B) don't mean *grow*. (C) looks good. (D) and (E) contain hard words that you may not know. You can't cross them out just because you don't know what *beatify* and *bedaub* mean. However, you can guess (C) over (D) and (E) because you know that (C) definitely works. Most of the time when you see an antonym that has an easy word like DECAY, the correct answer will also have an easy word.

QUICK QUIZ #1

For each of the following questions, make a simple opposite for the stem word. The answers are on page 174.

1. CALLOUS:

2. HAPHAZARD:

3. INDOLENCE:

4. AUSTERE:

5. ANNUL:

QUICK QUIZ #2

For each of the following questions, make a simple opposite for the stem word. Then pick the answer that is the best match. The answers are on page 174.

1. BESTOW:

   ○ condense
   ○ dispossess
   ○ contribute
   ○ disregard
   ○ accuse

2. AUTHENTICATE:

   ○ restore
   ○ misrepresent
   ○ disallow
   ○ invalidate
   ○ demolish

3. DECREPIT:

   ○ powerful
   ○ nurturing
   ○ just
   ○ impressive
   ○ conspicuous

4. PUNGENT:

   ○ benevolent
   ○ meek
   ○ bland
   ○ harmful
   ○ piercing

5. PINNACLE:

   ○ moderation
   ○ underestimation
   ○ lowest point
   ○ suppression
   ○ unvalued object

A WORD YOU SORT OF KNOW

So far, so good. Things start getting a little trickier, though, when the stem word is one that you only sort of know. If you come across a stem word you sort of know, there are three possible ways to attack it:

1. Opposites for the answer choices
2. Positive/Negative
3. Word Association

OPPOSITE ANSWER CHOICES

Since you can't define the stem word exactly—and so can't make a simple opposite for it—try starting with the answer choices instead. Make a simple opposite for each answer choice and then ask yourself if the opposite could be the meaning of the stem word. Let's try this technique with the example we looked at earlier.

INCENSED:

○ mollified
○ ecstatic
○ entertained
○ peeved
○ satisfied

Let's say that you're not sure what INCENSED means. Therefore, take a look at the answer choices.

What's a simple opposite for (A), *mollified*? *Mollified* means appeased, so a good opposite would be along the lines of *provoked* or *irritated*. Does INCENSED mean *provoked* or *irritated*? No. So eliminate (A).

What's a simple opposite for (B), *ecstatic*? Since *ecstatic* means very happy, a good opposite is *very angry*. Does INCENSED mean *very angry*? Yes. (B) looks good, but be sure to check the remaining answer choices.

What's a simple opposite for (C), *entertained*? *Bored*, maybe. Well, does INCENSED mean *bored*? No. Get rid of (C).

What's a simple opposite for (D), *peeved*? *Peeved* means annoyed, so a good opposite would be along the lines of *made happy*. Does INCENSED mean *made happy*? No. Eliminate (D).

What's a simple opposite for (E), *satisfied*? *Unsatisfied* works. Does INCENSED mean *unsatisfied*? No. Throw out (E).

Once again, we've proved that (B) is the best answer.

Let's try another one. For each blank line, write a word that is a good opposite for the answer choice.

UNADULTERATED:

○ mismanaged   _____
○ consecrated   _____
○ persecuted   _____
○ reprieved   _____
○ defiled   _____

A good opposite for *mismanaged* is *managed well*. Does UNADULTERATED mean *managed well*? No.

A good opposite for *consecrated* is *profaned*. Does UNADULTERATED mean *profaned*? No.

A good opposite for *persecuted* is *treated well*. Does UNADULTERATED mean *treated well*? No.

A good opposite for *reprieved* is *condemned*. Does UNADULTERATED mean *condemned*? No.

A good opposite for *defiled* is *pure*. Does UNADULTERATED mean *pure*? Yes.

The best answer, then, is (E). Notice how important it is to go through each answer choice. Also notice that distracting answer choices are those that mean the same thing as the stem word—not the opposite.

Okay, one more:

SANCTION:

- credit _____
- disapprove _____
- inform _____
- elaborate _____
- devalue _____

A good opposite for *credit* is *discredit*. Is that what SANCTION means? No.

A good opposite for *disapprove* is *approve*. Is that what SANCTION means? Looks good.

A good opposite for *inform* is—well, is there really a good opposite for *inform*? If an answer choice doesn't have an opposite, then it can't be right. *Inform* doesn't work, then.

Does *elaborate* have a good opposite? Not really.

A good opposite for *devalue* is *value*. Is that what SANCTION means? No. So the best answer is (B). Once again, make sure you check out (A) through (E). And be aggressive—challenge the words in the answer choices. Do they really have opposites or not? You may find that some of them don't.

Positive/Negative

Making opposites for the answer choices works well when you sort of know the stem word pretty well. There are other times when the stem word is one that you sort of know, just barely. In this case, try using Positive/Negative. Positive/Negative takes advantage of the fact that certain words have connotations. For example, we all would say the word *intelligent* has a positive connotation while the word *boastful* has a negative one.

Well, if you sort of know that the stem word is positive, then what do you know about the correct answer? It has to be negative. Similarly, if you sort of know that the stem word is negative, then you know the correct answer has to be positive. Finally, if you sort of know that the stem word is either positive or negative, then what else do you know? That any answer choice that is neutral can't be right. Try the example on the next page:

CENSURE:

○ speak in praise of
○ increase the value of
○ shy away from
○ take without consent
○ leave in its original state

If you know that CENSURE is a negative word, then you can eliminate any answer choice that is negative as well. (A) is positive, so leave it in. (B) is also positive, so leave it in, too. (C) and (D), however, are both negative, so eliminate them. (E) isn't really positive or negative. Possibly, it's slightly positive, but CENSURE is a very negative word, so it probably isn't right. You're left with (A) and (B). At this point, just guess. You have a 50 percent chance of getting the question right. As it turns out, the best answer is (A). CENSURE means to blame.

As you can see from this example, Positive/Negative won't necessarily get you to the right answer, but it can do some effective POE. And when you only sort of know a word, it can be pretty helpful.

WORD ASSOCIATION

Sometimes you only sort of know a word because you've heard it used in a sentence or a phrase. In other words, you associate that word with something. Take a look at the following example:

BOYCOTT:

○ negate
○ deflect
○ engender
○ patronize
○ entitle

Probably you've heard the word BOYCOTT used before, as in "to BOYCOTT the Olympics." Well, let's use "BOYCOTT the Olympics" to our advantage. Let's substitute each answer choice for BOYCOTT in the phrase.

Does "*negate* the Olympics" make sense? Not unless you can kill a sporting event.

Does "*deflect* the Olympics" make sense? Definitely not.

Does "*engender* the Olympics" make sense? Not really.

Does "*patronize* the Olympics" make sense? Sure.

Does "*entitle* the Olympics" make sense? Nope.

So the best answer is (D).

Word Association is a great technique to use if you've heard a word used before in a specific way. Also, keep in mind that sometimes Word Association can help you determine whether a word is positive or negative. In other words, you can use Positive/Negative and Word Association in conjunction to do some good POE.

QUICK QUIZ #3

For each of the following questions, determine whether the word is positive or negative. The answers are on page 174.

1. PEREMPTORY:

2. CAPTIOUS:

3. ABSTEMIOUS:

4. TORTUOUS:

5. PROPAGATE:

6. VITUPERATE:

7. PROFLIGATE:

8. SPURIOUS:

9. SATURNINE:

10. ALACRITY:

11. DELETERIOUS:

12. OBVIATE:

13. NOISOME:

14. REDOUBTABLE:

15. SEDULOUS:

QUICK QUIZ #4

For each of the following questions, pretend that you sort of know the stem word. Try to do some POE by making opposites for the answer choices or by using Positive/Negative or Word Association. The answers are on page 175.

1. UNREQUITED:
   - ○ beneficial
   - ○ attractive
   - ○ indulgent
   - ○ ethical
   - ○ reciprocated

2. IMPUGN:
   - ○ forestall
   - ○ commend
   - ○ extend
   - ○ conspire
   - ○ attribute

3. CAPITULATE:
   - ○ accomplish
   - ○ lament
   - ○ endorse
   - ○ stand fast
   - ○ demand

4. NIGGARDLY:
   - ○ vexing
   - ○ potent
   - ○ magnanimous
   - ○ accommodating
   - ○ prudish

5. SALIENT:
   - ○ inconspicuous
   - ○ disdainful
   - ○ attentive
   - ○ empty
   - ○ informative

6. ABDICATE:
   - ○ flourish
   - ○ subdue
   - ○ struggle
   - ○ disperse
   - ○ appropriate

7. HALCYON:
   - ○ arousing
   - ○ explicit
   - ○ insinuating
   - ○ disquieted
   - ○ bemoaning

8. HACKNEYED:
   - ○ ornamental
   - ○ uncertain
   - ○ faithful
   - ○ unprecedented
   - ○ winning

9. ABEYANCE:
   - ○ restoration of activity
   - ○ acquiescence to authority
   - ○ toleration of depravity
   - ○ insistence on decorum
   - ○ preservation of honor

10. ABERRATION:
    - ○ idleness
    - ○ clarification
    - ○ allusion
    - ○ refinement
    - ○ conformity

11. PHLEGMATIC:
- ○ contrary
- ○ unsettled
- ○ informed
- ○ duplicated
- ○ lively

12. PROBITY:
- ○ yield
- ○ indecency
- ○ cowardice
- ○ expediency
- ○ renown

13. PERFUNCTORY:
- ○ uncommitted
- ○ compelling
- ○ thorough
- ○ arbitrary
- ○ fostering

14. PRODIGAL:
- ○ besmirched
- ○ virtuous
- ○ pompous
- ○ unaffected
- ○ economical

15. VOLUBLE:
- ○ untalkative
- ○ fleeting
- ○ unqualified
- ○ suave
- ○ emphatic

A WORD YOU DON'T KNOW AT ALL

A word you don't know at all is one that you hate. If you ever come across a stem word that you've never seen before, don't waste your time. Be aggressive and guess. Then move on. The worst thing you can do is agonize over which answer choice is best when you haven't any clue what the stem word means.

To guide you in guessing, here are some last resorts:

1. Eliminate answer choices that contain words without opposites.

2. Pick an answer choice that is extreme—that is, very positive or very negative.

Probably the most effective POE tool is the first one: Eliminate words that don't have opposites. Always start off here, and then once you've done all the POE you can, just guess—pick the most extreme.

QUICK QUIZ #5

On the following questions, pretend that you don't know the stem word at all. Use your guessing techniques to eliminate bad answer choices. Then be aggressive and guess—pick the answer choice that is the most extreme. The answers are on page 177.

1. CANARD:

   ○ an improper gesture
   ○ a concealed object
   ○ a defined position
   ○ a true story
   ○ a casual lie

2. INFRANGIBLE:

   ○ breakable
   ○ mixable
   ○ aggressive
   ○ transitory
   ○ violating

3. CAVIL:

   ○ patronize
   ○ denounce
   ○ approve
   ○ consummate
   ○ fabricate

4. MACERATE:

   ○ concur
   ○ reflect
   ○ harden
   ○ officiate
   ○ liquefy

5. FRIABLE:

   ○ tactile
   ○ durable
   ○ wavering
   ○ conventional
   ○ disheveled

SECONDARY MEANINGS

Before we wrap up antonyms, a quick note. Often, ETS tests the secondary meanings of words. For example, look at the following antonym:

RAIL:

- ⬭ consolidate
- ⬭ extol
- ⬭ substantiate
- ⬭ encourage
- ⬭ emote

Is ETS talking about a RAIL that you can sit on? No. It's talking about the verb RAIL. You can tell ETS wants the verb definition of RAIL by looking at the answer choices. They're all verbs. The part of speech used in the answer choices can help you determine if ETS is testing a secondary meaning.

QUICK QUIZ #6

The following words have both primary definitions and secondary definitions. Provide the two meanings for each word. The answers are on page 178.

1. novel
   _____
   _____

2. table
   _____
   _____

3. color
   _____
   _____

4. plastic
   _____
   _____

5. convention
   _____
   _____

6. individual
   _____
   _____

7. industry
   _____
   _____

8. secrete
   _____
   _____

9. gauge
   _____
   _____

10. marshal
    _____
    _____

IN SUMMARY

Antonyms, once again, are largely a vocabulary test. Either you know the words or you don't. Still, there are some techniques to help you eliminate wrong answer choices. What's most important is that you take enough time to get an antonym right when it's a word you know or sort of know—and that you be aggressive and guess when it's a word you don't know at all. So be honest with yourself while working on antonyms. What kind of word is it: one you know, sort of know, or have never seen in your life?

When you know the stem word . . .

1. Make a simple opposite for the stem word. Then pick the answer choice that best matches your opposite. Watch out for answer choices that have the same meaning as the stem, and make sure to go through all of the choices.

When you sort of know the stem word . . .

1. Make opposites for the answer choices and see which opposite has the same meaning as the stem word. Remember, if a word doesn't have an opposite, it can't be right.

2. Use Positive/Negative or Word Association.

When you don't know the stem word at all . . .

1. Eliminate words with no opposites.

2. Pick the answer choice that is the most extreme.

PRACTICE QUESTIONS #1

Directions: Each question below consists of a word printed in capital letters, followed by five lettered words or phrases. Choose the lettered word or phrase that is most nearly <u>opposite</u> in meaning to the word in capital letters.

Since some of the questions require you to distinguish fine shades of meaning, be sure to consider all the choices before deciding which one is best. The answers are on page 179.

1. VARIEGATED:

   ○ uniform
   ○ unprecedented
   ○ infrequent
   ○ incomprehensible
   ○ presumable

2. SOLICITOUS:

   ○ belittling
   ○ ardent
   ○ indicative
   ○ inattentive
   ○ aspiring

3. CONFORMITY:

   ○ fluctuation
   ○ diminution
   ○ inflexibility
   ○ differentiation
   ○ disparity

4. BLASPHEME:

   ○ anticipate
   ○ reprimand
   ○ mollify
   ○ revere
   ○ revel

5. PIQUANT:

   ○ effervescent
   ○ insipid
   ○ obsolete
   ○ hoary
   ○ irksome

6. GERMANE:

   ○ irrepressible
   ○ circuitous
   ○ sumptuous
   ○ avaricious
   ○ extraneous

7. EFFRONTERY:

   ○ effacement
   ○ chasteness
   ○ audacity
   ○ malaise
   ○ banter

8. FACTITIOUS:

   ○ objective
   ○ erroneous
   ○ genuine
   ○ problematic
   ○ partial

9. VAGARIOUS:

   ○ predictable
   ○ stringent
   ○ widespread
   ○ affluent
   ○ sociable

10. VIM:

    ○ commotion
    ○ despondency
    ○ discord
    ○ lethargy
    ○ potency

11. CABAL:

    ○ well-disciplined unit
    ○ revered society
    ○ public organization
    ○ legal party
    ○ united front

PRACTICE QUESTIONS #2

Directions: Each question below consists of a word printed in capital letters, followed by five lettered words or phrases. Choose the lettered word or phrase that is most nearly opposite in meaning to the word in capital letters.

Since some of the questions require you to distinguish fine shades of meaning, be sure to consider all the choices before deciding which one is best. The answers are on page 182.

1. COMMENSURATE:

   ○ unimpressive
   ○ inconclusive
   ○ insignificant
   ○ uneven
   ○ inconvenient

2. REVILE:

   ○ welcome
   ○ spurn
   ○ compliment
   ○ utilize
   ○ demean

3. EXHUME:

   ○ investigate
   ○ return
   ○ air out
   ○ bury
   ○ grieve over

4. TACIT:

   ○ reluctant
   ○ unabashed
   ○ dour
   ○ flirtatious
   ○ spoken

5. REALIZE:

   ○ disclose
   ○ thwart
   ○ misrepresent
   ○ collapse
   ○ coerce

6. FLOTSAM:

   ○ valuable object
   ○ cherished memento
   ○ unusual antique
   ○ common item
   ○ creative endeavor

7. INCIPIENCY:

   ○ dispersion
   ○ detachment
   ○ extrusion
   ○ cessation
   ○ misrepresentation

8. QUOTIDIAN:

   ○ arousing
   ○ holy
   ○ manic
   ○ exceptional
   ○ methodical

9. JADED:

   ○ humorous
   ○ original
   ○ jovial
   ○ blessed
   ○ enlivened

10. VACUITY:

    ○ spaciousness
    ○ repleteness
    ○ fruition
    ○ rotundity
    ○ maturity

11. NUBILE:

    ○ emaciated
    ○ not marriageable
    ○ inactive
    ○ lacking in taste
    ○ awkward

PRACTICE QUESTIONS #3

Directions: Each question below consists of a word printed in capital letters, followed by five lettered words or phrases. Choose the lettered word or phrase that is most nearly <u>opposite</u> in meaning to the word in capital letters.

Since some of the questions require you to distinguish fine shades of meaning, be sure to consider all the choices before deciding which one is best. The answers are on page 184.

1. WILLFUL:

   ○ yielding
   ○ pleasant
   ○ calculated
   ○ rational
   ○ indirect

2. DORMANCY:

   ○ sluggishness
   ○ adaptability
   ○ boldness
   ○ consciousness
   ○ enthusiasm

3. ACUITY:

   ○ callousness
   ○ full of criticism
   ○ arrogance
   ○ shortsightedness
   ○ lack of insight

4. PROMULGATE:

   ○ diminish
   ○ revise
   ○ dismiss
   ○ truncate
   ○ revoke

5. EMASCULATE:

   ○ invigorate
   ○ incite
   ○ scour
   ○ purge
   ○ appropriate

6. ROUT:

   ○ uneasy stalemate
   ○ desperate act
   ○ unconditional surrender
   ○ joyous union
   ○ organized attack

7. SPECULATIVE:

   ○ destitute
   ○ confirmed
   ○ concrete
   ○ magnanimous
   ○ governable

8. DILATORY:

   ○ retracting
   ○ closed up
   ○ overextended
   ○ speeding up
   ○ cutting

9. NUGATORY:

   ○ having many consequences
   ○ possessing great worth
   ○ tending toward simplicity
   ○ free from guilt
   ○ deserving of blame

10. TYRO:

   ○ a philanthropist
   ○ an expert
   ○ a lackey
   ○ a miser
   ○ a prodigy

11. HAUTEUR:

   ○ adulation
   ○ gravity
   ○ humbleness
   ○ amicability
   ○ frivolity

PRACTICE QUESTIONS #4

Directions: Each question below consists of a word printed in capital letters, followed by five lettered words or phrases. Choose the lettered word or phrase that is most nearly <u>opposite</u> in meaning to the word in capital letters.

Since some of the questions require you to distinguish fine shades of meaning, be sure to consider all the choices before deciding which one is best. The answers are on page 187.

1. DISTEND:

   ○ restrict
   ○ limit
   ○ wrinkle
   ○ contract
   ○ reject

2. ARTLESS:

   ○ immodest
   ○ deceptive
   ○ demonstrative
   ○ common
   ○ delightful

3. PROCRASTINATE:

   ○ respond remorsefully
   ○ work rapidly
   ○ reject entirely
   ○ address immediately
   ○ complete fully

4. AFFABLE:

   ○ penitent
   ○ stubborn
   ○ retiring
   ○ languishing
   ○ disconsolate

5. INFINITESIMAL:

   ○ brief
   ○ eternal
   ○ powerful
   ○ huge
   ○ limited

6. DUCTILE:

   ○ infirm
   ○ imperceptible
   ○ unmalleable
   ○ climactic
   ○ perilous

7. APTNESS:

   ○ inexperience
   ○ timeliness
   ○ disinclination
   ○ unsuitability
   ○ virtuosity

8. CALLOW:

   ○ full-fledged
   ○ worn-out
   ○ somber
   ○ reflective
   ○ unproblematic

9. IGNOMINY:

   ○ honorable conduct
   ○ faithful adherence
   ○ careful exposition
   ○ vague suggestion
   ○ vigorous action

10. CELERITY:

   ○ dishonesty
   ○ cheerfulness
   ○ vividness
   ○ slowness
   ○ infamy

11. ABJURATION:

   ○ impotence
   ○ odiousness
   ○ fickleness
   ○ affirmation
   ○ vitality

PRACTICE QUESTIONS #5

Directions: Each question below consists of a word printed in capital letters, followed by five lettered words or phrases. Choose the lettered word or phrase that is most nearly <u>opposite</u> in meaning to the word in capital letters.

Since some of the questions require you to distinguish fine shades of meaning, be sure to consider all the choices before deciding which one is best. The answers are on page 190.

1. ARREST:

   ○ indulge
   ○ replace
   ○ speed up
   ○ go forth
   ○ initiate

2. DISCOUNT:

   ○ throw into confusion
   ○ simplify for convenience
   ○ declare with emphasis
   ○ gather one's composure
   ○ maintain as important

3. STANCH:

   ○ distill
   ○ commingle
   ○ make impure
   ○ increase the flow of
   ○ diminish in value

4. BEATIFY:

   ○ canonize
   ○ condemn
   ○ purge
   ○ pillage
   ○ debilitate

5. COMELY:

   ○ boorish
   ○ generous
   ○ unattractive
   ○ moderate
   ○ petty

6. IMPORTUNATE:

   ○ unimpressive
   ○ argumentative
   ○ not well-schooled
   ○ not urgent
   ○ vindicated

7. SANGUINE:

   ○ pallid
   ○ extenuated
   ○ impalpable
   ○ openness
   ○ protuberant

8. CATHOLIC:

   ○ irreligious
   ○ obstinate
   ○ close-minded
   ○ brazen
   ○ disreputable

9. SECRETE:

   ○ disclose
   ○ emit
   ○ enclose
   ○ attract
   ○ filter

10. CONDIGN:

    ○ undeserved
    ○ permissible
    ○ legitimate
    ○ disfavored
    ○ endorsed

11. SOPHISTIC:

    ○ sound
    ○ opportune
    ○ possible
    ○ coherent
    ○ merciful

ANSWERS AND EXPLANATIONS

Quick Quiz #1

1. sensitive

2. not random; ordered

3. working hard; diligence

4. not strict

5. reinstate

Quick Quiz #2

1. **B** Simple opposite: *take away*

2. **D** Simple opposite: *prove false*

3. **A** Simple opposite: *strong*

4. **C** Simple opposite: *flavorless*

5. **C** Simple opposite: *bottom*

Quick Quiz #3

1. −

2. −

3. +

4. −

5. +

6. −

7. −

8. −

9. −

10. +

11. −

12. −

13. −

14. +

15. +

Quick Quiz #4

1. **E** Try Word Association. Have you heard of the phrase "UNREQUITED love"? Use this phrase with each answer choice. Does *beneficial* love make sense? Not really. *Attractive* love? Not great. *Indulgent* love? Not great. *Ethical* love? No. *Reciprocated* love? Yes. The best answer is (E).

2. **B** Try Positive/Negative. IMPUGN is a negative word, so its opposite has to be positive. (A) is negative, so cross it out. (B) is positive, so leave it in. (C) is neither positive nor negative, so cross it out. (D) is negative, so cross it out. (E) could be either positive or negative, so it's probably not a good choice. The best answer is (B).

3. **D** Try Positive/Negative. CAPITULATE is a negative word, so its opposite has to be positive. (A) is positive, so leave it in. (B) is negative, so cross it out. (C) is positive, as is (D), so leave both in. (E) is negative, so cross it out. Now try making opposites for each answer choice. A simple opposite for (A) is *fail*. Is that what CAPITULATE means? Not quite. A simple opposite for (C) is *not support*. Is that what CAPITULATE means? No. A simple opposite for (D) is *give in*. Is that what CAPITULATE means? Yes. The best answer is (D).

4. **C** Try Positive/Negative. NIGGARDLY is a negative word, so its opposite has to be positive. (A) is negative, so cross it out. (B), (C), and (D) are all positive, so leave them in. (E) is negative, so cross it out. Now try Word Association. Have you heard of the phrase "NIGGARDLY sum of money"? Use that phrase with each remaining answer choice. Does *potent* sum of money make sense? Not really. Does *magnanimous* sum of money make sense? Sort of. Does *accommodating* sum of money make sense? No. The best answer is (C).

5. **A** Try Positive/Negative. SALIENT is a positive word, so its opposite must be negative. (A) is negative, so keep it. (B) is negative, too, so leave it in. (C) is positive, so cross it out. (D) is negative, so it's okay. (E) is positive, so cross it out. Now use Word Association. Have you heard of the phrase "Go over the SALIENT points"? Test that phrase on the remaining answer choices. Does *inconspicuous* points make sense? Sort of. What about *disdainful* points? No. *Empty* points? Maybe. At this point, you have two answer choices left—(A) and (D). If that's all you know about SALIENT, then just guess. You have a 50 percent chance of getting the question right. The best answer is (A).

6. **E** Try Word Association. Have you heard of the phrase "ABDICATE the throne"? Does *flourish* the throne make sense? No. Does *subdue* the throne? Maybe. Does *struggle* the throne? No. Does *disperse* the throne? No. Does *appropriate* the throne. Yes. Between (B) and (E), which makes more sense? (E). It's the best answer.

7. **D** Try Positive/Negative. HALCYON is a positive word, so its opposite must be negative. (A) is positive, so cross it out. (B) could be either positive or negative, so it's probably not right. (C), (D), and (E) are all negative, so leave them in. If you don't know anything else about HALCYON, then just guess—you have a one-in-three chance of getting the question right. The best answer is (D).

8. **D** Try making simple opposites for the answer choices. A simple opposite for (A) is *plain*. Does HACKNEYED mean *plain*? No. A simple opposite for (B) is *certain*. Does HACKNEYED mean *certain*? No. A simple opposite for (C) is *unfaithful*. Does HACKNEYED mean *unfaithful*? No. A simple opposite for (D) is *done before*. Does HACKNEYED mean *done before*? Sort of. A simple opposite for (E) is *losing*. Does HACKNEYED mean *losing*? No. The best answer is (D).

9. **A** Try making simple opposites for the answer choices. A simple opposite for (A) is *cessation of activity*. Is that what ABEYANCE means? (Think of the phrase "held in ABEYANCE.") Maybe. A simple opposite for (B) is *challenge to authority*. Is that what ABEYANCE means? No. A simple opposite for (C) is *refusing to tolerate depravity*. Is that what ABEYANCE means? No. A simple opposite for (D) is *disregard of decorum*. Is that what ABEYANCE means? No. A simple opposite for (E) is *wasting away of honor*. Is that what ABEYANCE means? No. The best answer is (A).

10. **E** Try making simple opposites for the answer choices. A simple opposite for (A) is *activity*. Is that what ABERRATION means? No. A simple opposite for (B) is *confusion*. Is that what ABERRATION means? No. There's not a strong opposite for (C), so it can't be the right answer. A simple opposite for (D) is *vulgarity*. Is that what ABERRATION means? No. A simple opposite for (E) is *deviancy*. Is that what ABERRATION means? Yes. The best answer is (E).

11. **B** Try Positive/Negative. PHLEGMATIC is a positive word, so its opposite must be negative. (A) and (B) are negative, so leave both in. (C) is positive, so cross it out. (D) could be slightly negative, so leave it in. (E) is positive, so cross it out. If that's all you know about PHLEGMATIC, then just guess. You have a one-in-three chance of getting the question right. The best answer is (B).

12. **B** Try Positive/Negative. PROBITY is a positive word, so its opposite must be negative. (A) is neither positive nor negative, so it can't be right. (B) is negative, so leave it in. (C) is negative, so leave it in. (D) is positive, as is (E), so cross them out. Now make simple opposites for each answer choice. A simple opposite for (B) is *decency*. Is that what PROBITY means? Yes. A simple opposite for (C) is *bravery*. Is that what PROBITY means? No. The best answer is (B).

13. **C** Try Word Association. Have you heard of the phrase "PERFUNCTORY kiss"? Use that phrase on the answer choices. Does *uncommitted* kiss make sense? Maybe. Does *compelling* kiss make sense? Yes. Does *thorough* kiss make sense? Yes. Does *arbitrary* kiss make sense? Not really. Does *fostering* kiss make sense? No. If that's all you know about PERFUNCTORY, then just guess. You have a one-in-three chance of getting the question right. The best answer is (C).

14. **E** Try Word Association. Have you heard of "the PRODIGAL son" in the Bible? If you have, that tells you PRODIGAL has a negative meaning. Its opposite, then, must be positive. (A) is negative, so cross it out. (B) is positive, so keep it. (C) is negative, so cross it out. (D) and (E) are positive, so keep them. If that's all you know about PRODIGAL, then just guess. You have a pretty good chance of getting the question right. The best answer is (E).

15. **A** Try Positive/Negative. VOLUBLE is a negative word, so its opposite must be positive. (A) is positive, so keep it. (B) is negative, so eliminate it. (C) can be either positive or negative, depending on context, so keep it. (D) is positive, so keep it. (E) is positive, so keep it. Now what? You weren't able to do any POE. Try making opposites for the answer choices. A simple opposite for (A) is *talkative*. Is that what VOLUBLE means? Yes. Still, check out the remaining answer choices. A simple opposite for (B) is *permanent*. Is that what VOLUBLE means? No. A simple opposite for (C) is *qualified*. Is that what VOLUBLE means? No. A simple opposite for (D) is *clumsy*. Is that what VOLUBLE means? No. A simple opposite for (E) is *indecisive*. Is that what VOLUBLE means? No. The best answer is (A).

Quick Quiz #5

1. **D** Improper gesture probably wouldn't have a good opposite. Neither would concealed object. What would the opposite of a casual lie be? A serious lie? A well-planned truth? You would probably want to guess between (C) and (D).

2. **A** Violating doesn't seem to have a good opposite. The others could all work. Take a guess and move on. Don't waste time.

3. **C** Consummate doesn't really have a good opposite. Take your best guess from what's left.

4. **C** There's no real good opposite for officiate. Reflect doesn't have a strong opposite. Guess between (A), (C), and (E).

5. **B** Tactile has no real opposite. Guess from the remaining four and move along. Save that time for questions that contain more words you know.

QUICK QUIZ #6

1. noun: prose narrative
   adjective: new; strange

2. noun: a piece of furniture
   verb: to put aside for an indefinite amount of time

3. noun: tint; hue
   verb: exaggerate

4. noun: synthetic material
   adjective: capable of being molded

5. noun: meeting; assembly
   noun: custom

6. noun: single member or person
   adjective: separate

7. noun: manufacturing activity
   noun: diligence

8. verb: emit
   verb: hide; conceal

9. noun: instrument for measuring
   verb: estimate; judge

10. noun: high official
    verb: arrange in order

Practice Questions #1

1. **A** If you know what the stem word means, make a simple opposite for it. VARIEGATED means varied, so a simple opposite might be something like *unvaried*. Does (A) mean *unvaried*? Yes. Does (B)? No. Does (C)? No. Does (D)? No. Does (E)? No. The best answer is (A).

2. **D** If you're not sure what the stem word means, you can do one of three things: (1) make simple opposites for the answer choices, (2) try Positive/Negative, or (3) try Word Association. Go with Positive/Negative. SOLICITOUS is a positive word, so its opposite must be negative. (A) is negative, so leave it in. (B) is positive, so eliminate it. (C) doesn't really have an opposite, so it can't be right. (D) is negative, so leave it in. (E) is positive, so cross it out.

   You're left with (A) and (D). Try making a simple opposite for each answer choice. A simple opposite for *belittling* is *praising*. Does SOLICITOUS mean *praising*? No. A simple opposite for *inattentive* is *attentive*. Does SOLICITOUS mean *attentive*? Yes. (D) is the best answer.

3. **E** When you know the stem word, make a simple opposite for it. CONFORMITY means agreement, so a simple opposite for it might be *disagreement*. Does (A) mean *disagreement*? No. Does (B)? No. Does (C)? Not really. Does (D)? Not quite. Does (E)? Yes. Looking at every answer choice is important because (D) is a close second.

4. **D** If you're not sure what the stem word means, you can do one of three things: (1) make simple opposites for the answer choices, (2) try Positive/Negative, or (3) try Word Association. Go with Positive/Negative. BLASPHEME is a negative word, so its opposite must be positive. (A) is sort of positive, so leave it in. (B) is negative, so cross it out. (C) is positive, so leave it in. (D) is positive, as is (E), so leave both in.

   Now what? Try making simple opposites for the answer choices. *Anticipate* in (A) means give advance thought to. A simple opposite, then, might be *put off*. Does BLASPHEME mean *put off*? No. *Mollify* in (C) means pacify, so a simple opposite might be *incite*? Does BLASPHEME mean *incite*? No. *Revere* in (D) means honor. A simple opposite, then, might be *dishonor*. Does BLASPHEME mean *dishonor*? Yes—but don't forget (E). *Revel* in (E) means take pleasure in, so a simple opposite might be *displease*. Does BLASPHEME mean *displease*? No. The best answer is (D).

   Note that you can also approach this question by using Word Association. You might have heard a form of BLASPHEME before (*blasphemous* or *blasphemy*) used in a religious way—e.g., to commit *blasphemy*.

5. **B** If you're not sure what the stem word means, you can do one of three things: (1) make simple opposites for the answer choices, (2) try Positive/Negative, or (3) try Word Association. Go with Word Association. Have you heard PIQUANT used before to describe food? If so, use this knowledge to your advantage. Is it possible to have *effervescent* food? *Effervescent* means bubbly, so (A) isn't likely. Is it possible to have *insipid* food? Sure—*insipid* means tasteless. Leave (B) in. Is it possible to have *obsolete* food? No—food can go bad, but it can't be outdated. Eliminate (C). Is it possible to have *hoary* food? If you don't know what *hoary* means, you can't cross (D) out. Is it possible to have *irksome* food? Probably not. Cross out (E).

    The remaining answer choices are (B) and (D). Go with what works. (B) is the best answer.

6. **E** If you're not sure what the stem word means, you can do one of three things: (1) make simple opposites for the answer choices, (2) try Positive/Negative, or (3) try Word Association. Go with Positive/Negative. GERMANE is a positive word, so its opposite must be negative. (A) is negative, so leave it in. (B) is somewhat negative, so leave it in, too. (C) is positive, so eliminate it. Don't cross out (D) if you don't know what *avaricious* means. (E) is negative, so leave it in.

    Now what? Try making simple opposites for the answer choices. A simple opposite for (A) is *repressible*. Does GERMANE mean *repressible*? No. A simple opposite for (B) is *straightforward* or *direct*. Is that what GERMANE means? No. (D) you have to skip if you don't know what *avaricious* means. A simple opposite for (E) is *relevant*. Does GERMANE mean relevant? Yes. Between an answer choice that contains a word you don't know and an answer choice that works, go with the one that works. (E) is the best answer.

7. **A** If you're not sure what the stem word means, you can do one of three things: (1) make simple opposites for the answer choices, (2) try Positive/Negative, or (3) try Word Association. Go with Positive/Negative. Since EFFRONTERY is a negative word, its opposite has to be positive. (A) and (B) are both positive, so leave them in. (C) and (D), though, are both negative, so eliminate them. (E) is positive, so it's okay.

    Now what? Try making opposites for the answer choices. A simple opposite for (A) is *boldness*. Is that what EFFRONTERY means? Yes. Still, check the remaining answer choices. A simple opposite for (B) is *impurity* or *indecency*. Does that match EFFRONTERY? No. A simple opposite for (E) is *serious talk*. Is that what EFFRONTERY means? No. The best answer is (A).

8. **C** When you don't know the stem word at all, don't waste time. Look at the answer choices and see if you can eliminate any that don't have opposites. Then guess —pick the answer choice that is the most extreme. For this question, each of the answer choices does have an opposite. So guess. The most extreme answer choices are (B) and (C). The best answer, as it turns out, is (C). FACTITIOUS means false.

9. **A** If you're not sure what the stem word means, you can do one of three things: (1) make simple opposites for the answer choices, (2) try Positive/Negative, or (3) try Word Association. Go with Word Association. You've probably seen a form of VAGARIOUS before: *vagary*. The phrase you might have heard using *vagary* is "*vagaries* of fortune." From the phrase, you can divine that VAGARY is a negative word. Therefore, its opposite is positive. (A) is positive, so leave it in. (B) is negative, so cross it out. (C) is slightly positive, so leave it in. (D) and (E) are both positive so leave them in, too.

    Go back to the phrase "*vagaries* of fortune." Try using the phrase with the answer choices. Does *predictable* fortune make sense? Sure. Does *widespread* fortune make sense? Perhaps. Does *affluent* fortune make sense? No. Does *sociable* fortune make sense? No.

    You're down to (A) and (C). In other words, you've got a 50 percent chance of getting this question right, so just guess. The best answer is actually (A).

10. **D** If you're not sure what the stem word means, you can do one of three things: (1) make simple opposites for the answer choices, (2) try Positive/Negative, or (3) try Word Association. Go with Word Association. Have you ever heard of the phrase "VIM and vigor"? This should tell you that VIM is a positive word. Its opposite, then, must be negative. (A), (B), (C), and (D) are all negative, so they could be right. (E) is positive, so it can't work. Cross it out. What does the phrase "VIM and vigor" indicate about VIM? Sounds like it means something to do with energy. The opposite of energy is *lack of energy*, so *lethargy* in (D) is the best answer.

11. **C** When you have no idea what the stem word means, don't waste time. Look at the answer choices and see if you can eliminate any that don't have opposites. Then guess—pick the answer choice that is the most extreme. For this question, each of the answer choices does have an opposite. So guess. The most extreme answer choice is (B). As it turns out, however, the best answer is (C). A CABAL is a secret group, usually one engaged in intrigue.

PRACTICE QUESTIONS #2

1. **D** When you know the stem word, make a simple opposite for it. COMMENSURATE means *equal*, so a simple opposite is *unequal*. Does (A) mean *unequal*? Not quite. (B)? No. (C)? Not quite. (D)? Yes. (E)? No. The best answer is (D).

2. **C** When you know the stem word, make a simple opposite. REVILE means *abuse*, so a simple opposite might be *treat well*. Does (A) match? Not really. Does (B)? No. (C)? Sure. (D)? No. (E)? No. The best answer is (C).

3. **D** EXHUME is probably a word you sort of know. If you can't provide a definition for EXHUME, then you have one of three options: (1) make simple opposites for the answer choices, (2) try Positive/Negative, or (3) try Word Association. Go with Word Association. Have you heard of the phrase "EXHUME a dead body"? Use that phrase with the answer choices. In (A): *investigate* a dead body? Maybe. In (B): *return* a dead body? No. In (C): *air out* a dead body? Not likely. In (D): *bury* a dead body. Sure. In (E): *grieve over* a dead body? Yes.

    You're left with (A), (D), and (E). What now? Make simple opposites for the answer choices. A simple opposite for (A) might be *ignore*. Is that what EXHUME means? No. A simple opposite for (D) is *unearth*. Is that what EXHUME means? Yes. A simple opposite for (E) is *celebrate*. Is that what EXHUME means? No. The best answer is (D).

4. **E** When you sort of know the stem word, you have one of three options: (1) make simple opposites for the answer choices, (2) try Positive/Negative, or (3) try Word Association. Go with Word Association. Have you heard of the phrase "TACIT approval"? Use that phrase with the answer choices. In (A): *reluctant* approval? Maybe. In (B): *unabashed* approval? Maybe. In (C): *dour* approval? No. In (D): *flirtatious* approval? No. In (E): *spoken* approval? Maybe.

    You're left with (A), (B), and (E). Try making simple opposites for the answer choices. A simple opposite for (A) is *eager*. Does TACIT mean *eager*? No. A simple opposite for (B) is *embarrassed*. Is that what TACIT means? No. A simple opposite for (E) is *silent*. Is that what TACIT means? Close. (E) is the best answer.

5. **B** REALIZE isn't too hard a word, but be careful—REALIZE is often used to mean *understand*. But just because it's used that way doesn't mean that *understand* is the definition of REALIZE. What does REALIZE actually mean? Pretty much what it sounds like—*make real*. In other words, REALIZE means *accomplish*. A

simple opposite for REALIZE, then, is *not accomplish*. Does (A) give you that? No. What about (B)? Sort of. (C)? No. (D)? No. (E)? Definitely not. The best answer is (B).

6. **A**   FLOTSAM is the type of word that you either know or you don't know at all. Unless you sail a lot, you probably don't know the word. Since you don't know the word, you basically have to guess. But before you guess, look at the answer choices and see if you can eliminate any because the word it contains doesn't have an opposite. (B) doesn't really have a strong opposite, nor does (C).

    You're left with (A), (D), and (E). At this point, guess—choose the one that is the most extreme. (D) isn't very extreme, nor is (E). A good guess, therefore, is (A). And it is the best answer. FLOTSAM is debris, usually the floating wreckage of a ship.

7. **D**   When you know the stem word, make a simple opposite for it. If something is *incipient* (a form of INCIPIENCY), it's about to happen. So a simple opposite for INCIPIENCY is *something not happening*. Does that match (A)? No. (B) doesn't work either. (C) isn't a good match, but (D) is okay. Finally, (E) doesn't work. Therefore, the best answer is (D).

8. **D**   When you don't know the stem word at all, just guess. Don't waste a lot of time on a question like this. However, do try to do some POE. Are there any answer choices you can eliminate that don't have opposites? No. Each answer choice could have an opposite. Therefore, guess—pick the answer choice that is the most extreme. (A) is pretty extreme, as are (B), (C), and (D). So pick—it doesn't really matter which one. Just be aggressive and don't waste time. As it turns out, the best answer is (D) because QUOTIDIAN means common or ordinary.

    This question is a great example of why it's a good idea to improve your vocabulary. Antonyms are basically a vocabulary test: If you know the stem word, an antonym is easy; if you don't, good luck.

9. **E**   JADED is a word that you probably sort of know. You can't provide a definition of it, but you do know that it's negative. The right answer, then, must be positive. Unfortunately, (A), (B), (C), (D), and (E) are all positive, so you can't do any POE.

    What now? Try making simple opposites for the answer choices. A simple opposite for (A) is *not funny*. Is that what JADED means? No. A simple opposite for (B) is *unoriginal*. Is that what JADED means? No. A good opposite for (C) is *very sad*. Is that what JADED means? No. A good opposite for (D) is *condemned*. Is that what JADED means? No. A good opposite for (E) is *tired*. Is that what JADED means? Yes. The best answer is (E).

10. **B** You may not have seen VACUITY before, but you probably have seen a form of it: *vacuous*. Don't let the noun form of *vacuous* throw you. You know that *vacuous* means empty, so a good opposite for VACUITY is *fullness*. (A) doesn't quite work. (B) does, however. (C) doesn't quite fit, and (D) definitely doesn't. Finally, (E) isn't a good match. The best answer, then, is (B).

This question is easy to miss if you work too quickly. (A) and (C) are both attractive if you don't take the time to think and consider all the answer choices. Remember, accuracy is more important than speed.

11. **B** Even though you've probably heard the word NUBILE before, make sure you *don't* treat it as a word you know. Can you provide a solid definition for NUBILE? If you can't, then it's a word that you only sort of know. For a word you sort of know, you can (1) make opposites for the answer choices, (2) use Positive/Negative, or (3) use Word Association. Go with Word Association. Have you heard the phrase "NUBILE young woman" before? If so, then you associate the word NUBILE with attractiveness. A good opposite for the stem word, then, is *unattractiveness*. Does (A) work? Not really. *Emaciated* means overly thin. What about (B)? It could work. (C)? No. (D)? No. (E)? Maybe.

You're left with (B) and (E). Since you have a 50 percent chance of getting this question right, just guess. The best answer is actually (B). Though you might associate NUBILE with attractiveness, it actually means marriageable.

Practice Questions #3

1. **A** When you know the stem word, make a simple opposite for it. WILLFUL means stubborn, so a simple opposite might be *docile*. Does (A) match *docile*? Yes. Still, check the remaining answer choices just in case. (B) doesn't match, so eliminate it. (C) doesn't work, nor does (D), so cross them both out. Finally, (E) doesn't match, so the best answer is (A).

2. **D** When you know the stem word, make a simple opposite for it. DORMANCY is a state of sleep, so a simple opposite might be a *state of awakeness*. (A) is a synonym of DORMANCY—not an antonym—so cross it out. (B) doesn't match, nor does (C), so eliminate both. (D) looks pretty good, but check out (E) just in case. (E) isn't quite right, so the best answer is (D).

3. **E** You may think you don't know the word ACUITY, but you probably do. ACUITY is just a form of *acute*. What does *acute* mean? Perceptive. So a simple opposite for ACUITY is *no perception*. Does (A) match *no perception*? No. Does (B)? No. (C)? No. (D) isn't quite right, so check out (E). (E) is a good match— therefore, it's the best answer.

4. **E** PROMULGATE is one of those words that you hear used all the time, but you probably don't know the definition for. Since PROMULGATE is a word you only sort of know, you can't make an opposite for it. Instead, you have one of three ways to attack this question: (1) make simple opposites for the answer choices, (2) use Positive/Negative, or (3) use Word Association. Go with simple opposites for the answer choices. A simple opposite for (A) is *increase*. Does PROMULGATE mean *increase*? No. A simple opposite for (B) is *leave alone*. Does PROMULGATE mean *leave alone*? No. A simple opposite for (C) is *pay attention to*. Is that what PROMULGATE means? No. A simple opposite for (D) is *lengthen*. Is that what PROMULGATE means? No. A simple opposite for (E) is *put forth*. Is that what PROMULGATE means? It's the closest out of the five choices. (E) is the best answer.

5. **A** You've probably heard the word EMASCULATE used before, but you might not know its definition. If that's the case, don't make a simple opposite for EMASCULATE. Instead, you can (1) make simple opposites for the answer choices, (2) use Positive/Negative, or (3) use Word Association. Go with Positive/Negative. EMASCULATE is a negative word, so its opposite must be positive. (A) is positive, so it's okay. (B) and (C) are negative, so eliminate them. (D) could be either positive or negative, depending on context. Leave it in for now. (E) is positive, so leave it in, too.

    Now what? Try Word Association. You've probably heard of men being EMASCULATED in the sense that they somehow lose power. So EMASCULATE means something like take power away. A simple opposite, then, might be *give power*. Does (A) match? It could. Does (D)? No. What about (E)? No. The best answer is (A).

6. **E** If you only sort of know the stem word, you can do one of three things: (1) make simple opposites for the answer choices, (2) use Positive/Negative, or (3) use Word Association. Try Word Association. You might have heard ROUT used before in sports when one team completely defeats another—as in "it was a ROUT." ROUT, then, has something to do with being defeated, so a simple opposite might be something like *victory*. (A) isn't a good match, nor is (B) or (C). (D) is a bit too much. (E) isn't a perfect match, but it's the best one. ROUT is the opposite of an *organized attack*, or a *disorderly retreat*. The best answer is (E).

7. **C** SPECULATIVE is another one of those words that you've probably heard a lot, but you can't give a definition for. Since that's the case you can (1) make simple opposites for the answer choices, (2) use Positive/Negative, or (3) use Word Association. Try Positive/Negative. SPECULATIVE is slightly negative, so its opposite has to be slightly positive. (A) is negative, so eliminate it. (B) is

positive, so leave it in. (C) is also positive, so it's okay. Finally, (D) and (E) are positive, so leave them in.

What now? How about Word Association. Have you heard of the phrase "SPECULATIVE thought"? Try applying this phrase to the answer choices. Does a *confirmed* thought make sense? It could. Does a *concrete* thought make sense? Yes. Does a *magnanimous* thought make sense. Maybe. Does a *governable* thought make sense? Not really.

You're left with (B), (C), and (D). At this point, just guess. (D) probably isn't a good pick—*magnanimous* thought is okay, but it's not great. So choose either (B) or (C). You have a 50 percent chance of getting the question right. As it turns out, the best answer is (C). SPECULATIVE means *theoretical*.

8. **D** If you don't know DILATORY at all, don't waste time on this question. Try to use POE by eliminating answer choices without opposites, and then guess—pick the answer choice that is most extreme. Each answer choice for this question does have an opposite, so you can't do any POE. Pick, then, the most extreme. (C), (D), and (E) are the most extreme, so choose one of them. As it turns out, the best answer is (D). DILATORY means delaying.

This question is a good example of why you should improve your vocabulary. If you do know what DILATORY means, it doesn't take very long to do the question and get it right. If you don't know what DILATORY means, then you're pretty much stuck. What's important is that you don't spend too much time on any antonym if you don't know the word at all.

9. **B** NUGATORY is a word that you might sort of know. Since it's a word that you only sort of know, you can (1) make simple opposites for the answer choices, (2) use Positive/Negative, or (3) use Word Association. Try Positive/Negative. NUGATORY is a negative word, so its opposite must be positive. (A) and (E) are both negative, so eliminate them.

You're left with (B), (C), and (D). Each answer choice has an opposite, so you can't do any more POE. Therefore, guess—pick the choice that is the most extreme. That would probably be (B)—and (B) is the best answer.

10. **B** TYRO is probably a word you sort of know. Therefore, you have three options: (1) make simple opposites for the answer choices, (2) use Positive/Negative, or (3) use Word Association. Try Positive/Negative. TYRO is a negative word, so its opposite must be positive. (C) and (D) are both negative, so cross them out.

If you don't know anything else about TYRO, then you just have to guess. But before you do that, try to do some POE. Are there any answer choices left that don't really have opposites? (E) possibly. A *prodigy* is a young person who is very talented. So you're left with (A) and (B). Pick the choice that is the most extreme. (B) is more extreme than (A), and guess what? It's the best answer.

11. **C** Most likely, HAUTEUR is a word you sort of know. Therefore, you have three options: (1) make simple opposites for the answer choices, (2) use Positive/ Negative, or (3) use Word Association. Try Positive/Negative. HAUTEUR is negative, so its opposite must be positive. (B) is slightly negative, so eliminate it. (E) is slightly negative, too, so cross it out.

You're left with (A), (C), and (D). You can't do any more POE because each of the answer choices has an opposite. Therefore, just pick the answer choice that is the most extreme. (A) is the most extreme, so it's a good guess. As it turns out, though, the best answer is (C). HAUTEUR means arrogance.

Even though you missed this question, don't despair. You had only a very slight knowledge of HAUTEUR, and yet you were able to get the question down to three choices. A one-in-three chance of getting a question right isn't bad. In fact, it's quite good.

PRACTICE QUESTIONS #4

1. **D** When you know the stem word, make a simple opposite for it. DISTEND means swell out, so a simple opposite might be *shrink*. Does (A) match *shrink*? Not quite. What about (B)? No. (C)? Not quite. (D)? Yes. (E)? No. The best answer is (D).

2. **B** When you know the stem word, make a simple opposite for it. ARTLESS means something along the lines of natural, so a simple opposite might be *unnatural*. Does (A) match *unnatural*? No. What about (B)? Possibly. What about (C)? No. (D)? Not quite. (E)? No. The best answer is (B).

3. **D** When you know the stem word, make a simple opposite for it. PROCRASTINATE means to put off, so a simple opposite might be *do right away*. Is (A) a good match? No. What about (B)? Not quite. (C)? No. (D)? Looks good, but still, check out (E). (E) isn't quite right, so the best answer is (D). This question is easy—as long as you don't work too quickly and look at all the answer choices.

4. **C** If you're not entirely sure what AFFABLE means, then you have three options: (1) make simple opposites for the answer choices, (2) use Positive/Negative, or (3) use Word Association. Start off with Positive/Negative. AFFABLE is a positive word, so its opposite must be negative. (A) is positive, so eliminate it. (B) through (E) are all negative, so leave them in.

Now try making simple opposites for the answer choices. A simple opposite for (B) might be *yielding*. Is that what AFFABLE means? No. A simple opposite for (C) might be *outgoing*. Is that what AFFABLE means? Sort of. A simple opposite for (D) might be *active*. Is that what AFFABLE means? No. A simple opposite for (E) might be *happy*. Is that what AFFABLE means? Not quite. The best answer is (C).

5. **D** If you're not sure what INFINITESIMAL means, then you have three options: (1) make simple opposites for the answer choices, (2) use Positive/Negative, and (3) use Word Association. Start off with Positive/Negative. INFINITESIMAL is a slightly negative word, so its opposite must be positive. (A) is negative, so cross it out. (B) through (D) are all positive, so leave them in. (E) is negative, so eliminate it.

Now what? If Positive/Negative is the extent of your knowledge of INFINITESIMAL, then don't waste time. Each of the remaining answer choices has an opposite, so you can't do any POE. So just guess—pick the answer choice that is the most extreme. In this case, (B) or (D) are the most extreme possibilities. The best answer is actually (D) because INFINITESIMAL means very, very small.

6. **C** If you aren't entirely sure what DUCTILE means, then you have three options: (1) make simple opposites for the answer choices, (2) use Positive/Negative, or (3) use Word Association. Start off with Positive/Negative. DUCTILE is a slightly positive word, so its opposite must be negative. (A), (B), and (C) are all negative, so leave them in. (D) is positive, so cross it out. (E) is negative, so keep it.

Now what? If you don't know anything else about DUCTILE, then don't waste time. See if you can eliminate any answer choice because it doesn't have an opposite; then, just guess. For this question, each answer choice remaining does have an opposite, so you can't do any POE. So guess—pick the answer choice that is the most extreme. (E) is the most extreme, so it's a good guess. However, the best answer is actually (C) because DUCTILE means flexible or able to be shaped.

7. **D** You probably know a form of APTNESS: *apt*. Use this knowledge to your advantage. If something is *apt*, then it's appropriate. A simple opposite for APTNESS, then, is *inappropriateness*. (A) isn't a good match, nor is (B). (C) doesn't work, but (D) looks good. Finally, (E) isn't quite what you're looking for. The best answer is (D).

8. **A** If you aren't sure what CALLOW means, then you have three options: (1) make simple opposites for the answer choices, (2) use Positive/Negative, or (3) use Word Association. Try Word Association. Have you ever heard of the phrase "CALLOW youth"? Apply this phrase to each answer choice. Does *full-fledged* youth make sense? It could. What about *worn-out* youth? Not quite. *Somber* youth? Maybe. *Reflective* youth? Again, maybe. *Unproblematic* youth? Sure.

So you're left with (A), (C), (D), and (E). Try making simple opposites for each answer choice. A simple opposite for (A) might be *immature*. Is that what CALLOW means? Yes. Still, check out the remaining answer choices. A simple opposite for (C) might be *happy*. Is that what CALLOW means? No. A simple opposite for (D) might be *headstrong*. Is that what CALLOW means? No. A simple opposite for (E) might be *problematic*. Is that what CALLOW means? No. The best answer is (A).

9. **A** If you aren't sure what IGNOMINY means, then you have three options: (1) make simple opposites for the answer choices, (2) use Positive/Negative, or (3) use Word Association. Start off with Positive/Negative. IGNOMINY is a negative word, so its opposite must be positive. Each answer choice is positive, except (D), so get rid of (D). Now what? If Positive/Negative is the limit of what you know about IGNOMINY, then don't waste time. Make sure that each remaining answer choice does have an opposite; then just guess. In this case, the remaining answer choices do have opposites, so you can't do any more POE. So guess. Pick the answer choice that is the most extreme. (A) and (B) are both pretty extreme, so either one is a good guess. As it turns out, the best answer is (A). IGNOMINY means disgrace.

10. **D** If you aren't sure what CELERITY means, then you have three options: (1) make simple opposites for the answer choices, (2) use Positive/Negative, and (3) use Word Association. Start off with Positive/Negative. CELERITY is a positive word, so its opposite must be negative. (A) is negative, so keep it. (B) and (C) are positive, so eliminate them. (D) is negative, so it's okay, as is (E).

At this point, if you don't know anything else about CELERITY, check the remaining answer choices to ensure each has an opposite. Then, just guess. For this question, each answer choice left does have an opposite, so guess. Pick the one that is the most extreme. (A), (D), and (E) are all pretty extreme, so any one is a good guess. As it turns out, the best answer is (D). CELERITY means speediness.

11. **D** If you aren't sure what ABJURATION means, then you have three options: (1) make simple opposites for the answer choices, (2) use Positive/Negative, and (3) use Word Association. Start off with Positive/Negative. ABJURATION is a negative word, so its opposite has to be positive. Eliminate (A), (B), and (C) because each is negative.

You're left with (D) and (E). (D) and (E) each have an opposite, so you can't do any more POE. Therefore, just guess—you have a 50 percent chance of getting the question right. Pick the answer choice that is more extreme. Either (D) or (E) is a good guess because each is pretty extreme. As it turns out, the best answer is (D). ABJURATION means renunciation.

PRACTICE QUESTIONS #5

1. **E** When you know the stem word, make a simple opposite for it. ARREST means stop, so a simple opposite might be *start*. Does (A) mean *start*? No. Does (B)? No. Does (C)? Not quite. Does (D)? No. Does (E)? Yes. The best answer is (E).

2. **E** When you know the stem word, make a simple opposite for it. DISCOUNT means to disregard, so a simple opposite might be *regard well*. Does (A) match? No. What about (B)? No. (C)? Not quite. (D)? No. (E)? Yes. The best answer is (E).

3. **D** If you're not quite sure what STANCH means, then you have three options: (1) make simple opposites for the answer choices, (2) use Positive/Negative, or (3) use Word Association. Try Word Association. Have you heard of the phrase "STANCH the flow of blood"? Use that phrase on the answer choices. Does *distill* the flow of blood make sense? No. Does *commingle* the flow of blood make sense? Not quite. Does *make impure* the flow of blood make sense? Maybe. Does *increase the flow of* blood make sense? Yes. Does *diminish in value* the flow of blood make sense? No. Between (C) and (D), which makes more sense? Definitely (D). The best answer is (D).

4. **B** If you don't know for sure what BEATIFY means, then you have three options: (1) make simple opposites for the answer choices, (2) use Positive/Negative, or (3) use Word Association. Try Positive/Negative. BEATIFY is a positive word, so its opposite has to be negative. (A) is positive, so cross it out. (B) is negative, so leave it in. (C) is slightly positive, so cross it out. (D) is negative, so leave it in. (E) is negative, so leave it in.

You're left with (B), (D), and (E). Try making simple opposites for the answer choices. A simple opposite for (B) is *bless*. Is that what BEATIFY means? Yes.

Still, check out (D) and (E). It's hard to come up with a good opposite for *pillage* in (D), which means plunder. Therefore, (D) probably isn't right. A simple opposite for (E) is *strengthen*. Is that what BEATIFY means? No. Therefore, the best answer is (B).

5. **C** If you don't know for sure what COMELY means, then you have three options: (1) make simple opposites for the answer choices, (2) use Positive/Negative, or (3) use Word Association. Try Positive/Negative. COMELY is a positive word, so its opposite must be negative. (B) and (D) are both positive, so eliminate them. (A), (C), and (E) are all negative, so keep them.

   At this point, if you don't know anything else about COMELY, just guess. If you pick the answer choice that is most extreme, you might pick (A) or (C). As it turns out, (C) is the best answer. COMELY means having a pleasing appearance.

6. **D** If you don't know for sure what IMPORTUNATE means, then you have three options: (1) make simple opposites for the answer choices, (2) use Positive/Negative, or (3) use Word Association. Try Positive/Negative. IMPORTUNATE is a negative word, so its opposite must be positive. (A), (B), and (C) are all negative, so cross them out. (D) is positive, as is (E), so leave them in.

   You're left with (D) and (E). What now? Try making simple opposites for the answer choices. A simple opposite for (D) is *urgent*. Is that what IMPORTUNATE means? Yes—still, check (E). A simple opposite for (E) is *blamed*. Is that what IMPORTUNATE means? No. The best answer is (D).

7. **A** If you don't know for sure what SANGUINE means, then you have three options: (1) make simple opposites for the answer choices, (2) use Positive/Negative, or (3) use Word Association. Try Word Association. You might have heard SANGUINE used before as a color—red. Therefore, the opposite of SANGUINE should have something to do with color. *Pallid* in (A) means pale, so leave it in. (B) doesn't have anything to do with color, so cross it out. (C) doesn't either, nor does (D) or (E), so cross them all out. The best answer is (A).

8. **C** If you don't know for sure what CATHOLIC means, then you have three options: (1) make simple opposites for the answer choices, (2) use Positive/Negative, or (3) use Word Association. Try Positive/Negative. CATHOLIC is a positive word, so its opposite must be negative. Unfortunately, (A) through (E) are all negative, so you can't do any POE.

   What now? If you really don't have any idea what CATHOLIC means, then just guess. Don't waste time—pick the one that is the most extreme. As it turns out, the best answer is (C) because CATHOLIC means liberal or universal.

9. **A** When you know the stem word, make a simple opposite. SECRETE means give off, so a simple opposite might be *suck in*. Do any of the answer choices match? No. Does this mean there is no right answer? No—it means that it's the secondary definition of SECRETE that's being tested.

What's the secondary definition of SECRETE? If you don't know, then don't waste time. Just guess—pick the answer choice that is the most extreme. But if you know the secondary definition, then this question is easy. SECRETE means to conceal (as in to make secret), so a simple opposite might be *reveal*. Does (A) match *reveal*? Yes. What about (B)? No. (C)? No. (D)? No. (E)? No. The best answer is (A).

10. **A** CONDIGN, most likely, is a word you just don't know at all. If that's the case, don't waste time. Make sure each answer choice has an opposite and then guess—pick the one that is the most extreme. As it turns out, the best answer is (A). CONDIGN means deserved or appropriate.

11. **A** If you don't know for sure what SOPHISTIC means, then you have three options: (1) make simple opposites for the answer choices, (2) use Positive/Negative, or (3) use Word Association. Try Positive/Negative. SOPHISTIC is a negative word, so its opposite must be positive. Unfortunately, (A) through (E) are all positive, so you can't do any POE.

What now? How about Word Association? Have you heard of the phrase "SOPHISTIC reasoning" before? Try using that phrase on the answer choices. Does *sound* reasoning make sense? Yes. Does *opportune* reasoning? Not really. Does *possible* reasoning? Sure. Does *coherent* reasoning? Yes. Does *merciful* reasoning? Not really.

You're left with (A), (C), and (D). If you don't know anything else about SOPHISTIC, then don't waste time. Make sure the remaining answer choices have opposites and then pick the one that is the most extreme. As it turns out, the best answer is (A). SOPHISTIC means false or faulty.

Analytical Writing

WELCOME TO ANALYTICAL WRITING

So, as you are aware, one of the tasks that ETS has deemed essential for evaluating your grad school potential is writing two short essays. You won't be writing these essays on a topic in your graduate field. In fact, you won't be writing these essays on any academic topic at all. There will be no research involved, no careful consideration of evidence, no peer review, no faculty supervision. In short, it's about as far away from the type of academic writing you'll be doing in grad school as you can imagine. But don't worry. With the right knowledge and some practice, you can learn to score higher on the Analytical Writing section. It's no different from the rest of the GRE in that regard.

HOW MUCH DOES ANALYTICAL WRITING MATTER?

We asked this question about the GRE as a whole in the Introduction chapter, and the answer here is fundamentally the same: It depends. However, it's probably safe to say that right now the Analytical Writing section will matter the least of the three sections. This is partly because it's the newest section, having been administered for the first time in October 2002. Grad schools are still figuring out how useful it is, and many don't want to weight it too heavily until they have more experience with it.

A second reason is that it doesn't distinguish between candidates as well as the multiple-choice sections do. About 60 percent of test takers score between 4 and 5.5 on the Analytical Writing section, which means most people get a 4, 4.5, 5, or 5.5. In contrast, on the GRE Verbal section, for example, 60 percent of test takers score between 410 and 620, which gives a much wider range of possible scores.

The best way to be certain, however, is to call the schools you're interested in, and ask them directly. Some will tell you that they don't really care about the Analytical Writing section at all, and some will tell you that they want a minimum score of 5. It's important to find out what the situation is at the schools you intend to apply to, so you can determine how much time and effort to devote to this chapter.

STRUCTURE

First, let's review the basics of the Analytical Writing section. This section contains two parts. The first part lasts 45 minutes and is officially titled "Present Your Perspective on an Issue." You are presented with two essay prompts and must choose one. The second part lasts 30 minutes and is officially titled "Analyze an Argument." You are presented with only one essay prompt here. For ease of reference, we'll continue to refer to the two tasks as the Issue essay and the Argument essay. The Analytical Writing section will always be the first section on your test, and will never be experimental.

SCORING

Each essay will be scored from 0 to 6 by two readers. If the scores are within one point of each other, they will be averaged. If the scores are not within one point of each other (this is rare) then an expert reader will be brought in to read and score the essay. The final scores for the two essays are then averaged and rounded to the nearest half point.

For example, your Argument essay may receive a 5 from both readers, so your average for that essay would be a 5. Your Issue essay may receive a 5 from one reader and a 4 from the other, so your average for that essay would be a 4.5. The average of 5 and 4.5 is 4.75, which rounds up to 5. Thus, you would get a 5 as your Analytical Writing score.

The essays are scored "holistically," which means the readers assign a score based on their overall impression of the essay. There's no checklist that they use to sum up the points (e.g., half a point for good grammar, one point for a good conclusion, etc.). It's okay to make minor grammatical or spelling errors as long as the essay as a whole is strong. The readers aren't going to examine your essays carefully enough or long enough to notice all the details. They have a lot of essays to grade and are probably not going to spend more than two or three minutes reading each one. Later, we'll talk about how to make your essay cater to a short attention span.

What You'll See on the Screen

Don't expect to get a fancy word processor on the Analytical Writing section. In fact, what you get barely deserves the name "word processor." There's no spell check, no grammar check, no italics, no underlining—basically no formatting features at all. Here's what your screen will look like:

> Discuss how well-reasoned you find this argument.
>
> The director of the International Health Foundation recently released this announcement:
> "A new medical test that allows the early detection of a particular disease will prevent the deaths of people all over the world who would otherwise die from the disease. The test has been extremely effective in allowing doctors to diagnose the disease six months to a year before it would have been spotted by conventional means. As soon as we can institute this test as routine procedure in hospitals around the world, the death rate from this disease will plummet."
>
> The argument that this new medical test |
>
> Cut
>
> Paste
>
> Undo

As you can see, it's not much. The essay prompt will stay in front of you the whole time at the top of your screen. You type your essay into the field at the bottom. You'll have to scroll eventually to see everything you've written, because the field isn't very big. To navigate in the text field you can use the arrow keys or click with the mouse. There are also three editing buttons on the right side of your screen: cut, paste, and undo. By highlighting text in your essay, you can move it around with the cut-and-paste feature. You shouldn't need to use these buttons, however. In fact, if you're using the cut-and-paste feature heavily, it's already a bad sign: a pretty clear indicator that your essay isn't well planned. By the way, you have to type your essays—no writing them by hand—so brush up on your typing if it's a little rusty.

TOPICS

The topics are about issues of general interest and don't require any special knowledge. Make sure to read the directions for each essay prompt. In the past, the directions have been the same on every exam. However, ETS has hinted that the directions might have subtle differences in the near future. Visit the ETS website at **www.gre.org** for a complete list of all the potential essay topics and directions. (Yes, you really get to see this information in advance of the test!) Practice responding to these essay prompts and check to see if different sets of instructions are provided on ETS's website. If so, be sure to mix it up; the prompt/directions pairings you see on the ETS website are not necessarily the duos you will see on the real test. Practicing with a variety of these essays will prepare you for whatever comes your way on test day.

There are nearly 250 topics listed for each essay, so the point isn't to memorize them to be ready for your actual GRE topic in advance. Rather, by browsing through the lists, you'll get an idea of what kinds of topics you'll be asked to write about.

UNDERSTANDING THE TWO TASKS

The two essays that ETS requires you to write have distinct features, and it's important to know exactly how they differ. The simplest way to understand the distinction is that the Issue essay requires you to present your own opinion and support it with examples, while the Argument essay requires you to evaluate someone else's opinion without giving your own. Another way to put it is that the Issue essay requires you to develop your own argument by making claims and providing evidence to support and explain those claims, while the Argument essay requires you to critique another person's argument by analyzing its claims and judging the evidence it presents.

This distinction is important, because if you don't understand clearly the task you're being asked to perform, you're not likely to do a good job on the essay. In particular, many people get confused about the Argument essay because they're not accustomed to breaking down an argument and analyzing its logic. Many people simply give their own opinion on the argument, which is a sure way to score poorly. We'll be covering all the details of how to break down arguments and write a strong Argument essay later in this chapter.

ESSAY WRITING BASICS

It's important to understand that the essays you write for the GRE are not going to be masterpieces. We're not redefining the craft of writing here. You have limited time to write and revise, so what we're talking about is a quickly produced first-draft essay.

In order to score well, there are several components your essay should have. The following are some of the most important:

- **Length.** This is a good example of the difference between GRE writing and real writing. In the real world, good, vigorous writing is concise. Unnecessary things are cut out. On the GRE, you want to write as much as you can. That doesn't mean that you're filling the screen with blather or repeating yourself a hundred times, but you do want to expand on your ideas as much as possible and explore as many of their ramifications as you can. Be thorough. However, in your quest for length, know that depth is better than breadth. It's much better to have a few well-chosen examples that you explore in depth than many examples that you discuss only superficially. The bottom line is that high-scoring essays are usually long, and low-scoring essays are usually short. Make it as long as time permits. Aiming for about 500 words is a good guideline.

- **Organization.** Remember, the readers are going to go through your essay very quickly, and they're grading holistically. You need to make a good overall impression. No brilliant example, no amazing turn of phrase will save your essay if it is disorganized. One of the primary things the readers are looking for is a well-structured, well-organized piece of writing. In a sense the structure is much more important than the content. No one *really* cares what you say—they're not reading your essay to decide whether they agree with you. They care how you say it—whether you write a well-planned, logical response to the prompt. The easiest way to organize your essay is to use the old boring four- or five-paragraph essay format that you first learned in sixth grade: introduction, two or three body paragraphs, and a conclusion. Hard to believe something so basic could work on the GRE? Believe it. We're not writing real essays here, we're learning how to tackle a standardized test.

- **Introduction and Conclusion.** This is really part of organization, but it's important enough to discuss separately. Your essay must have an introduction and a conclusion. You can't simply launch into an example in the first sentence of your essay—the reader will be jolted. You have to ease the reader into the essay by spreading out a road map of where the essay is going. A good introduction can do a lot for you, because a reader who comes away with a good impression from the introduction is more likely to keep that good impression throughout the rest of your essay. Think of it as building good will. A conclusion is also crucial, because you don't want your essay to just en—. Wow. See how jarring that was? Now you probably wouldn't end in mid-word, but the point is that you have to bring your reader home with some kind of summation. The essay needs closure. A strong introduction gives the reader a good first impression; a strong conclusion leaves the reader with a good last impression.

- **Clear Point of View.** Unlike the other points mentioned so far, this one is not structural but rather content-based. It should always be clear to someone reading your essay exactly where you stand. Whether you're presenting your opinion in the Issue essay or critiquing the argument in the Argument essay, your own position should always be clear. When a clear point of view isn't present, your essay is weak and abstract, and the reader doesn't know why you wrote it—you clearly had nothing to say. When this situation arises, most of the time it's because you haven't actually figured out what you think. You're hoping to uncover it by writing about it, but that rarely works. Instead you end up with an essay that reads as though you were trying to discover your point of view along the way—which is exactly what you are doing. In order to write a high-scoring essay, you need to know what it is you want to say. And that means that you have to think before you write. Writing is just thinking on paper, but the thinking has to come first. We'll discuss this in more detail shortly.

- **Proper Grammar and Effective Language.** To some degree, of course, your essay score will be affected by how well you write. If your sentences are all the same length and same structure, your writing will be monotonous. If you make numerous or prominent grammatical errors, it will seem careless and unsophisticated. Using language well is part of good essay writing. We can't really teach you in this book to be a better writer (that's an entire book in itself), but we'll try to give you some helpful guidance along the way. In general, try to write as well as you can, but don't think that you need complicated syntax or fancy rhetorical flourishes to be successful on the Analytical Writing section. Use language that you're comfortable with and you should be fine. This is the GRE. You don't need the essay-writing skills of E. B. White to score well.

THE FOUR STEPS

There are lots of ways to construct a high-scoring essay. We're going to use a four-step process that has the benefits of simplicity and effectiveness. First, we'll lay out the four steps, and then we'll look at each one in more detail.

1. Brainstorm
2. Outline
3. Write
4. Proof

Brainstorm

After you read the prompt, it's time to brainstorm. You need ideas to write about: theories, examples, counterexamples, and reasons. What might you say to support your position? What can you point to? What assumptions is the argument making? Where can you attack the prompt or the argument?

Write down all your ideas on your scratch paper—even the stupid ones. The idea is just to get your thoughts down without inhibition. Play devil's advocate. Think about the other side of the issue or argument. Don't try to tailor your ideas to fit a particular point of view. Let this process be wide-ranging.

Outline

You should have lots of ideas written down from brainstorming. Here is where you impose order on the chaos. Look over your ideas to see which ones grab you, which ones seem promising. In order to achieve the organization and clarity you need, it's important to plan your essay. This is not the place for stream-of-consciousness writing. Outlining allows you to decide what you're going to write about, and what you're going to say. You need to decide what your perspective is and which examples will best support it. Writing things down on your scratch paper is a good idea here as well. It will help you organize your thoughts and create a paragraph-by-paragraph plan.

Many people will shortchange these first two steps because they feel they're wasting time. We'll discuss time guidelines later, but for now here are two reasons why these initial steps are so important. First, saving time isn't helpful to you if you end up writing a poorly thought-out, disorganized mess in the end. Think of an essay like a building: You could dispense with the architect to save time, and just have the construction team show up at the site and start building. But would you want to? Without blueprints or a plan, it would probably be a disaster. The same is true of writing. Your essay may be a disaster if you haven't done the initial work of brainstorming and outlining.

The second reason for outlining is time. Skipping the planning stage doesn't actually save you time in the end. The writing will go much faster and smoother if you already know what you're going to say, just as the construction of a building will go much faster when there are blueprints to follow. Writing without a plan is a frustrating, protracted experience. Outlining will lay the foundation for your essay. If the foundation is solid, the essay built upon it will be too.

Write

Well, eventually you're going to have to actually write the thing. As you write, remember the elements of high-scoring essays. Try to say a lot about each of your examples to add depth and length. Write a solid introduction and make sure you leave time to write a conclusion. You could even write the conclusion immediately after the introduction and then write the body paragraphs in between. (After all, you should already know what your conclusion is, and you're working on a word processor.) Make sure that your point of view always comes through clearly and that you're saying what you want to say. Keep it organized with a clear structure, good transitions, and a logical flow of ideas. Try to write well, but don't stop and correct yourself too much, even when you write things that aren't as smooth or graceful as you'd like. You need to get the essay written. There will be time to look it over afterward.

Proof

In your final minutes, you want to look over your essay and proofread for grammar, spelling, typos, awkward sentences, and anything that you might be able to clean up quickly. You're not looking to do heavy editing or substantial revision, but just to polish the essay before you wrap up.

THE ISSUE ESSAY

The first essay that we're going to look at is the Issue essay. We've already discussed the basic tasks for an essay. Now we're going to look at how you do it.

THE PROMPT

Remember, the Issue essay actually gives you two prompts from which to choose. Don't spend time going back and forth trying to decide which one is better. You're on the clock and it won't matter which prompt you choose. Just pick whichever one strikes you as easier to write about. In this chapter, we'll be working with single prompts because it's simpler and because you want to be able to write about any topic ETS gives you.

So let's take a look at a sample prompt.

> *In order to accomplish anything great, one must seek unpopularity. Few things of importance are ever achieved by those who want to be liked.*

One thing you want to notice about this prompt is that it not only presents an issue, but it takes a side. The prompt will always take a position; it's never neutral. You won't see, "School vouchers: discuss." Instead you'll see, "School vouchers are good. They give parents educational choices. Discuss." Or "School vouchers are bad. They drain money from our public schools. Discuss." This means that you can start brainstorming by thinking about ways in which you might agree with the prompt, and ways in which you might disagree with it.

Let's start applying our steps to this prompt.

APPLYING THE FOUR STEPS TO THE ISSUE ESSAY

1. Brainstorm

Let's think about this prompt and start generating some ideas. First, let's think of some situations in which we might agree. Can we think of some people who accomplished great things by courting unpopularity? How about Martin Luther King, Jr.? Malcolm X? Margaret Sanger? Galileo?

Why did they have to be unpopular? Perhaps because they wanted to accomplish unpopular things that their societies weren't ready for. The struggle is what made their accomplishments great in the first place.

Now, let's also think about how we might disagree with the prompt. Can we think of circumstances in which great things were accomplished by people seeking popularity? Or by people who were neither popular nor unpopular? Perhaps you could point to FDR, who used his own popularity and political skills to rally the American people and defeat the Axis in World War II. Or to Gandhi, who became a beloved figure for the people of India and led them to freedom from British colonial rule. You could point to medical or scientific discoveries: Jonas Salk curing polio, or Albert Einstein developing relativity theory, in which popularity wasn't really an issue either way.

Now we have some ideas to play with.

2. Outline

Okay, now we need to look at the ideas we came up with during brainstorming and make some decisions. We have to figure out where we stand on the issue. What is our point of view? And further, which examples are we going to cite and discuss in order to develop our position?

There are a few ways we could go with this essay. We could agree with the prompt and write the entire essay from that perspective. If we chose this position, we would use examples like Martin Luther King, Jr., or whomever seemed to best support our view and whom we felt most competent to talk about. We would probably devote one body paragraph to each example. And in our introduction and conclusion we would try to explain in general why we believed the statement to be true—why unpopularity is necessary to do great things.

We could also go in the exact opposite direction and disagree with the prompt and use the other examples we came up with.

And finally, we could discuss both sides of the issue and incorporate examples from each side into our essay to show when the prompt is true, when it isn't, and why. You can write a perfectly acceptable essay by taking one side. But the highest-scoring essays on the GRE tend to examine both sides and explore the pros and the cons of each. That's what we're going to do with this example. We're going to give examples of both situations in the body of the essay, and use the introduction and conclusion to discuss why unpopularity is sometimes necessary to accomplish great things, and sometimes not.

3. Write

Next, it's time to write. Remember the things we're looking to do here. We want to write a well-organized essay with a clear introduction and conclusion. We want it to be long enough, and to discuss several examples thoroughly. It needs to have a clear point of view, and has to be written without major errors of grammar and syntax. We'll take a look at a sample essay in a moment.

4. Proof

Always give yourself a few minutes to look over your essay and proofread for errors. There shouldn't be any substantial errors in this essay (that's the beauty of having book editors) so we probably won't have to do much with it.

SAMPLE ESSAY

Many people who have achieved important objectives have done so at the cost of being unpopular. It is sometimes argued that unpopularity is necessary in order to accomplish anything great and that nothing important is achieved by those who worry about being liked. While this may be true in some situations, many great things have been achieved by people who needed to court popularity in order to do them. In other cases, great things have been achieved by people for whom popularity or unpopularity were irrelevant. The key factor is the particular nature of the objective.

When the goal is to accomplish a change in society, unpopularity is probably inevitable. Most people resist large changes, and therefore the people who are pushing for the changes are bound to be unpopular with the section of the population that wants to keep things the way they are. For example, when civil rights leaders such as Malcolm X and Martin Luther King, Jr., were pushing for equal civil rights for black Americans, they were despised by much of the country. The goals they were advancing were controversial and confrontational and this made them deeply unpopular with millions of Americans. Despite this, the cause of civil rights was undoubtedly a great and noble one.

In other situations, however, great things can be accomplished and sometimes can only be accomplished by people with popular support. For example, when Britain was in danger of being defeated by Germany in 1940, Franklin Roosevelt was able to use his popularity and political skill to gather support for programs such as the Lend-Lease Act, which gave badly needed supplies to the British military. Without Roosevelt's skill in rallying the American people, the necessary support might not have been there to defeat the Axis powers and win the war. Victory in World War II is an example of a great thing that could only have been accomplished by a popular leader.

Finally, in some circumstances popularity is irrelevant to the achievement of an important task. Some examples of this would be scientific and medical research. When Jonas Salk developed the polio vaccine, a dangerous disease was eradicated, which is a great thing. Salk's accomplishment, however, did not depend on whether he was popular. Similarly, when Einstein wrote his 1905 paper on the photoelectric effect, his achievement in recognizing that the speed of light is constant for all observers did not depend on whether other scientists liked him. A scientific advance is not judged by the popularity of the scientist who discovers it. It just doesn't really matter either way.

In the end, to know whether unpopularity will be a necessary component of achieving something great, you need to know the type of achievement under discussion. Achievements that require large-scale social change will probably make those who fight for them unpopular, but other types of achievements will only be possible when their supporters are popular. And with still other types of achievements, such as scientific ones, it doesn't matter if their proponents are well liked or not. It's all a question of circumstance.

Now let's discuss a few things about this essay. First, this is not a flawless essay. It's not supposed to be perfect. However, this would get a high score on the GRE. Here are some of its features.

Introduction

The introduction accomplishes a few things, all of which you want to do in your essays. First, it establishes what the issue under discussion is. It does this by paraphrasing the prompt in the second sentence. Paraphrasing is usually better than quoting it verbatim, because it's less boring to the reader, and even seems less lazy. (If the prompt is very short, you may have a hard time paraphrasing it; if this is so, don't worry about it.) There are other ways to make it clear to the reader what issue is under discussion, but paraphrasing is the simplest.

Second, the introduction clearly establishes the point of view of the essay. After reading this introduction, you know quite clearly that the writer believes the prompt is sometimes true, but not always. And it leads you to believe that the following paragraphs will back up those assertions by providing examples of the different types of situations.

Body Paragraphs

The body paragraphs follow the implicit promise of the introduction to back up the writer's position. The first paragraph not only explains *why* the prompt is sometimes true, but presents concrete examples in Malcolm X and Martin Luther King, Jr., to support the point. You always want to make sure that your body paragraphs have concrete detail. Abstractions are not persuasive. Specifics and particulars are needed to back up your thesis.

The third paragraph logically follows by discussing an example of the opposite situation, exactly as the introduction has led you to expect. It gives a concrete example backed up by historical details.

The fourth paragraph continues the logical structure and organization of the essay by giving concrete examples of the last situation described in the introduction. Thus, all the body paragraphs give details and examples that support the basic point of view of the essay.

Conclusion

The most important thing about the conclusion is that it's there. You'll notice that it doesn't really say anything that wasn't already said in the introduction. The purpose of the conclusion is to tie a bow on the essay and give it the feeling of closure. It's a matter of ending the essay on the right note, with the right tone.

TIME GUIDELINES

You have 45 minutes to write the Issue essay. How should you spend your time? Here are some guidelines.

Brainstorm } Outline	10 – 12 minutes
Write	30 – 32 minutes
Proof	3 minutes

These are only rough estimates, but they should give you a sense of how to apportion your time. You should develop your own essay-pacing plan by writing some practice essays and adjusting your timing if necessary.

THE ARGUMENT ESSAY

Now it's time to take a look at the Argument essay. You'll find that even though the Argument essay is the more unfamiliar of the two essay types, once you learn how arguments are constructed, it's actually not that difficult to write one. If you read and practice the material in this section, you'll be able to bang out a high-scoring essay on any Argument topic ETS throws at you. Let's begin.

WHAT IS AN ARGUMENT?

On the GRE, an argument isn't about you and your roommate yelling at each other over whose turn it is to buy toilet paper. An argument is a short paragraph that attempts to convince you of something by providing evidence. Your job on the GRE is to analyze that argument and discuss how well-reasoned it is—whether it's logical and persuasive.

THE *REAL* TASK OF THE ARGUMENT ESSAY

The directions on the GRE describe your task as "analyzing" the argument. There's a simpler way to understand what you're really supposed to do, however. Your job is to *criticize* the argument. "Analyzing" sounds like an even-handed evaluation of the argument. That's not what you're doing here. On the Issue essay, there's no right answer; you can take any position you like. On the Argument essay, however, there *is* a right answer. How well-reasoned will you find the argument? The answer will always be, "Not very well. In fact, rather poorly. This argument is terrible."

If the argument were a well-reasoned piece of writing, there wouldn't be much to say about it. "Great argument! Airtight logic! The reasoning is ironclad! The conclusion must certainly be true!" That wouldn't make for much of an essay. So the first thing you need to do is reorient yourself to understand the real situation: ETS provides you with a weak, badly reasoned argument, and your job is to rip it apart and demonstrate why it's so bad. We'll be showing you how to do exactly that in the following pages.

The Parts of an Argument

Arguments consist of three basic parts:

- Conclusion
- Premises
- Assumptions

Let's look at each of these components in detail.

Conclusion

The conclusion is the most basic part of an argument. There's no point in writing an argument unless there's some conclusion you're trying to reach. The conclusion is simply the main point of the argument, the primary thing that the author is trying to convince you of.

Let's look at a simple argument.

> *Bobby needs to watch the Red Sox game. His TV is broken. Therefore, he should buy a new TV.*

What is the conclusion of the above argument? Pretty clearly, the ultimate point the author is trying to make is that Bobby should buy a new television. In addition to the general thrust of the argument, the tip-off we have here is the word "therefore." Certain words tend to indicate that the conclusion is about to follow. Among them are *therefore, thus, so, clearly, hence, consequently,* and *in conclusion.*

The first thing you should always do is identify the conclusion of the argument.

Premises

Think of premises as the reasons that the author gives to make you believe the conclusion. An argument can't simply assert something without backing it up. That wouldn't be an argument at all. The author of an argument needs to provide evidence to support the conclusion. Those pieces of evidence are the premises. Let's take another look at our sample argument.

> *Bobby needs to watch the Red Sox game. His TV is broken. Therefore, he should buy a new TV.*

We know that the conclusion is that Bobby should buy a new television. What are the premises of this argument? What evidence did the author provide to support the conclusion? This time it's pretty clear that the premises are the other two sentences in the argument: Bobby needs to watch the Red Sox game; his TV is broken.

After identifying the conclusion, you should always identify the premises of an argument.

The "Why?" Test

There's a simple way to determine if you've correctly identified the conclusion and premises of an argument. It's called the "Why?" test, and this is how it works. After you have identified what you believe to be the conclusion of the argument, ask yourself, "Why should I believe this is true?" The premises should answer that question. For example, ask, "Why should I believe that Bobby should buy a new TV?" The answer here is clearly, "Because he needs to watch the Red Sox, and his TV is busted." That means we've correctly identified the conclusion and premises. What if we'd misidentified them?

Let's say we had thought that the conclusion was the first sentence. When we ask, "Why should I believe that Bobby needs to watch the Red Sox?" there's nothing to point to. Nothing in the argument provides any support for that statement. The argument just says so. We just have to accept it as given.

So the "Why?" test helps us to make sure we've correctly broken down the argument into its basic pieces.

Assumptions

So far, we've seen how to find conclusions and premises. Assumptions are the third part of arguments. Assumptions are similar to premises in that they also provide reasons to support the conclusion. But they have a key difference. While the premises are explicitly stated in the argument, the assumptions are by definition *unstated*.

Assumptions are things that must be true in order for the conclusion to make sense, but that the author left out of the argument. Instead of establishing the truth of those facts, the author simply *assumed* that they were true. Let's go back one more time to our sample argument.

> *Bobby needs to watch the Red Sox game. His TV is broken. Therefore, he should buy a new TV.*

What must the author be assuming in order for the argument to make sense? What else must be true for the conclusion to follow properly from the premises?

Well, for one, we have to assume that Bobby can't get his TV fixed, or can't get it fixed soon enough to watch the game. If he could get it fixed, then he wouldn't have to buy a new one.

Second, we have to assume that there's no other way Bobby can watch the Red Sox game. For example, he can't go over to his friend Johnny's house and watch the game there. Or he can't go to Fenway Park and see the game live. If he could do either of these things he wouldn't have to buy a new TV.

So, let's summarize the breakdown of this argument:

Conclusion: Bobby should buy a new TV.

Premises: He needs to watch the Red Sox Game. His TV is broken.

Assumptions: He can't get his TV fixed. He can't watch the game some other way.

Why Assumptions Are So Important

It's important to understand that assumptions are necessary for an argument to work. If the assumptions aren't true, the argument falls apart. In the argument above, if Bobby can fix his TV, or watch the game another way, then he doesn't have to buy a new TV. The conclusion is effectively destroyed. This is the key because, as we said, your task on the Argument essay is to weaken the argument. You do that by identifying the assumptions of the argument and attacking them.

Here are a few more tips to help you spot assumptions:

- **Focus on the gap in the argument.** There is always a gap between the premises of an argument and the conclusion, some unjustified leap of logic that needs to be filled by the assumptions. If you look for the gap in the reasoning, and think about what information will bridge that gap, it will be easier to find the assumptions.

- **Look for new stuff in the conclusion.** If the conclusion talks about things that weren't mentioned at all in the premises, then the author must have simply assumed there was a connection.

- **Think about weaknesses in the argument.** What are the possible flaws? An argument is always weakest at its unstated parts. Pretend you're a lawyer in a courtroom and your job is to raise doubt in the minds of the members of the jury about the truth of the argument's conclusion. What could you say? What counterexamples and alternative possibilities could you suggest?

QUICK QUIZ #1

Try to break down the following arguments. Write down the conclusion and premises, using the "Why?" test to check yourself. Then write down any assumptions you spot. The answers are on page 215.

1. All the classrooms in the Dover school district have computers. The children in Dover have higher standardized test scores than the children in Wilmington, where there are no computers in the classrooms. Clearly, Wilmington should put computers in its classrooms to raise students' scores.

   Conclusion: _____

   _____

   Premises: _____

   _____

   Assumptions: _____

   _____

2. Tony's Macaroni is the best-selling brand of macaroni and cheese at FreshStar supermarket. Therefore, more people in town must prefer its taste to that of any other brand.

   Conclusion: _____

   _____

   Premises: _____

   _____

   Assumptions: _____

   _____

3. *This new food additive has been shown to cause cancer in laboratory rats. Consequently, any product that uses it will be dangerous for humans.*

Conclusion: _____

_____

Premises: _____

_____

Assumptions: _____

_____

All of the examples we've looked at so far are much shorter and simpler than the arguments you'll get as prompts for the Argument essay, but you break them down in the exact same way. The arguments you'll actually be writing about have a lot more than two assumptions. There will be more things wrong with them than you'll have time to write about. This is good because it means you don't have to find every assumption in order to write a high-scoring essay. You only have to find a few.

THE PROMPT

Now we're ready to tackle a sample prompt for the Argument essay. Remember, you only get one prompt (unlike the Issue essay). Let's take a look.

The following is a memo from the circulation manager of National Newsletter, Inc.

"To make the home delivery service of our national newsletter more profitable, we should focus on Holden County rather than Plymouth County. First, the residents of Plymouth County are more geographically spread out, which would require us to spend more money per customer delivering the newsletter to them than to the residents of Holden County. Furthermore, a study by a nearby university indicates that Plymouth County residents prefer local news to national news, since they spend 50 percent more time watching local television news broadcasts than national broadcasts. Lastly, because Holden County has a higher average income per resident than Plymouth County, we can expect to make more money delivering newsletters in Holden County than in Plymouth County."

Applying the Four Steps to the Argument Essay

1. Brainstorm

On the Argument essay, brainstorming is all about breaking down the argument and finding the assumptions. Your body paragraphs will be devoted to discussing the assumptions, so if you haven't found any, you won't have anything to write about. Let's break down the argument.

The conclusion is that National Newsletter, Inc.'s home delivery service will be more profitable if they concentrate on Holden County rather than Plymouth County. The premises are: 1) Plymouth residents are spread out so it will cost more to deliver the newsletter to them; 2) A study suggests that Plymouth residents care more about local news because they watch local news programs more than national programs; and 3) Holden residents have more money on average than Plymouth residents.

So far this is not too difficult because the structure of the argument is fairly straightforward. But now comes the important part: spotting assumptions. So let's think about what else must be true for this argument to work, and what implicit facts are being left out. Where is the gap in the reasoning? How might we challenge this argument? What possibilities could we suggest that would cast doubt on the conclusion?

First, we might notice that they're assuming that the higher per-customer cost of delivering to Plymouth County (due to geographical spread) won't be compensated for by higher sales there, or by a slightly higher subscription rate, or by some other factor.

Second, we can point out that the argument assumes that this university study is valid and accurate.

Third, they're assuming that although the residents of Plymouth County may watch more local TV news than national news (according to the study), the residents of Holden County *don't*. (Remember, the argument is making a comparison between two counties, so the claim about Plymouth County's TV news preferences is only helpful to the argument if Holden County's preferences are different.)

Fourth, the argument assumes that because Plymouth County residents aren't interested in national TV news programs (compared with local programs), they won't be interested in a national newsletter. In other words, it assumes that their television preferences are the same as their newsletter preferences.

Fifth, we can point to the assumption that higher income leads to higher home-delivery subscription sales.

We could probably find a few more if we kept looking, but five assumptions are more than enough to write the Argument essay. It's time to move on to the next step.

2. Outline

Now we have to make some decisions. We've identified more assumptions than we can write about. Remember, you only have 30 minutes for the Argument essay, not 45 as for the Issue essay. So we want to pick our three best assumptions and turn them into three strong body paragraphs. Don't spend much time deciding which are your best three. Just pick the ones you like best and go with them.

It's also important during this step to think about some concrete counterexamples you can use in your essay to attack the assumptions. Being specific and using concrete details is just as important in the Argument essay as in the Issue essay. It's not enough to just say, "The argument assumes [insert assumption], but maybe that's not true." You have to demonstrate why it might not be true, why it's a bad assumption.

Let's come up with some specific criticisms of the assumptions we identified for this argument.

Assumption 1: Higher cost of delivery to spread-out people means less profit.

Why it's a bad assumption: Because higher costs can be counterbalanced by higher revenue. If they sell more subscriptions, they could make more money. Or maybe they can charge a higher rate because of the extra delivery distance.

Assumption 2: The university study is valid.

Why it's a bad assumption: We have no idea how it was conducted. We don't know that the sample it used was representative of the Plymouth County population. Maybe it only surveyed people who watch television, rather than people who read to get their news.

Assumption 3: The preference for local TV news by Plymouth County residents does not apply to residents of Holden County.

Why it's a bad assumption: Because maybe residents of Holden County also watch 50 percent more local TV news than national TV news. In fact, perhaps they watch 150 percent more local news than national news. Perhaps they don't watch any national news at all.

Assumption 4: The preference of Plymouth County residents for local television news over national television news indicates that they won't want to read a national newsletter.

Why it's a bad assumption: Because people's preferences for written material may be very different from their television preferences. Perhaps people really like seeing local events covered on television, but prefer to read about national events in newspapers and newsletters.

Assumption 5: Higher average income means more sales and more profits.

Why it's a bad assumption: Because we don't know what the difference in income actually is. It could be $5 a year, which would be insignificant. Furthermore, we have no evidence that the newsletter is expensive and therefore more likely to be bought by wealthier people.

Remember, we're not going to write about all of these assumptions. We only have to pick a few of them.

3. Write

Once you have your outline, you're ready to write. The essay itself will be based on a template, so it will almost be automatic. We're still looking for the same basic qualities, though: length, organization, introduction and conclusion, clear point of view, and good writing.

4. Proof

Don't forget to give the essay a quick proofread to find any obvious typos and other errors. We hope there are none left in the following essay.

SAMPLE ESSAY

The argument concludes that in order to increase the profitability of the home delivery service for its national newsletter, National Newsletter, Inc., should concentrate on Holden County rather than Plymouth County. This conclusion is based on the premises that Plymouth County is more geographically spread out than Holden County, that people in Plymouth County watch more local TV news than national TV news, and that Holden County residents have a higher average income than residents of Plymouth County. The reasoning in the argument is logically flawed, however, because it relies on numerous assumptions that appear to be wholly unsupported.

First, the argument assumes that because the residents of Plymouth County are spread out geographically, making delivery more costly, there is less potential for profit. However, higher costs could be compensated for with higher revenues. For example, if more home delivery subscriptions were sold in Plymouth County than Holden County, the revenue from higher sales would lead to more profit. People in Plymouth County may even be more likely to order home delivery precisely because they live in far-out places. Furthermore, Plymouth County residents might be willing to pay a higher subscription rate because of the distance, compensating for the extra cost of delivery. The argument fails to address any of these potential situations.

Second, the argument ignores the possibility that residents of Holden County watch the same amount of local television news as do the residents of Plymouth County. The argument mentions a university study that says Plymouth County residents watch 50 percent more local TV news than national TV news. However, no information is provided about television viewing in Holden County at all. For all we know, everyone in Holden County also watches 50 percent more local TV news than national TV news. In fact, Holden County residents might not watch any national TV news at all. If any of this is true, it would severely weaken the argument.

Finally, the argument fails to take into account that the higher average income of Holden County does not necessarily mean more sales and more profit. We don't even know how much higher the average income is, for one thing. It could be higher by an insignificant amount. Moreover, there's no reason to believe that higher income will lead to more newsletter subscriptions. A newsletter isn't a luxury item like a yacht that can only be afforded by the wealthy.

In conclusion, the argument that focusing on Holden County rather than Plymouth County will make home delivery of the newsletter more profitable is rather weak. If the author demonstrated that higher delivery costs couldn't be balanced with higher revenues, that Holden County residents watch more national news than residents of Plymouth County, and that higher incomes lead to higher subscription sales, the argument would be greatly strengthened. Without this additional support, however, there is no reason to accept the conclusion of the argument.

As was true of the sample Issue essay earlier, this is not a perfect essay. It's not a particularly creative essay, but it gets the job done and would rate a high score on the GRE. Let's look a little closer.

Introduction

The introduction accomplishes a few things. It demonstrates understanding of the argument (and of arguments in general), and it establishes the point of view of the essay very clearly. This introduction follows a very easy template that you can use for your essays.

The argument concludes [paraphrase conclusion]. This conclusion is based on the premises [paraphrase premises]. The reasoning in the argument is logically flawed, however, because it relies on assumptions that appear to be wholly unsupported.

The first two sentences of the introduction demonstrate that you understand the argument and that you understand how arguments work. You're using the jargon of arguments such as "conclusion" and "premises" and later "assumptions." You're not giving your own opinion at all. Instead, you're showing the reader that you understand the task of the Argument essay. The final sentence of the introduction establishes your point of view, which will always be the same: This argument is terrible because of its unsupported assumptions.

Body Paragraphs

The body paragraphs logically follow the introduction and proceed to systematically address major assumptions of the argument and show them to be dubious. Each body paragraph does two things. First, it identifies an assumption, and then, it criticizes that assumption with specific, concrete details and counterexamples.

There are many ways to introduce assumptions. Here are a few good ones.

> The argument assumes [assumption]. However ...

> The argument fails to consider that [assumption may be false]. For example ...

> The argument ignores the possibility that [assumption may be false]. For example ...

> The argument does not take into account that [assumption may be false]. For example...

Notice that the body paragraphs make heavy use of structure words to indicate the overall organization of the essay and the organization of the paragraphs themselves—words like, *first, second, finally, last, furthermore, in addition, moreover, for example.*

Also notice that the body paragraphs use specific details and counterexamples to attack the assumptions. If the assumption is false, then something else must be true, and you should always suggest what that alternative could be. Otherwise your argument will be too abstract and too vague.

Conclusion

As in the Issue essay, the conclusion is really just restating the basic perspective of the introduction. Here it recaps the three assumptions from the point of view of how the argument could be improved. After all, if you're ripping the argument to shreds, it's only polite to suggest ways that the author could begin to fix it. Ultimately, though, your goal is to wrap up the essay with a final restatement of your position and end the whole thing on a conclusive note.

TIME GUIDELINES

You have 30 minutes to write the Argument essay. Here are some guidelines on how to use your time.

Brainstorm } Outline	5–7 minutes
Write	20–22 minutes
Proof	3 minutes

Again, these are only suggestions. You have to find something that works for you. With practice, you'll become better and faster at producing these essays, so you'll feel less pressed for time.

FINAL THOUGHTS

Now you have the knowledge you need in order to raise your score on the Analytical Writing section. The only thing missing is the experience. Practice writing these essays and you'll find that they become easier and easier. Writing GRE essays is a craft, not an art, and anyone can learn how to do it. Work hard, and when your real test comes you'll finish the first 75 minutes with confidence. Those essays aren't going to hold you back.

ANSWERS AND EXPLANATIONS

Quick Quiz #1

1. The conclusion is that putting computers into Wilmington classrooms will raise students' test scores. Why should we believe that? Because Dover has higher scores and there are computers in all of its classrooms. Those are the premises. Lastly, what are the assumptions? First, that the computers are the actual explanation for the higher test scores in Dover, rather than something else such as better teachers or access to Princeton Review books. Second, even if the computers are the cause of the higher test scores, you have to assume that the two towns are similar enough so that what works in one town will work in the other. Maybe the students in Wilmington don't know how to use computers and so computers won't help them.

2. The conclusion is that Tony's Macaroni is the best-tasting brand of mac and cheese in town. The evidence for this conclusion (in other words, the premises) is that it's the best-selling brand at FreshStar supermarket. What are the big assumptions here? One is that the sales at FreshStar are representative of the sales at all other supermarkets in town. Maybe Tony's Macaroni sells very poorly at other stores. (If you were thinking that FreshStar is the only supermarket in town, you were just assuming that. The argument never says it.) The second big assumption is that best sales = best taste. In other words, the argument assumes that Tony's Macaroni sells well because it tastes better than other brands. But that's not necessarily true. Maybe it's just cheaper.

3. The conclusion is that any product using the food additive will be dangerous for humans. The premise is that it caused cancer in lab rats. The assumptions? Well, for one, they're assuming that humans are like lab rats (kind of like how ETS views you when you're working on the multiple-choice experimental section). More precisely, they're assuming that something that is dangerous to lab rats will also be dangerous to humans—that humans and lab rats are similar in this way. The second assumption is that any product using the additive will use similar quantities to those that were given to the lab rats. After all, if the rats were fed 20 grams of the additive per day, and a typical product for human consumption would only use .05 grams, maybe we shouldn't be as concerned (especially given the difference in body weight between rats and humans).

SAMPLE ESSAYS

The following essays are intended to give you additional exposure to the points that were made in this chapter. They are not models of perfection and are not supposed to be. Despite their flaws, however, they do the important things well enough to receive high scores on the GRE. Remember, reading these essays is not a substitute for practicing writing essays yourself. Ultimately, you're the one who has to sit at the computer and type out two essays—this book can't do it for you. But these essays will help you get a better feel for what the graders are looking for.

ISSUE ESSAYS

Issue Essay #1

> *A good decision is one that takes into account its future consequences more than its present benefits.*

When trying to decide a course of action, it is important to consider both its short-term and long-term consequences. Looking at only one of these factors may lead to sound decisions sometimes, but in other cases will bring on disaster. Some argue that the future ramifications of a decision are more important than whatever present advantages it may have, but that will not always be true. Sometimes, the immediate benefits of a choice are important so that steps should be taken to achieve them even at the cost of future problems. Two examples from history demonstrate that neither present benefits nor future consequences are enough to justify a decision by themselves.

First, consider the compromise that British Prime Minister Neville Chamberlain struck with Nazi Germany. The Munich Compromise was supposed to accomplish "peace in our time," but Hitler soon seized more territory and invaded Poland. Seeking to avoid war is a good thing, and Chamberlain's actions kept Britain out of the war longer than it otherwise would have been. However, all it really did was postpone the day when appeasement would no longer be possible and confrontation would become necessary. In the meantime, Hitler became stronger and solidified his hold over more and more of Europe. Britain would likely have lost far fewer men in the war had it been more willing to sacrifice the short-term benefits of appeasing Hitler for the longer-term necessity of defeating him. In this case, the future costs far outweighed the present advantages.

In contrast, however, sometimes the immediate benefits of a decision are so great that they outweigh future problems.

For example, when the U.S. Constitution was being drafted, a controversy arose over how representatives would be apportioned. The southern states wanted black slaves to be counted for population purposes, because this would give them more representatives in Congress. The northern states did not want to do this and argued that only free men should be counted. Eventually, the 3/5 compromise was adopted, which determined that a slave would count as three fifths of a free man. Condoning and recognizing slavery in the Constitution led to tremendous problems, culminating 75 years later in the Civil War. However, without that compromise the Constitution would never have been ratified and the states would never have been able to form a unified country. In this situation, the importance of establishing a new country and government was high enough that making such a compromise was necessary. Despite the terrible future consequences that almost destroyed the country, at least there was a country to be preserved.

In conclusion, as the above examples demonstrate, neither the long-term consequences nor the short-term benefits of a decision can determine definitively whether that decision was proper. Rather, it is the relative importance of the benefits and consequences themselves that determine the best course of action. In some situations, the immediate advantages will be great enough to justify future problems. In others, short-sighted decisions will lead to terrible costs down the road. Good decisions must be based on circumstances, not principles alone.

Analysis

The introduction of this essay makes clear that the author believes that the prompt is sometimes true, and sometimes not. The point of view is clear. Furthermore, it gives some general description of why that might be. There are two solid body paragraphs that back up the author's thesis, contrasting the importance of focusing on long-term consequences vs. short-term benefits. The body paragraphs also use concrete, specific examples rather than vague assertions or hypothetical situations. The body paragraphs are well developed, giving the essay depth and length. Finally, the conclusion restates the point of view and ends with a good sentence to give the essay a proper note of closure. This is an example of a well-organized essay that uses only two examples, but uses them well to support its point.

Issue Essay #2

> *Progress is impossible without failure and mistakes.*

Throughout history, progress has not followed a straight road. It has not been a string of pure successes, going from okay to good to better in an unbroken line. Instead, progress has been achieved in fits and starts, with steps back and then steps forward. Some believe that if we changed our approach or followed a different and wiser plan, we would be able to avoid the errors and steps backward, and move forward with success. However, all experience tells us that mistakes and failures are the unavoidable price we pay for progress.

For example, during the Great Depression, Franklin Roosevelt instituted numerous programs as part of the New Deal to try to stimulate the economy and keep up the spirits of the public. Many of these programs failed and were scrapped. Some were declared unconstitutional by the Supreme Court. However, if Roosevelt had attempted to avoid all possibility of failure, many of these programs would never have been tried in the first place. Without allowing for such failures, we might not have certain things today that were begun in that era such as FDIC deposit insurance or Social Security. Franklin Roosevelt knew that he would make many mistakes as he tried to tackle the Depression, but he also knew that without those mistakes, progress would never be made.

Another example of the price of failure for progress is the early days of the space program. In the late fifties, it was deemed exceedingly important to keep up with the Russians in space. Project Mercury was developed as an ambitious way to launch astronauts into space as soon as possible. The great priority and ambition of the project meant that NASA would be pushing the envelope trying to develop the necessary capsule and rockets. Failures were inevitable, given the scope of the project. Several test rockets blew up on national television. However, the engineers at NASA learned from their mistakes and were able to anticipate ways to avoid them in the future. By the early sixties Alan Shepard had become the first American in space, and John Glenn had become the first American to orbit Earth. This was not in spite of the early failures of the space program—it was because of them. That was how we eventually succeeded.

To sum up, failure and mistakes are the inevitable by-products of our quest for progress. We are not perfect, and it is unrealistic to expect that significant progress can be made without trial and error. In the abstract, it seems nice to imagine that if we were only a little smarter, or had a little more time to plan, or put the right people in charge, that we would be able to make progress without the pain and inconvenience of making mistakes along the way. Unfortunately, that's just a fantasy. Failure is part of the human condition, and we can only hope that progress is too.

Analysis

This essay shows an example of an author taking one position on the issue, rather than trying to look at both sides. The introduction makes it clear that this author firmly agrees with the prompt and is writing the essay from that one perspective. That assertion is then supported in the body paragraphs with good, specific examples. The first paragraph doesn't just mention the Depression, but mentions some particular details of Roosevelt's ideas. The second paragraph doesn't just say that we failed and then succeeded in space, but gives specific facts like the name of the program and the names of some of the astronauts involved. The conclusion brings it all together, suggesting that the author's view is reality, while the opposing view is a fantasy. The point of view is clear. The examples are solid. It's well organized. It's long enough. It does what it needs to do.

Issue Essay #3

> The arts (music, dance, visual arts) are much less important to students' futures than academic subjects such as Math, History, English, and Science. The arts should be deemphasized in schools.

The question of how to use limited time and resources in schools is a contentious one. Schools are where kids learn the basic skills and knowledge they will need in life, like reading and math. Schools traditionally are also where kids are exposed to other important aspects of a well-rounded education, such as sports and the arts. Many people believe that academic subjects like history and science are much more important than music, dance, or the visual arts, and therefore that the arts should not receive much emphasis in schools. However, the arts are an important aspect of what gives life beauty and meaning. Depriving kids of exposure to the arts would leave them less able to understand and enjoy one of the primary things that can give their lives satisfaction and purpose.

For example, music education gives a tremendous number of benefits to students. Nearly all students listen to music, but far fewer know much about how it actually works.

Studying music gives one a new appreciation for composers and songwriters that enhances the experience of listening to music. Furthermore, studying music gives students the chance to make music themselves, by singing or learning to play an instrument. The ability to play music even gives some students career opportunities, but more often it gives students the opportunity to find a life-long passion and hobby. The joys of having music in one's life are hard to calculate.

Another reason why the arts should be taught in school is that students will develop skills that are not emphasized in academic subjects. For instance, students that practice drawing and painting develop hand-eye coordination and the ability to translate things from the imagination to the reality of paper. Students that practice dance learn about their own bodies and how to express themselves with body language and gestures. These are all useful skills that are neglected in regular classroom subjects.

Finally, studying the arts taps into students' inborn sense of creativity and stimulates their work in other academic subjects. Someone who studies painting or photography is likely to be able to write in a more visually descriptive way. Someone who has learned about the history of sculpture and tried to make pottery will have a greater appreciation for the history of ancient civilizations and their cultural artifacts. Studying the arts can in fact enhance the study of academic subjects.

In conclusion, it would be a terrible mistake to de-emphasize the arts in schools. While no one can deny that it is important for students to learn math and English and history, ways should be found to teach these subjects better, rather than simply giving them more time at the expense of the arts. Students who get no exposure to the arts in school are likely never to be exposed to them later. Without the arts, their lives will not be as full and fulfilling as they would otherwise have been, and that would be a terrible loss.

Analysis

This essay also shows an author arguing one side of a prompt, but unlike the previous essay, this one disagrees with the prompt. The introduction begins by outlining the problem, pointing out one perspective on the problem, and then clearly rejecting that perspective to argue that the arts are important. We know what the issue is and we know where this author stands. The three body paragraphs use clear transition words (*for example, another reason, finally*) to make the structure and organization obvious. They show three specific ways that the arts are beneficial to students, thus providing solid support to back up the thesis of the essay. The conclusion paragraph reiterates the main point and sums up the author's argument, ending on the right kind of conclusory note.

Issue Essay #4

> *Today's world offers many ways to learn; reading books is no longer necessary to become a well-educated person.*

For centuries, books were the primary means of passing on knowledge. There was no television, no radio, no Internet, no study-at-home videotapes. Now that all these things exist, books no longer have a monopoly on information. This leads some to the conclusion that reading books isn't necessary for becoming educated anymore. There is some truth to this. Today, people learn things in other ways and from other sources. However, much of the world's knowledge is still only available in books, and therefore reading them will continue to be an important part of people's education. How important will depend to some degree on what exactly we mean by education.

For example, if we consider an educated person to be one who knows the basic facts of history, then there are many sources for this information outside of books. Much information about world history can be found online and can help a person learn about the basic facts and dates and people that we believe educated people should know. History is also available on CD-rom encyclopedias. Beyond the computer, there are many historical documentary films that can educate people about the realities of the past. Even some Hollywood movies convey accurate historical information that can properly be called educational.

However, many kinds of information that we feel educated people should know are not available anywhere but in books. Literature is an obvious example. Most people would not consider an education complete if it did not include exposure to some of the world's great literature. Shakespeare and Milton and Dickens and Austen have much to teach us through their stories and characters. And right now, experiencing literature still means reading books. Despite such things as books on tape and e-books, reading books is still the only realistic way for people to become knowledgeable about literature.

Finally, if we believe that being a well-educated person means having some special knowledge about a particular field, then reading books will also be essential. Becoming a lawyer requires reading case books on contracts and evidence in law school. Becoming a doctor requires reading textbooks on anatomy and neurology. Being a scientist requires reading scientific journals to learn about new scientific discoveries. For almost any "major" in college, the information that one would need to study is only available in books, whether you want to study sociology, religion, anthropology, philosophy, or something else.

In conclusion, while there are many sources outside of books for some types of information, many other types of information are still largely restricted to books. Radio, movies, television, the Internet, and other sources of knowledge are certainly places where you can educate yourself, but their scope is limited. Whether the reading of books is truly "necessary" to be a well-educated person will depend on how exactly you define "well-educated," but most people will probably define it in a way that will make the reading of books essential still.

Analysis

This essay is finding truth in both sides of the issue, similar to the way the first essay did, although the introduction shows it to be leaning somewhat toward the claim that reading books will still be necessary. The first body paragraph describes one situation that could support the idea that education can be obtained outside of books, but the second and third suggest two other definitions of education that indicate that books are still necessary. So this essay entertains the thesis of the prompt, but ultimately moves in the direction of rejecting it. Remember, there is no right answer, no correct perspective to take. As long as you support your opinion, your essay will be fine. The conclusion here recaps the points made in the introduction and body paragraphs, which is the main thing it needs to do.

ARGUMENT ESSAYS

Argument Essay #1

> *The following appeared in a memo circulated to the Benden town council.*
>
> "Super Fit *magazine frequently sells out, according to the owner of Eastern Circle newsstand.* Super Fit *features photographs of star athletes working out with personal trainers. In order to satisfy the fitness desires of Benden residents, we should hire personal trainers to work at our community fitness center."*

The argument concludes that the town council of Benden should hire personal trainers for its community fitness center to satisfy the fitness desires of its residents. This conclusion is based on the premises that *Super Fit* magazine sells out frequently at Eastern Circle newsstand, and that it features photos of elite athletes exercising with personal trainers. The reasoning of the argument is flawed, however, because it depends on many unsupported assumptions. The following paragraphs will explore those weaknesses in depth.

To begin, the argument assumes that because *Super Fit* magazine sells out at Eastern Circle newsstand, this must be representative of its sales at other newsstands in town, indicating its popularity with the residents of Benden. However, there is no evidence to support that idea. At other newsstands in town there might be dozens of copies of *Super Fit* left on the stand each month. Eastern Circle newsstand might be located near a gym, which would explain why a fitness magazine sells out there, but most of the population of Benden could be totally indifferent to the magazine. With just one newsstand as evidence, there is no way to properly draw the conclusion that the residents of Benden have any special interest in the contents of *Super Fit* magazine.

Furthermore, the argument does not take into account that those people who buy *Super Fit* magazine from Eastern Circle newsstand might do it for reasons totally unrelated to the photos of athletes exercising with trainers. They may be purchasing *Super Fit* for the articles because they want to learn more about exercising on their own. Or they may want to look at the classified ads or the general advertisements. Even if they buy it for the pictures, they may want to look at pictures other than the ones featuring star athletes and personal trainers. The argument has said nothing that would rule out any of these plausible alternatives.

Finally, the argument fails to consider that what is appropriate and useful to professional athletes will not be useful to or desired by ordinary town residents. The fitness needs and desires of ordinary people are far different from those of star athletes. Star athletes devote themselves 100 percent to their athletic pursuits and need the attention of a personal trainer to succeed on the highest levels of competition. Ordinary people often do not have the time or inclination to devote themselves so seriously to fitness. Thus, personal trainers may not at all be what Benden town residents desire for their fitness center.

In conclusion, the argument that hiring personal trainers will satisfy the fitness desires of Benden town residents is weak. If the author of the argument demonstrated that *Super Fit*'s sales at Eastern Circle were representative of sales at other newsstands, that the people who buy *Super Fit* are buying it primarily because of the photos of athletes with trainers, and that the needs of professional athletes would be appropriate for typical town residents, the argument would be strengthened. Without that support, however, there is little reason to accept the conclusion.

Analysis

This essay follows the basic template that was laid out in the Analytical Writing chapter. It begins by breaking down the argument into its components and then criticizes it because of its unsupported assumptions. The body paragraphs proceed to identify three key assumptions made by this argument, and then give concrete reasons and counterexamples to suspect that those assumptions aren't true. Clear transition words make the structure logical and clear. The conclusion simply restates the author's point, recaps the assumptions quickly, and ends with a final assertion of the fundamental weakness of the argument.

Argument Essay #2

The following is from a state report on safety procedures in various towns.

The Peabody health department requires that all mine workers be screened at least once every four months for health problems that may arise from working underground. However, this requirement may be unnecessary and of no benefit to workers. In the town of Orange, the health department has no such requirement, and surveys show that workers are screened on average only once every three years. Not only is the reported number of workers with job-related illnesses lower in Orange, but the number of deaths known to be the result of exposure to harmful agents on the job is half as large. Clearly, increased frequency of health screenings neither prevents illness nor saves lives.

The argument concludes that more frequent screenings for job-related health problems don't reduce illness or save lives. The conclusion is based on the premises that although Peabody screens workers every four months and workers in Orange are screened on average every three years, the reported number of sick workers is lower in Orange and the number of deaths is half as much. The argument is not logically persuasive, however, because it relies on numerous shaky assumptions for which no evidence has been given.

First, the argument does not address the possibility that the populations of Peabody and Orange may be very different. The argument claims that half as many people die in Orange from exposure to harmful agents as do in Peabody. But comparisons of absolute numbers are only valid if the populations are similar. For example, say the population of Peabody was 1,000 and 10 people died, while the population of Orange was 100 and 5 people died. Even though twice as many people died in Peabody as in Orange, Peabody's rate was only 1 percent while Orange's rate was 5 percent. The argument fails to address this issue.

Moreover, the argument assumes that the condition of mine workers is identical in Peabody and Orange except for the difference in frequency of screening. However, there are many other potential explanations for the reported differences. Perhaps the mine workers in Orange have better protective equipment, which means they get sick less often. Or perhaps they work in less toxic mines. There could even be differences in screening procedures that account for the differences. No information has been presented to show that other plausible explanations have been ruled out.

Lastly, the argument fails to consider that workers in Orange may be screened more often than the averages suggest. Averages can be deceptive because they are subject to distortion by extreme values. For example, most workers in Orange could be screened every few months, but if there were a minority who refused to be screened at all, and hadn't been screened for, say, 20 years, then the average of once every three years would not truly be representative.

In sum, the argument that frequent screening does not prevent illness or save lives is logically unsound. If the author showed that the populations of Peabody and Orange are similar, that there are no other significant differences between the towns other than the frequency of screening, and that the average frequency of screening in Orange is actually representative, the argument would be much stronger. In the absence of this additional evidence, however, we should be wary about accepting the truth of the argument's conclusion.

Analysis

Again, this essay begins by identifying the conclusion and premises of the argument and taking the position that the argument is flawed because of its shaky assumptions. Remember, this is always our position. The argument is always weak because of its assumptions. Each body paragraph follows the pattern of identifying an assumption made by the argument, and then criticizing that assumption with concrete objections. The argument essay is almost a mechanical exercise once you learn how to find the assumptions, so these essays will sound very much alike. The conclusion follows the exact same plan as did the first essay, restating the main point and recapping the assumptions.

Argument Essay #3

> A recent study reported that people who own dogs live healthier and longer lives than people who are not dog owners. In particular, people who own dogs have much lower rates of strokes than the general population. Therefore, the city of Weston should create a program that selects dogs from the Weston animal shelter and gives them to stroke patients when they return home to convalesce. Not only will this speed their recovery, but it will save the city money by reducing the number of return visits to the hospital. Furthermore, the stroke patients will tell their friends, which means that more people will become dog owners, reducing the number of people who have strokes in the future.

The argument concludes that the city of Weston will save money and reduce the number of people who suffer strokes by creating a program that selects dogs from the local animal shelter and giving them to recently discharged stroke patients as pets. This conclusion is based on the premises that dog owners have lower rates of strokes than the general population does, according to a recent study. The logic of the argument is not convincing, however, because it assumes the truth of many things that have not in fact been demonstrated.

To start with, the argument assumes that dog ownership is in fact the cause of the lower incidence of stroke among dog owners, rather than a mere correlated fact. But noting that people who have dogs also have low rates of stroke does not demonstrate that the former is the cause of the latter. It's quite possible that both of these facts are explained by something the argument does not mention. For example, perhaps energetic people who like to lead active lives are less likely to have strokes because of the exercise they get, and are also more likely to own dogs that they run with and take to the park to play frisbee. If that is the case, then it is the active lifestyle that is the real cause of better health, and giving a dog to an inactive person will do nothing to prevent a stroke.

In addition, the argument assumes that giving dogs to people after they have had strokes will have healing benefits. But the evidence provided by the study does not support that idea. The study says that people who own dogs have lower rates of strokes than most people. It suggests that owning a dog may be a good measure to prevent strokes. But once a person has actually had a stroke, there is no evidence that a dog will help them get better. Brushing your teeth may help prevent cavities, but once you have one, brushing won't do anything to fix it.

Finally, the argument fails to address the possibility that the program will not save money after all. The program itself will cost money to implement and no figures have been presented that show that there will be a net savings to the town of Weston once the program has been put in place. It might turn out to be quite expensive to find the right dog for each stroke patient. The patients might have to be driven to the shelter to see the dogs first. The dogs would have to be transported to their homes. People would have to be hired to make all of this happen. Furthermore, we have no idea how many return visits will be prevented by this program. It could be very few, or even none at all. Without some evidence that allows us to at least estimate these numbers, it's difficult to have any confidence in this claim.

In conclusion, the argument that giving dogs to stroke patients will save money and reduce the number of strokes in Weston is dubious. If the author demonstrated that dog ownership was the actual cause of the lower rate of strokes in dog owners, showed that owning a dog could heal a stroke as well as prevent one, and provided some evidence to back up the claim of saving money, the argument would be substantially stronger. As it currently stands, however, there is little reason to follow its recommendation.

Analysis

The introduction presents the components of the argument and establishes our permanent point of view: The argument is terrible. The first body paragraph identifies a very common assumption, namely that a correlation of two things implies a causal relationship. The second body paragraph criticizes a common unjustified leap of logic and uses a comparison with brushing teeth to make the criticism easier to understand. The third body paragraph addresses a third claim that the argument makes, and gives concrete reasons why that claim might not be true. Finally, the conclusion wraps it all up. The argument has been thoroughly demolished.

Argument Essay #4

> *Excelsior Corporation provides subsidized daycare to its employees and is usually ranked among the top 10 companies for employee satisfaction. Excelsior's competitor, Sigma corporation, is hoping to boost its productivity and take some market share from Excelsior. Sigma intends to provide free daycare for its employees as the cornerstone of this strategy. Clearly, Sigma will soon command a bigger piece of market share than Excelsior.*

The argument concludes that Sigma Corporation will soon have a greater share of the market than Excelsior Corporation. The evidence provided for this conclusion is that Excelsior gives subsidized daycare to its employees and is highly ranked in employee satisfaction, and Sigma plans to give its employees free daycare. The argument's logic is faulty, however, since it relies on several unsupported assumptions to bridge the gap between its premises and conclusion.

First of all, the argument does not address the possibility that the high employee satisfaction rating enjoyed by Excelsior is due to factors unrelated to its subsidized daycare. No direct causal relationship has been established between subsidized daycare and employee satisfaction. The author simply mentions the former and assumes a connection to the latter. But the high employee satisfaction rating could be caused by excellent salaries, health benefits, a good working environment, respectful treatment by company management, or a host of other factors. There is no reason to assume that subsidized daycare is the main explanation for employee satisfaction.

Furthermore, the argument fails to take into account that the market share currently possessed by Excelsior may have nothing to do with its high employee satisfaction ranking. We know nothing about Excelsior's business—what it does or how it does it. Excelsior's market share could be caused by patented designs, or excellent branding, or attractive pricing, or exceptional management. Nothing indicates that the satisfaction of the employees is directly responsible for the company's market share, and that Sigma could take some of that market share or boost its productivity by raising the satisfaction level of its employees.

Finally, the argument assumes that giving free daycare to Sigma's employees will increase their level of satisfaction and raise productivity. However, we don't know anything about the current levels of satisfaction of Sigma employees. The employees could be so demoralized by horrible working conditions, low salaries, and other negatives that free daycare won't be nearly enough to satisfy them. Or, alternatively, Sigma's employees might already be extremely satisfied, so much so that adding free daycare won't change things much. Perhaps Sigma is already ranked among the top five companies in employee satisfaction. All of these possibilities remain unexamined by the author.

To sum up, the argument that Sigma will steal market share from Excelsior by giving free daycare to its employees is quite weak. If the author demonstrated that Excelsior's level of employee satisfaction is due to its subsidized daycare, that Excelsior's current market share is caused by the satisfaction of its employees, and that free daycare will raise the level of satisfaction for Sigma employees, the argument would be on much firmer ground. Without additional support, however, there isn't much reason to believe the conclusion.

Analysis

Are you bored yet? Yet again, we have an essay that follows a very clear template. But more important, we have an essay that accomplishes the task, and would receive a high score on the GRE. This is an example of an argument that has a few tricky assumptions because they seem quite natural. For example, you might not have thought at first to criticize the idea that Excelsior's high employee satisfaction is the reason for its current market share, because that idea seems so natural. In other words, you yourself may have made that assumption. It's often difficult to identify the assumptions we ourselves are making. However, this essay did take that into account, and a solid paragraph of criticism resulted. Two other key assumptions were also identified and criticized, and the conclusion ties a bow on the essay, giving it the right tone of completion. Length is good. Transitions and organization are good. Do something similar on your GRE, and you'll score well on the Analytical Writing section.

7
Vocabulary

WORDS, WORDS, WORDS

As we mentioned in the Strategies chapter, one of the most important things you need to do to improve your score on the GRE Verbal section is to improve your vocabulary. There is simply no getting around it. It's also very important that you learn the techniques and apply them on the test, but relying on technique alone is like relying on exercise alone to keep you healthy. Exercise is great, but to be as healthy as possible you also have to focus on nutrition and eating the right things. Likewise, think of words as your GRE verbal nutrition. You need a healthy diet of vocabulary as well as good technique to get your maximum score on the Verbal section.

The best way to learn words is to read good books and magazines and newspapers throughout your life. However, since you presumably can't put off the GRE for a few more years while you beef up your reading, we need to find other ways.

THE HIT PARADE

The Hit Parade is a list of about 300 words that appear with great frequency on the GRE. It was compiled by analyzing every written GRE available, as well as dozens of computer-based GREs. This is the first task in your vocabulary preparation: Learn the Hit Parade cold. We have split the list into four groups, and each group of words is followed by quizzes, drills, and some sample questions that make use of those words. Make sure to spend some time learning each group before you tackle the practice material. Use the drills and questions to see how well you've mastered that particular group. When you have the first group down, move on to the second, and so on.

The Hit Parade also appears in our book *Cracking the GRE*, but the drills in this book are slightly different. You can use these drills as extra practice if you already own *Cracking*.

BEYOND THE HIT PARADE

The Hit Parade is the beginning, not the end, of your vocabulary workout. Once you've mastered all the words in the Hit Parade, you should move on to the additional vocabulary lists we've provided. Remember, every new word you learn makes it more likely you'll score higher on the GRE Verbal section. Furthermore, learning vocabulary is the only part of your GRE preparation that is actually useful to you in grad school and in life.

HOW TO LEARN NEW WORDS

Before we give you the lists, we're going to talk a bit about how to learn words. There are many different ways because everyone is a little different, and what works well for someone else might not work well for you. In the end, you'll have to find the method that helps you the most. However, there are several things that most people find useful. Here are some suggestions.

- **Write them down.** In order to learn words, you have to make them your own. One of the first ways you do that is by writing them and their definitions down, rather than just reading them on a list. Whether you write them in a notebook or on flash cards or on the palm of your hand is your call, but write them down somewhere.

- **Use a dictionary.** You probably have a dictionary, but you might not have a paperback dictionary that you can carry with you easily. Get one. You're much more likely to look up a word and check its definition if you have easy access to a dictionary. A dictionary will also give you secondary meanings of words that you might not have known, as well as information about their history and etymology that may make it easier to remember them.

- **Say them out loud.** This is related to writing them down, because saying them aloud is another way that you make words your own. It also brings another sense into play (hearing) and makes it more likely that you'll remember the meaning of the word. (Just don't say words aloud during your test. The other test takers in the room may hurt you.)

- **Create mnemonic devices.** A mnemonic device is a memory trick that helps you remember something by tying it to a rhyme, story, sentence, song, acronym, or anything that you already know or can remember more easily. A simple example of a mnemonic device that many students are taught is the sentence "My very educated mother just sliced up nine pickles," used to remember the order of the planets from the sun. Making a mnemonic is one of the best ways to nail down those words that keep eluding you no matter how many times you seem to read their definitions.

- **Visualize.** Another great way to remember words is to visualize them—to associate them with some image. One of the more creative visualizations we've heard in our classes involved the word *sycophant*, which is someone who attempts to win advancement by flattering influential people—basically, a brownnoser. This student imagined a psychotic elephant putting its trunk into a giant puddle of mud—brownnosing—and then, every time she saw the word *sycophant*, she thought of her "psycho-elephant." We doubt she'll ever forget the meaning of that word.

- **Look at word roots.** You can also help yourself remember words by learning a little bit about their etymology. Many English words have prefixes and suffixes that come from Latin and Greek. So perhaps you remember the word *anachronism* (something out of its proper time, like an automobile showing up in a movie about the eighteenth century) by remembering that *chron* is a root that means time. For example, think of the words *chronology*, *synchronize*, *chronic*, and others.

- **Make sentences with them.** One of the hard things about learning words from lists is that the words have no context. Writing down a sentence for each word not only ensures that you understand the definition, it gives you context for the meaning of the word, which makes it easier to remember. When you make a sentence like, "My grandfather was from a small, bucolic town in Kansas," it's easier to remember that bucolic means "rustic, pastoral, rural."

- **Use them.** Try to incorporate as many new words as you can into your writing and your conversation. Not only will you impress people with your superior command of language (unless they want to smack you for showing off), you'll truly be internalizing these words and making them part of your permanent vocabulary. Ultimately, it's through constant reinforcement that you expand your vocabulary.

- **Make it a priority.** This is just one final reminder that in order to increase your vocabulary you have to work at it. If you don't put effort into learning words, don't expect to get results. You'll just be wasting your time. Remember, there is no way to get a high score on the GRE Verbal section without a strong vocabulary, and there is no way to get a huge improvement in your score without expanding your vocabulary.

So, bring on the words!

HIT PARADE GROUP 1

aberrant	adjective	deviating from the norm (noun form: *aberration*)
abscond	verb	to depart clandestinely; to steal off and hide
alacrity	noun	eager and enthusiastic willingness
anomaly	noun	deviation from the normal order, form, or rule; abnormality (adj. form: *anomalous*)
approbation	noun	an expression of approval or praise
arduous	adjective	strenuous; taxing; requiring significant effort
assuage	verb	to ease or lessen; to appease or pacify
audacious	adjective	daring and fearless; recklessly bold (noun form: *audacity*)
austere	adjective	without adornment; bare; severely simple; ascetic (noun form: *austerity*)
axiomatic	adjective	taken as a given; possessing self-evident truth (noun form: *axiom*)
canonical	adjective	following or in agreement with accepted, traditional standards (noun form: *canon*)
capricious	adjective	inclined to change one's mind impulsively; erratic; unpredictable
censure	verb	to criticize severely; to officially rebuke
chicanery	noun	trickery or subterfuge
connoisseur	noun	an informed and astute judge in matters of taste; expert
convoluted	adjective	complex or complicated
disabuse	verb	to undeceive; to set right
discordant	adjective	conflicting; dissonant or harsh in sound
disparate	adjective	fundamentally distinct or dissimilar
effrontery	noun	extreme boldness; presumptuousness
eloquent	adjective	well-spoken; expressive; articulate (noun form: *eloquence*)
enervate	verb	to weaken; to reduce in vitality
ennui	noun	dissatisfaction and restlessness resulting from boredom or apathy
equivocate	verb	to use ambiguous language with a deceptive intent (adj. form: *equivocal*)

erudite	adjective	very learned; scholarly (noun form: *erudition*)
exculpate	verb	exonerate; to clear of blame
exigent	adjective	urgent; pressing; requiring immediate action or attention
extemporaneous	adjective	improvised; done without preparation
filibuster	noun	intentional obstruction, esp. using prolonged speechmaking to delay legislative action
fulminate	verb	to loudly attack or denounce
ingenuous	adjective	artless; frank and candid; lacking in sophistication
inured	adjective	accustomed to accepting something undesirable
irascible	adjective	easily angered; prone to temperamental outbursts
laud	verb	to praise highly (adj. form: *laudatory*)
lucid	adjective	clear; easily understood
magnanimity	noun	the quality of being generously noble in mind and heart, esp. in forgiving (adj. form: *magnanimous*)
martial	adjective	associated with war and the armed forces
mundane	adjective	of the world; typical of or concerned with the ordinary
nascent	adjective	coming into being; in early developmental stages
nebulous	adjective	vague; cloudy; lacking clearly defined form
neologism	noun	a new word, expression, or usage; the creation or use of new words or senses
noxious	adjective	harmful; injurious
obtuse	adjective	lacking sharpness of intellect; not clear or precise in thought or expression
obviate	verb	to anticipate and make unnecessary
onerous	adjective	troubling; burdensome
paean	noun	a song or hymn of praise and thanksgiving
parody	noun	a humorous imitation intended for ridicule or comic effect, esp. in literature and art
perennial	adjective	recurrent through the year or many years; happening repeatedly
perfidy	noun	intentional breach of faith; treachery (adj. form: *perfidious*)
perfunctory	adjective	cursory; done without care or interest

perspicacious	adjective	acutely perceptive; having keen discernment (noun form: *perspicacity*)
prattle	verb	to babble meaninglessly; to talk in an empty and idle manner
precipitate	adjective	acting with excessive haste or impulse
precipitate	verb	to cause or happen before anticipated or required
predilection	noun	a disposition in favor of something; preference
prescience	noun	foreknowledge of events; knowing of events prior to their occurring (adj. form: *prescient*)
prevaricate	verb	to deliberately avoid the truth; to mislead
qualms	noun	misgivings; reservations; causes for hesitancy
recant	verb	to retract, esp. a previously held belief
refute	verb	to disprove; to successfully argue against
relegate	verb	to forcibly assign, esp. to a lower place or position
reticent	adjective	quiet; reserved; reluctant to express thoughts and feelings
solicitous	adjective	concerned and attentive; eager
sordid	adjective	characterized by filth, grime, or squalor; foul
sporadic	adjective	occurring only occasionally, or in scattered instances
squander	verb	to waste by spending or using irresponsibly
static	adjective	not moving, active, or in motion; at rest
stupefy	verb	to stun, baffle, or amaze
stymie	verb	to block; thwart
synthesis	noun	the combination of parts to make a whole (verb form: *synthesize*)
torque	noun	a force that causes rotation
tortuous	adjective	winding; twisting; excessively complicated
truculent	adjective	fierce and cruel; eager to fight
veracity	noun	truthfulness; honesty
virulent	adjective	extremely harmful or poisonous; bitterly hostile or antagonistic
voracious	adjective	having an insatiable appetite for an activity or pursuit; ravenous
waver	verb	to move to and fro; to sway; to be unsettled in opinion

QUICK QUIZ #1
Define the following words.

Assuage: _____

_____

Axiomatic: _____

_____

Ennui: _____

_____

Paean: _____

_____

Perspicacious: _____

_____

Voracious: _____

_____

Capricious: _____

_____

Precipitate: _____

_____

Virulent: _____

_____

Prevaricate: _____

_____

Equivocate: _____

_____

Obviate: _____

Tortuous: _____

Laud: _____

Mundane: _____

QUICK QUIZ #2

Match the following words to their definitions. The answers are on page 278.

A.	Aberrant	_____	Urgent; pressing
B.	Disabuse	_____	To babble meaninglessly
C.	Prescience	_____	Truthfulness; honesty
D.	Solicitous	_____	Harmful; injurious
E.	Veracity	_____	To undeceive; to set right
F.	Audacious	_____	Deviating from the norm
G.	Noxious	_____	Misgivings; reservations
H.	Qualms	_____	Coming into being
I.	Nascent	_____	To stun, baffle, or amaze
J.	Enervate	_____	Daring and fearless; recklessly bold
K.	Exigent	_____	Foreknowledge of events
L.	Prattle	_____	To loudly attack or denounce
M.	Fulminate	_____	To weaken; to reduce in vitality
N.	Stupefy	_____	Concerned and attentive

QUICK QUIZ #3

Try the following analogies, antonyms, and sentence completions. The answers are on page 278.

1. EXTEMPORANEOUS : REHEARSED ::
   ○ valid : refuted
   ○ eloquent : delighted
   ○ delectable : explained
   ○ pervasive : elaborated
   ○ luminous : elated

2. TRUCULENT : FIGHT ::
   ○ futile : exculpate
   ○ hungry : eat
   ○ slothful : save
   ○ duplicitous : inform
   ○ hasty : dawdle

3. BOLD : EFFRONTERY ::
   ○ healthful: anomaly
   ○ frugal : parsimony
   ○ somber : perfidy
   ○ novel : creativity
   ○ stealthy : blasphemy

4. PARODY : RIDICULE ::
   ○ postulate : believe
   ○ mendicant : plead
   ○ torque : rotate
   ○ filibuster : blame
   ○ conjecture : allege

5. ALACRITY:
   ○ depravity
   ○ approbation
   ○ reluctance
   ○ chicanery
   ○ precedent

6. NEBULOUS:
   ○ consummate
   ○ perfunctory
   ○ deleterious
   ○ irascible
   ○ concrete

7. NEOLOGISM:
   ○ faction
   ○ cliché
   ○ bequest
   ○ synthesis
   ○ predilection

8. INURED:
   ○ perennial
   ○ ironic
   ○ austere
   ○ unaccustomed
   ○ fraternal

9. Poverty can be a function not only of absolute wealth, but also of comparison in a community; in an area with _____ income levels, those at the very bottom will suffer cost-of-living increases brought on by those in the middle and top income brackets.
   ○ disparate
   ○ reticent
   ○ arduous
   ○ onerous
   ○ wavering

10. The priest was told to publicly ____ his religious views because they were revolutionary and certainly not ____.
   ○ expound . . official
   ○ squander . . authoritative
   ○ censure . . convoluted
   ○ retract . . erudite
   ○ recant . . canonical

HIT PARADE GROUP 2

abate	verb	to lessen in intensity or degree
accolade	noun	an expression of praise
adulation	noun	excessive praise; intense adoration
aesthetic	adjective	dealing with, appreciative of, or responsive to art or the beautiful
ameliorate	verb	to make better or more tolerable
ascetic	noun	one who practices rigid self-denial, esp. as an act of religious devotion
avarice	noun	greed, esp. for wealth (adj. form: *avaricious*)
axiom	noun	a universally recognized principle (adj. form; *axiomatic*)
bucolic	adjective	rustic and pastoral; characteristic of rural areas and their inhabitants
burgeon	verb	to grow rapidly or flourish
cacophony	noun	harsh, jarring, discordant sound; dissonance (adj. form: *cacophonous*)
canon	noun	an established set of principles or code of laws, often religious in nature (adj. form: *canonical*)
castigation	noun	severe criticism or punishment (verb form: *castigate*)
catalyst	noun	a substance that accelerates the rate of a chemical reaction without itself changing; a person or thing that causes change
caustic	adjective	burning or stinging; causing corrosion
chary	adjective	wary; cautious; sparing
cogent	adjective	appealing forcibly to the mind or reason; convincing
complaisance	noun	the willingness to comply with the wishes of others (adj. form: *complaisant*)
contentious	adjective	argumentative; quarrelsome; causing controversy or disagreement
contrite	adjective	regretful; penitent; seeking forgiveness (noun form: *contrition*)
culpable	adjective	deserving blame (noun form: *culpability*)
dearth	noun	smallness of quantity or number; scarcity; a lack
demur	verb	to question or oppose

didactic	adjective	intended to teach or instruct
discretion	noun	cautious reserve in speech; ability to make responsible decisions (adj. form: *discreet*)
disinterested	adjective	free of bias or self-interest; impartial
dogmatic	adjective	expressing a rigid opinion based on unproved or unprovable principles (noun form: *dogma*)
ebullience	adjective	the quality of lively or enthusiastic expression of thoughts and feelings (adj. form: *ebullient*)
eclectic	adjective	composed of elements drawn from various sources
elegy	noun	a mournful poem, esp. one lamenting the dead (adj. form: *elegiac*)
emollient	adjective/ noun	soothing, esp. to the skin; making less harsh; mollifying; an agent that softens or smoothes the skin
empirical	adjective	based on observation or experiment
enigmatic	adjective	mysterious; obscure; difficult to understand (noun form: *enigma*)
ephemeral	adjective	brief; fleeting
esoteric	adjective	intended for or understood by a small, specific group
eulogy	noun	a speech honoring the dead (verb form: *eulogize*)
exonerate	verb	to remove blame
facetious	adjective	playful; humorous
fallacy	noun	an invalid or incorrect notion; a mistaken belief (adj. form: *fallacious*)
furtive	adjective	marked by stealth; covert; surreptitious
gregarious	adjective	sociable; outgoing; enjoying the company of other people
harangue	verb/noun	to deliver a pompous speech or tirade; a long, pompous speech
heretical	adjective	violating accepted dogma or convention (noun form: *heresy*)
hyperbole	noun	an exaggerated statement, often used as a figure of speech (adj. form: *hyperbolic*)
impecunious	adjective	lacking funds; without money
incipient	adjective	beginning to come into being or to become apparent

inert	adjective	unmoving; lethargic; sluggish
innocuous	adjective	harmless; causing no damage
intransigent	adjective	refusing to compromise (noun form: *intransigence*)
inveigle	verb	to obtain by deception or flattery
morose	adjective	sad; sullen; melancholy
odious	adjective	evoking intense aversion or dislike
opaque	adjective	impenetrable by light; not reflecting light
oscillation	noun	the act or state of swinging back and forth with a steady, uninterrupted rhythm (verb form: *oscillate*)
penurious	adjective	penny-pinching; excessively thrifty; ungenerous
pernicious	adjective	extremely harmful; potentially causing death
peruse	verb	to examine with great care (noun form: *perusal*)
pious	adjective	extremely reverent or devout; showing strong religious devotion (noun form: *piety*)
precursor	noun	one that precedes and indicates or announces another
preen	verb	to dress up; to primp; to groom oneself with elaborate care
prodigious	adjective	abundant in size, force, or extent; extraordinary
prolific	adjective	producing large volumes or amounts; productive
putrefy	verb	to rot; to decay and give off a foul odor (adj. form: *putrid*)
quaff	verb	to drink deeply
quiescence	noun	stillness; motionlessness; quality of being at rest (adj. form: *quiescent*)
redoubtable	adjective	awe-inspiring; worthy of honor
sanction	noun/verb	authoritative permission or approval; a penalty intended to enforce compliance; to give permission or authority to
satire	noun	a literary work that ridicules or criticizes a human vice through humor or derision (adj. form: *satirical*)
squalid	adjective	sordid; wretched and dirty as from neglect (noun form: *squalor*)
stoic	adjective	indifferent to or unaffected by pleasure or pain; steadfast (noun form: *stoicism*)
supplant	verb	to take the place of; supersede
torpid	adjective	lethargic; sluggish; dormant (noun form: *torpor*)

ubiquitous	adjective	existing everywhere at the same time; constantly encountered; widespread
urbane	adjective	sophisticated; refined; elegant (noun form: *urbanity*)
vilify	verb	to defame; to characterize harshly
viscous	adjective	thick; sticky (noun form: *viscosity*)

QUICK QUIZ #4

Define the following words.

Pernicious: _____

Eulogy: _____

Aesthetic: _____

Castigation: _____

Prodigious: _____

Penurious: _____

Satire: _____

Ebullience: _____

Incipient: _____

Penurious: _____
_____

Quaff: _____
_____

Emollient: _____
_____

Harangue: _____
_____

Inveigle: _____
_____

Facetious: _____
_____

Caustic: _____
_____

Cogent: _____
_____

Quick Quiz #5

Match the following words to their definitions. The answers are on page 278.

A. Pious   _____ Drawn from different sources or styles

B. Intransigent   _____ Evoking intense aversion or dislike

C. Torpid   _____ To examine with great care

D. Eclectic   _____ To defame; to characterize harshly

E. Heretical   _____ Unwilling to compromise

F. Peruse   _____ Impenetrable by light

G. Culpable   _____ Lethargic; sluggish

H. Ascetic   _____ Extremely reverent or devout

I. Enigmatic   _____ Argumentative; quarrelsome

J. Supplant   _____ Mysterious; obscure

K. Opaque   _____ Deserving blame

L. Odious   _____ One who practices rigid self-denial

M. Vilify   _____ Violating accepted dogma or convention

N. Contentious   _____ To take the place of

QUICK QUIZ #6

Try the following analogies, antonyms, and sentence completions. The answers are on page 278.

1. DEMUR : ACQUIESCE ::

   ○ construe : determine
   ○ ameliorate : impugn
   ○ excuse : condemn
   ○ burgeon : delineate
   ○ inaugurate : elect

2. ACCOLADE : PRAISE ::

   ○ utopia : perfection
   ○ insult : disrespect
   ○ avarice : generosity
   ○ discretion : adulation
   ○ cacophony : sound

3. COMPLY : COMPLAISANT ::

   ○ socialize : gregarious
   ○ terminate : bucolic
   ○ ameliorate : dogmatic
   ○ fester : egalitarian
   ○ impede: officious

4. CATALYST : CHANGE ::

   ○ precept : happiness
   ○ oscillation : rhythm
   ○ precursor : event
   ○ mercenary : money
   ○ salve : healing

5. ABATE:

   ○ dissolve
   ○ dwindle
   ○ putrefy
   ○ preen
   ○ intensify

6. DISINTERESTED:

   ○ didactic
   ○ biased
   ○ fascinated
   ○ furtive
   ○ innocuous

7. DEARTH:

   ○ glut
   ○ foible
   ○ sanction
   ○ quiescence
   ○ nostalgia

8. REDOUBTABLE:

   ○ esoteric
   ○ ubiquitous
   ○ unimpressive
   ○ stoic
   ○ ephemeral

9. After failing to advance to the final round of the state spelling bee for the third year in a row, Heather's mood could only be described as

   _____.

   ○ morose
   ○ chary
   ○ contrite
   ○ impecunious
   ○ detestable

10. The chances of becoming _____ writer decrease substantially when one spends too much time alone; lack of human contact turns what should be a fast flowing stream of words into a _____ sludge.

    ○ an urbane : filthy
    ○ a creative : torrential
    ○ a popular : wasteful
    ○ a prolific : viscous
    ○ a wealthy : sticky

HIT PARADE GROUP 3

acumen	noun	keen, accurate judgment or insight
adulterate	verb	to reduce purity by combining with inferior ingredients
amalgamate	verb	to combine several elements into a whole (noun form: *amalgamation*)
archaic	adjective	outdated; associated with an earlier, perhaps more primitive, time
aver	verb	to state as a fact; to declare or assert
bolster	verb	to provide support or reinforcement
bombastic	adjective	pompous; grandiloquent (noun form: *bombast*)
diatribe	noun	a harsh denunciation
dissemble	verb	to disguise or conceal; to mislead
eccentric	adjective	departing from norms or conventions
endemic	adjective	characteristic of or often found in a particular locality, region, or people
evanescent	adjective	tending to disappear like vapor; vanishing
exacerbate	verb	to make worse or more severe
fervent	adjective	greatly emotional or zealous (noun form: *fervor*)
fortuitous	adjective	happening by accident or chance
germane	adjective	relevant to the subject at hand; appropriate in subject matter
grandiloquence	noun	pompous speech or expression (adj. form: *grandiloquent*)
hackneyed	adjective	rendered trite or commonplace by frequent usage
halcyon	adjective	calm and peaceful
hedonism	noun	devotion to pleasurable pursuits, esp. to the pleasures of the senses (a *hedonist* is someone who pursues pleasure)
hegemony	noun	the consistent dominance of one state or ideology over others
iconoclast	noun	one who attacks or undermines traditional conventions or institutions
idolatrous	adjective	given to intense or excessive devotion to something (noun form: *idolatry*)

impassive	adjective	revealing no emotion
imperturbable	adjective	marked by extreme calm, impassivity, and steadiness
implacable	adjective	not capable of being appeased or significantly changed
impunity	noun	immunity from punishment or penalty
inchoate	adjective	in an initial stage; not fully formed
infelicitous	adjective	unfortunate; inappropriate
insipid	adjective	without taste or flavor; lacking in spirit; bland
loquacious	adjective	extremely talkative (noun form: *loquacity*)
luminous	adjective	characterized by brightness and the emission of light
malevolent	adjective	having or showing often vicious ill will, spite, or hatred (noun form: *malevolence*)
malleable	adjective	capable of being shaped or formed; tractable; pliable
mendacity	noun	the condition of being untruthful; dishonesty (adj. form: *mendacious*)
meticulous	adjective	characterized by extreme care and precision; attentive to detail
misanthrope	noun	one who hates all other humans (adj. form: *misanthropic*)
mitigate	verb	to make or become less severe or intense; to moderate
obdurate	adjective	unyielding; hardhearted; intractable
obsequious	adjective	exhibiting a fawning attentiveness
occlude	verb	to obstruct or block
opprobrium	noun	disgrace; contempt; scorn
pedagogy	noun	the profession or principles of teaching, or instructing
pedantic	adjective	the parading of learning; excessive attention to minutiae and formal rules
penury	noun	poverty; destitution
pervasive	adjective	having the tendency to permeate or spread throughout
pine	verb	to yearn intensely; to languish; to lose vigor

pirate	verb	to illegally use or reproduce
pith	noun	the essential or central part
pithy	adjective	precise and brief
placate	verb	to appease; to calm by making concessions
platitude	noun	a superficial remark, esp. one offered as meaningful
plummet	verb	to plunge or drop straight down
polemical	adjective	controversial; argumentative
prodigal	adjective	recklessly wasteful; extravagant; profuse; lavish
profuse	adjective	given or coming forth abundantly; extravagant
proliferate	verb	to grow or increase swiftly and abundantly
queries	noun	questions; inquiries; doubts in the mind; reservations
querulous	adjective	prone to complaining or grumbling; peevish
rancorous	adjective	characterized by bitter, long-lasting resentment (noun form: *rancor*)
recalcitrant	adjective	obstinately defiant of authority; difficult to manage
repudiate	verb	to refuse to have anything to do with; disown
rescind	verb	to invalidate; to repeal; to retract
reverent	adjective	marked by, feeling, or expressing a feeling of profound awe and respect (noun form: *reverance*)
rhetoric	noun	the art or study of effective use of language for communication and persuasion
salubrious	adjective	promoting health or well-being
solvent	adjective	able to meet financial obligations; able to dissolve another substance
specious	adjective	seeming true, but actually being fallacious; misleadingly attractive; plausible but false
spurious	adjective	lacking authenticity or validity; false; counterfeit
subpoena	noun	a court order requiring appearance and/or testimony
succinct	adjective	brief; concise
superfluous	adjective	exceeding what is sufficient or necessary
surfeit	noun/verb	an overabundant supply; excess; to feed or supply to excess

tenacity	noun	the quality of adherence or persistence to something valued; persistent determination (adj. form: *tenacious*)
tenuous	adjective	having little substance or strength; flimsy; weak
tirade	noun	a long and extremely critical speech; a harsh denunciation
transient	adjective	fleeting; passing quickly; brief
zealous	adjective	fervent; ardent; impassioned; devoted to a cause (a *zealot* is a zealous person)

QUICK QUIZ #7

Define the following words.

Tirade: _____

_____

Solvent: _____

_____

Idolatrous: _____

_____

Opprobrium: _____

_____

Obsequious: _____

_____

Luminous: _____

_____

Tenuous: _____

_____

Reverent: _____

_____

Iconoclast: _____

_____

Fervent: _____

_____

Amalgamate: _____

_____

Repudiate: _____

_____

Specious: _____

_____

Pervasive: _____

_____

Surfeit: _____

_____

Hedonism: _____

_____

Quick Quiz #8

Match the following words to their definitions. The answers are on page 279.

A. Zealous   _____ The essential or central part

B. Malleable   _____ Tending to disappear like vapor

C. Grandiloquence   _____ Brief; concise

D. Proliferate   _____ Controversial; argumentative

E. Evanescent   _____ Lacking authenticity; false; counterfeit

F. Impassive   _____ Capable of being shaped or formed

G. Misanthrope   _____ Fervent; ardent; devoted to a cause

H. Tenacity   _____ Persistent determination

I. Spurious   _____ One who hates other human beings

J. Pith   _____ Revealing no emotion

K. Querulous   _____ Pompous speech or expression

L. Specious   _____ To grow or increase swiftly

M. Polemical   _____ Prone to complaining; whiny

N. Succinct   _____ Seemingly true, but actually false

QUICK QUIZ #9

Try the following analogies, antonyms, and sentence completions. The answers are on page 279.

1. RESENTMENT : RANCOROUS ::
   - ⟵ purification : inattentive
   - ⟵ irregularity : eccentric
   - ⟵ diatribe : hackneyed
   - ⟵ acumen : polemical
   - ⟵ hypocrisy : deliberate

2. IMPLACABLE : APPEASE ::
   - ⟵ insoluble : fathom
   - ⟵ archaic : date
   - ⟵ superfluous : occlude
   - ⟵ doleful : mourn
   - ⟵ bombastic : ingratiate

3. MITIGATE : SEVERITY ::
   - ⟵ rue : regret
   - ⟵ embellish : compassion
   - ⟵ slake : interlude
   - ⟵ adulterate : purity
   - ⟵ exacerbate : platitude

4. PENURY : WEALTH ::
   - ⟵ empathy : concern
   - ⟵ impunity : rhetoric
   - ⟵ hegemony : power
   - ⟵ gambit : advantage
   - ⟵ mendacity : candor

5. RECALCITRANT:
   - ⟵ untenable
   - ⟵ pedantic
   - ⟵ loquacious
   - ⟵ accommodating
   - ⟵ satiated

6. PLACATE:
   - ⟵ bolster
   - ⟵ antagonize
   - ⟵ soothe
   - ⟵ dissemble
   - ⟵ usurp

7. RESCIND:
   - ⟵ pirate
   - ⟵ pine
   - ⟵ enact
   - ⟵ aver
   - ⟵ attenuate

8. PROLIX:
   - ⟵ dispensable
   - ⟵ obdurate
   - ⟵ insipid
   - ⟵ minuscule
   - ⟵ pithy

9. Ellen and Suzanne had not planned to have lunch together on Friday, and thus running into each other at the sushi restaurant was simply _____ occurrence
   - ⟵ an infelicitous
   - ⟵ a fortuitous
   - ⟵ a profuse
   - ⟵ a transient
   - ⟵ a suggestive

10. Duane hoped that his retirement would be _____, but he suspected that the daily chaos _____ to city life, with its constant sense of crisis, would make that difficult.
    - ⟵ halcyon . . endemic
    - ⟵ meticulous . . related
    - ⟵ quiet . . offensive
    - ⟵ salubrious . . connected
    - ⟵ malevolent . . devoted

HIT PARADE GROUP 4

acerbic	adjective	having a sour or bitter taste or character; sharp; biting
aggrandize	verb	to increase in intensity, power, influence, or prestige
alchemy	noun	a medieval science aimed at the transmutation of metals, esp. base metals into gold (an *alchemist* is one who practices alchemy)
amenable	adjective	agreeable; responsive to suggestion
anachronism	noun	something or someone out of place in terms of historical or chronological context
astringent	adjective/noun	having a tightening effect on living tissue; harsh; severe
bombast	noun	self-important or pompous writing or speech (adj. form: *bombastic*)
contiguous	adjective	sharing a border; touching; adjacent
convention	noun	a generally agreed-upon practice or attitude
credulous	adjective	tending to believe too readily; gullible (noun form: *credulity*)
cynicism	noun	an attitude or quality of belief that all people are motivated by selfishness (adj. form: *cynical*)
decorum	noun	polite or appropriate conduct or behavior (adj. form: *decorous*)
derision	noun	scorn; ridicule; contemptuous treatment (adj. form: *derisive*; verb form: *deride*)
desiccate	verb	to dry out or dehydrate; to make dry or dull
dilettante	noun	one with an amateurish or superficial interest in the arts or a branch of knowledge
disparage	verb	to slight or belittle
divulge	verb	to disclose something secret
fawn	verb	to flatter or praise excessively
flout	verb	to show contempt for, as in a rule or convention
garrulous	adjective	pointlessly talkative, talking too much

glib	adjective	marked by ease or informality; nonchalant; lacking in depth; superficial
hubris	noun	overbearing presumption or pride; arrogance
imminent	adjective	about to happen; impending
immutable	adjective	not capable of change
impetuous	adjective	hastily or rashly energetic; impulsive and vehement
indifferent	adjective	having no interest or concern; showing no bias or prejudice
inimical	adjective	damaging; harmful; injurious
intractable	adjective	not easily managed or directed; stubborn; obstinate
intrepid	adjective	steadfast and courageous
laconic	adjective	using few words; terse
maverick	noun	an independent individual who does not go along with a group or party
mercurial	adjective	characterized by rapid and unpredictable change in mood
mollify	verb	to calm or soothe; to reduce in emotional intensity
neophyte	noun	a recent convert; a beginner; novice
obfuscate	verb	to deliberately obscure; to make confusing
obstinate	adjective	stubborn; hardheaded; uncompromising
ostentatious	adjective	characterized by or given to pretentious display; showy
pervade	verb	to permeate throughout (adj. form: *pervasive*)
phlegmatic	adjective	calm; sluggish; unemotional
plethora	noun	an overabundance; a surplus
pragmatic	adjective	practical rather than idealistic
presumptuous	adjective	overstepping due bounds (as of propriety or courtesy); taking liberties
pristine	adjective	pure; uncorrupted; clean
probity	noun	adherence to highest principles; complete and confirmed integrity; uprightness
proclivity	noun	a natural predisposition or inclination
profligate	adjective	excessively wasteful; recklessly extravagant (noun form: *profligacy*)

propensity	noun	a natural inclination or tendency, penchant
prosaic	adjective	dull; lacking in spirit or imagination
pungent	adjective	characterized by a strong, sharp smell or taste
quixotic	adjective	foolishly impractical; marked by lofty romantic ideals
quotidian	adjective	occurring or recurring daily; commonplace
rarefy	verb	to make or become thin, less dense; to refine
recondite	adjective	hidden; concealed; difficult to understand; obscure
refulgent	adjective	radiant; shiny; brilliant
renege	verb	to fail to honor a commitment; to go back on a promise
sedulous	adjective	diligent; persistent; hardworking
shard	noun	a piece of broken pottery or glass
soporific	adjective	causing drowsiness; tending to induce sleep
sparse	adjective	thin; not dense; arranged at widely spaced intervals
spendthrift	noun	one who spends money wastefully
subtle	adjective	not obvious; elusive; difficult to discern
tacit	adjective	implied; not explicitly stated
terse	adjective	brief and concise in wording
tout	verb	to publicly praise or promote
trenchant	adjective	sharply perceptive; keen; penetrating
unfeigned	adjective	genuine; not false or hypocritical
untenable	adjective	indefensible; not viable; uninhabitable
vacillate	verb	to waver indecisively between one course of action or opinion and another; waver
variegated	adjective	multicolored; characterized by a variety of patches of different color
vexation	noun	annoyance; irritation (noun form: *vex*)
vigilant	adjective	alertly watchful (noun form: *vigilance*)
vituperate	verb	to use harsh condemnatory language; to abuse or censure severely or abusively; berate
volatile	adjective	readily changing to a vapor; changeable; fickle; explosive (noun form: *volatility*)

Quick Quiz #10
Define the following words.

Soporific: _____
_____

Rarefy: _____
_____

Ostentatious: _____
_____

Variegated: _____
_____

Unfeigned: _____
_____

Terse: _____
_____

Glib: _____
_____

Disparage: _____
_____

Cynicism: _____
_____

Contiguous: _____
_____

Neophyte: _____
_____

Mercurial: _____

_____

Flout: _____

_____

Volatile: _____

_____

Phlegmatic: _____

_____

Mollify: _____

_____

Vexation : _____

_____

QUICK QUIZ #11

Match the following words to their definitions. The answers are on page 279.

A. Obstinate   _____ To go back on a promise

B. Sedulous   _____ Using few words; terse

C. Pungent   _____ One who spends money wastefully

D. Fawn   _____ To dry out or dehydrate

E. Vigilant   _____ An overabundance; a surplus

F. Shard   _____ Stubborn; uncompromising

G. Trenchant   _____ Alertly watchful

H. Desiccate   _____ Characterized by a strong, sharp smell

I. Spendthrift   _____ To flatter or praise excessively

J. Laconic   _____ To permeate throughout

K. Plethora   _____ Excessively wasteful

L. Renege   _____ A piece of broken pottery or glass

M. Profligate   _____ Diligent; hardworking; persistent

N. Pervade   _____ Sharply perceptive; keen; penetrating

QUICK QUIZ #12

Try the following analogies, antonyms, and sentence completions. The answers are on page 279.

1. RECONDITE : UNDERSTAND ::
   - ◯ inevitable : agitate
   - ◯ intractable : manage
   - ◯ protracted : propitiate
   - ◯ untenable : flout
   - ◯ imminent : occur

2. PROSAIC : IMAGINATION ::
   - ◯ credulous : skepticism
   - ◯ sparse : convention
   - ◯ mercurial : volatility
   - ◯ garrulous : exposure
   - ◯ taut : esteem

3. QUIXOTIC : PRAGMATIC ::
   - ◯ indifferent : acerbic
   - ◯ flamboyant : effete
   - ◯ subtle : elusive
   - ◯ impetuous : deliberate
   - ◯ venerable : timorous

4. PROUD : HUBRIS ::
   - ◯ unethical : probity
   - ◯ false : forgery
   - ◯ intrepid : recklessness
   - ◯ refulgent : alchemy
   - ◯ steady : turbulence

5. AGGRANDIZE:
   - ◯ savor
   - ◯ mollify
   - ◯ divulge
   - ◯ tout
   - ◯ belittle

6. PRISTINE:
   - ◯ equivocal
   - ◯ soiled
   - ◯ tacit
   - ◯ astringent
   - ◯ phlegmatic

7. PROPENSITY:
   - ◯ disinclination
   - ◯ decorum
   - ◯ vexation
   - ◯ presumption
   - ◯ proclivity

8. OBFUSCATE:
   - ◯ meander
   - ◯ engender
   - ◯ vacillate
   - ◯ illuminate
   - ◯ vituperate

9. Taking a few art classes had convinced Elaine that she was an expert in sculpture, but the museum curators viewed her instead as a mere _____.
   - ◯ bystander
   - ◯ fraud
   - ◯ dilettante
   - ◯ anachronism
   - ◯ maverick

10. Alastor's contempt for musical theater was _____; no matter how many times people tried to change his mind, he could only view it with _____.
    - ◯ amenable . . bombast
    - ◯ inimical . . scorn
    - ◯ legendary . . anger
    - ◯ quotidian . . disdain
    - ◯ immutable . . derision

EXTRA VOCABULARY

The 300 or so words on the Hit Parade are the most important part of your vocabulary building, but they shouldn't be the end. After you've mastered the Hit Parade, learn as many more words as you can. For you hardcore vocabulary students, here are another 200 good GRE words that you should study. Once you've learned them, test yourself with the exercises at the end. Remember, every new word you learn makes it more likely you'll score well on the GRE Verbal section. So keep it up!

abash	verb	to make ashamed; to embarrass
abject	adjective	hopeless; extremely sad and servile; defeated
abnegate	verb	to deny oneself things; to reject; to renounce
abrogate	verb	to abolish or repeal formally; to set aside; to nullify
abstemious	adjective	sparing or moderate, especially in eating and drinking
abstruse	adjective	hard to understand or grasp
abysmal	adjective	extremely hopeless or wretched; bottomless
accede	verb	to give in; to yield; to agree
accrete	verb	to increase by growth or addition
adduce	verb	to bring forward as an example or as proof; to cite
adroit	adjective	skillful; dexterous; clever; socially at ease
advent	noun	arrival; coming; beginning
affable	adjective	easy to talk to; friendly
affectation	noun	unnatural or artificial behavior, usually intended to impress
aggregate	noun	sum total; a collection of separate things mixed together
aghast	adjective	terrified; shocked
allege	verb	to assert without proof
allusion	noun	an indirect reference to something else; a hint
ambience	noun	atmosphere; mood; feeling
ambivalent	adjective	undecided; having opposing feelings simultaneously
amiable	adjective	friendly; agreeable
amorphous	adjective	shapeless; bloblike
anathema	noun	something or someone loathed or detested; a formal ecclesiastical curse and excommunication
ancillary	adjective	subordinate; providing assistance
animosity	noun	resentment; hostility; ill will

antecedent	noun	something that went before; a preceding cause or event
antipathy	noun	firm dislike; a strong feeling of aversion
antithesis	noun	the direct opposite
apex	noun	highest point
aphorism	noun	a brief, witty saying; a proverb
apocryphal	adjective	of dubious authenticity; fictitious
apostasy	noun	abandonment or rejection of faith or loyalty
apposite	adjective	distinctly suitable; pertinent
appropriate	verb	to take without permission; to set aside for a particular use
arbiter	noun	one who decides; a judge
arcane	adjective	mysterious; known only to a select few
archetype	noun	an original model or pattern
arrant	adjective	utter; unmitigated; very bad
astute	adjective	shrewd; keen in judgment
attrition	noun	a gradual wearing away, weakening, or loss; a natural decrease in numbers or size
augment	verb	to make bigger; to add to; to increase
auspicious	adjective	favorable; promising
avow	verb	to claim; to declare boldly; to admit
banal	adjective	unoriginal; ordinary
belabor	verb	to go over repeatedly or to an absurd extent
beleaguer	verb	to surround; to besiege; to harass
belie	verb	to give a false impression of; to contradict
benign	adjective	gentle; not harmful; kind; mild
bereave	verb	to deprive or leave desolate, especially through death
blithe	adjective	carefree; cheerful
broach	verb	to open up a subject for discussion, often a delicate subject
brook	verb	to bear or tolerate; to put up with something
callow	adjective	immature
cardinal	adjective	most important; chief
catholic	adjective	universal; embracing everything

cavil	verb	to quibble; to raise trivial objections
chagrin	noun	humiliation; embarrassed disappointment
choleric	adjective	hot-tempered; quick to anger
circumspect	adjective	cautious
coalesce	verb	to come together as one; to fuse; to unite
coda	noun	a passage concluding a musical composition
cognizant	adjective	fully informed; knowledgeable; aware
collusion	noun	conspiracy; secret cooperation
commensurate	adjective	equal; proportionate
conciliatory	adjective	making peace; attempting to resolve a dispute through goodwill
consecrate	verb	to make or declare sacred
consonant	adjective	harmonious; in agreement
consummate	adjective	perfect; complete; supremely skillful
contumely	noun	rudeness; insolence; arrogance
convivial	adjective	fond of partying; festive
copious	adjective	abundant; plentiful
corroborate	verb	to confirm; to back up with evidence
coterie	noun	a select group of close associates
countenance	noun	face; facial expression
covet	verb	to wish for enviously
cull	verb	to pick out from among many; to select; to collect
cursory	adjective	hasty; superficial
daunt	verb	to make fearful; to intimidate
debacle	noun	a sudden disastrous collapse, downfall, or defeat; a rout
debauchery	noun	corruption by sensuality; intemperance; wild living
decorous	adjective	in good taste; orderly; proper
deleterious	adjective	harmful
deluge	noun	a flood
deprecate	verb	to express disapproval of
dilapidated	adjective	broken-down; fallen into ruin
discomfit	verb	to confuse; to disconcert; to thwart the plans of; to defeat in battle

discourse	noun	to converse; to formally discuss a subject
doggerel	noun	comic, loose verse
egregious	adjective	extremely bad; flagrant
elucidate	verb	to explain; to make understandable
empirical	adjective	relying on experience or observation; not merely theoretical
endemic	adjective	native; belonging to a specific region or people
enormity	noun	extreme evil or wickedness
epicure	noun	a person with refined taste in wine and food
epitome	noun	the perfect example of something; a paradigm
equanimity	noun	composure; calm
eschew	verb	to avoid; to shun
espouse	verb	to support; to advocate
evince	verb	to show or demonstrate clearly; manifest
exhort	verb	to urge strongly
exposition	noun	a setting forth of meaning or intent; a discourse intended to explain
extol	verb	to praise highly
facile	adjective	fluent; skillful in a superficial way; easy
fatuous	adjective	foolish; silly; idiotic
fetter	verb	to restrain; to hamper
flag	verb	to weaken; to slow down
flippant	adjective	frivolously shallow and disrespectful
foment	verb	to stir up; to instigate
forbear	verb	to refrain from; to abstain
founder	verb	to fail; to collapse; to sink
fulsome	adjective	offensively flattering or insincere; repulsive
gainsay	verb	to deny; to speak or act against
gambit	noun	a scheme to gain an advantage; a ploy
genial	adjective	cheerful and pleasant; friendly; helpful
germane	adjective	applicable; pertinent; relevant
gratis	adjective	free of charge
gratuitous	adjective	given freely (said of something bad); unjustified; unprovoked; uncalled for

guile	noun	cunning; duplicity; artfulness
harbinger	noun	a forerunner; a signal of
hermetic	adjective	impervious to external influence; airtight
idyllic	adjective	charming in a rustic way; naturally peaceful
ignominy	noun	deep disgrace
impecunious	adjective	without money; penniless
impromptu	adjective	without preparation; on the spur of the moment
impugn	verb	to attack as false or questionable
incandescent	adjective	brilliant; giving off heat or light
incipient	adjective	beginning; emerging
incorrigible	adjective	incapable of being reformed
indolent	adjective	lazy
indulgent	adjective	lenient; yielding to desire
ineluctable	adjective	inescapable; unavoidable
inept	adjective	clumsy; incompetent
inert	adjective	inactive; sluggish; not reacting chemically
inexorable	adjective	relentless; inevitable; unavoidable
inherent	adjective	part of the essential nature of something; intrinsic
inundate	verb	to flood; to overwhelm
inveterate	adjective	habitual; deeply rooted
itinerant	adjective	moving from place to place
judicious	adjective	exercising sound judgment
lament	verb	to mourn
largess	noun	liberality in giving gifts; money or gifts bestowed; generosity of attitude
lascivious	adjective	lustful; obscene; lewd
latent	adjective	present but not visible or apparent; potential
levee	noun	an embankment designed to prevent the flooding of a river
levity	noun	lightness; frivolity; unseriousness
licentious	adjective	lascivious; lewd; promiscuous; amoral
magnate	noun	a rich, powerful, or very successful businessperson
manifest	adjective	visible; evident
maudlin	adjective	tearfully sentimental; silly or weepy

maxim	noun	a fundamental principle; an old saying
mendicant	noun	a beggar
motility	noun	spontaneous movement
noisome	adjective	offensive or disgusting; stinking; noxious
nominal	adjective	in name only; insignificant
novel	adjective	new; original
oblique	adjective	indirect; at an angle
palliate	verb	to make less severe or intense; to make an offense seem less serious
panacea	noun	something that cures everything
paradigm	noun	a model or example
paradox	noun	a true statement or phenomenon that seems to contradict itself
parsimonious	adjective	stingy; miserly
partisan	adjective	having a bias in support of a party, group, or cause
partisan	noun	one who supports a particular party, group, or cause
patina	noun	surface discoloration caused by age and oxidation
paucity	noun	scarcity
pedestrian	adjective	unoriginal; banal
perturb	verb	to disturb greatly
piquant	adjective	pleasantly pungent or tart
placid	adjective	pleasantly calm; peaceful
plaintive	adjective	expressing sadness or sorrow
plumb	verb	to measure the depth of something
portent	noun	an omen; a sign of something coming in the future
precipitous	adjective	steep
predilection	noun	a natural preference for something
presage	verb	to portend; to foreshadow; to forecast or predict
privation	noun	lack of comforts or necessities; poverty
provincial	adjective	limited in outlook to one's own small corner of the world; narrow
prurient	adjective	having lustful thoughts or desires; causing lust
putative	adjective	commonly accepted; supposed; reputed
quay	noun	a landing on the edge of the water; wharf; pier

queue	noun	a line of waiting people or things
queue	verb	to get in line
quintessential	adjective	being the most perfect example of
rampart	noun	a fortification; a bulwark of defense
redolent	adjective	fragrant; aromatic; suggestive or reminiscent
remonstrate	verb	to argue against; to protest; to raise objections
remuneration	noun	payment; recompense
renaissance	noun	a rebirth or revival
replete	adjective	completely filled; abounding
reproach	verb	to scold, usually in disappointment; to blame; to disgrace
reprobate	noun	a wicked, sinful, depraved person
reprove	verb	to criticize mildly
respite	noun	a period of rest or relief
ribald	adjective	characterized by vulgar, lewd humor
sagacious	adjective	wise
sagacity	noun	wisdom
sage	noun	a wise person
salutary	adjective	healthful; remedial; wholesome
sanguine	adjective	cheerful; optimistic; hopeful
surreptitious	adjective	sneaky; secret
sycophant	noun	one who sucks up to others; a servile, self-seeking flatterer
taciturn	adjective	untalkative by nature
temerity	noun	recklessness; audacity; foolhardy disregard of danger
turpitude	noun	shameful wickedness or depravity
unalloyed	adjective	undiluted; pure
usury	noun	lending money at an extremely high rate of interest
venal	adjective	capable of being bribed; corrupt
verdant	adjective	covered with green plants; leafy; inexperienced
vestige	noun	a remaining bit of something; a last trace
vitiate	verb	to make faulty or defective; impair; to corrupt morally
wizened	adjective	shriveled; withered; shrunken

QUICK QUIZ #13
Define the following words.

Quintessential: _____

Surreptitious: _____

Apex: _____

Affable: _____

Belie: _____

Inexorable: _____

Debacle: _____

Founder: _____

Gainsay: _____

Largess: _____

Mendicant: _____

Queue: _____

_____

Sycophant: _____

_____

Apostasy: _____

_____

Impugn: _____

_____

QUICK QUIZ #14

Match the following words to their definitions. The answers are on page 280.

A. Panacea   _____ Pleasingly pungent or tart

B. Cavil   _____ Rudeness; insolence; arrogance

C. Itinerant   _____ To explain; to make understandable

D. Aghast   _____ To make ashamed; to embarrass

E. Guile   _____ Moving from place to place

F. Piquant   _____ Extreme evil or wickedness

G. Banal   _____ Terrified; shocked

H. Enormity   _____ Cunning; duplicity

I. Abash   _____ Unoriginal; ordinary

J. Contumely   _____ Something that cures everything

K. Fetter   _____ To quibble; to raise trivial objections

L. Apposite   _____ To argue against; to protest

M. Elucidate   _____ Distinctly suitable; pertinent

N. Remonstrate   _____ To restrain; to hamper

Quick Quiz #15

Try the following analogies, antonyms, and sentence completions. The answers are on page 280.

1. CONSECRATE : SACRED ::

   ○ augment : ancillary
   ○ discomfit : facile
   ○ vitiate : defective
   ○ palliate : partisan
   ○ reproach : disgraceful

2. THRIFTY : PARSIMONIOUS ::

   ○ sentimental : maudlin
   ○ copious : adequate
   ○ empirical : nominal
   ○ taciturn : garrulous
   ○ noisome : decorous

3. ABSTRUSE : COMPREHEND ::

   ○ abysmal: reprove
   ○ provincial : presage
   ○ conciliatory : coalesce
   ○ cursory : foment
   ○ incorrigible : reform

4. ADROIT : DEXTERITY ::

   ○ judicious : ignominy
   ○ cognizant : awareness
   ○ indolent : harbinger
   ○ egregious : discourse
   ○ putative : chagrin

5. SALUTARY:

   ○ fatuous
   ○ manifest
   ○ prurient
   ○ deleterious
   ○ unalloyed

6. LICENTIOUS:

   ○ chaste
   ○ venal
   ○ inexorable
   ○ blithe
   ○ arcane

7. CALLOW:

   ○ inveterate
   ○ mature
   ○ benign
   ○ convivial
   ○ fulsome

8. SANGUINE:

   ○ ribald
   ○ verdant
   ○ ineluctable
   ○ morose
   ○ placid

9. Alice was shocked at her brother's _____ when he stood up in class and interrupted the teacher to disagree with her.

   ○ equanimity
   ○ debauchery
   ○ temerity
   ○ animosity
   ○ countenance

10. Despite her _____ for seeing movies, Rebecca _____ those films that starred child actors because she hated watching children on screen.

   ○ gambit . . shunned
   ○ inclination . . adduced
   ○ epitome . . exhorted
   ○ maxim . . abrogated
   ○ predilection . . eschewed

ADVANCED VOCABULARY

You want more? Wow, you really are a glutton for vocabulary. Congratulations, that's great! Here is a list of about 100 very challenging vocabulary words, followed by some exercises. If you've learned the Hit Parade and the Extra Vocabulary list, take a look at these.

abjure	verb	to repudiate; to take back; to refrain from
adumbrate	verb	to foreshadow vaguely; to suggest or outline sketchily; to obscure or overshadow
anodyne	adjective/ noun	soothing; something that assuages or comforts; something that allays pain
apogee	noun	the most distant point in the orbit of the moon or of an artificial satellite
apotheosis	noun	an exalted or glorified example; elevation to divine standard
artful	adjective	crafty; wily; sly
artless	adjective	completely without guile; natural, without artificiality
assay	verb	to examine by trial or experiment; to evaluate or assess
asseverate	verb	to aver; to allege; to assert
augur	verb	to serve as an omen or sign; to predict or foretell
baleful	adjective	sinister; pernicious; ominous
beatify	verb	to bless, make happy, or ascribe a virtue to; to regard as saintly
bilious	adjective	ill-tempered; cranky
calumny	noun	slander; a maliciously false statement
captious	adjective	disposed to point out trivial faults; calculated to confuse or entrap in argument
carapace	noun	a protective shell
celerity	noun	swiftness of action or motion; speed
coeval	adjective	of the same period; coexisting
contretemps	noun	an embarrassing occurrence; a mishap
contumacious	adjective	stubbornly rebellious or disobedient
corrigible	adjective	capable of being set right; correctable; reparable
denouement	noun	an outcome or solution; the unraveling of a plot
descry	verb	to discriminate or discern
desuetude	noun	disuse

desultory	adjective	moving or jumping from one thing to another; disconnected; occurring haphazardly
diaphanous	adjective	of such fine texture as to be transparent or translucent; delicate; insubstantial
diffident	adjective	reserved; shy; unassuming; lacking in self-confidence
diurnal	adjective	occurring every day; occurring during the daytime
dulcet	adjective	melodious; harmonious; mellifluous
egress	noun	exit
encomium	noun	a formal expression of praise; a tribute
essay	verb	to test or try; attempt; experiment
estimable	adjective	worthy; formidable
excoriate	verb	to censure scathingly; to upbraid
execrate	verb	to denounce; to loathe
exegesis	noun	critical examination; explication
expiate	verb	to make amends for; to atone
fecund	adjective	fertile; productive
fell	verb/ adjective	to cause to fall by striking; cruel; lethal; dire; sinister
fractious	adjective	quarrelsome; rebellious; unruly; irritable
hirsute	adjective	hairy; shaggy
hoary	adjective	gray or white with age; ancient; stale
husband	verb	to use sparingly or economically; conserve
imbroglio	noun	difficult or embarrassing situation
importune	verb	to urge with annoying persistence; to trouble
indefatigable	adjective	not easily exhaustible; tireless; dogged
insouciant	adjective	nonchalant; lighthearted; carefree
invidious	adjective	causing envy or resentment; offensively harmful
jejune	adjective	vapid; uninteresting; childish, immature, puerile
lachrymose	adjective	causing tears; tearful
lassitude	noun	exhaustion; weakness
ligneous	adjective	woodlike
limn	verb	to draw; to outline in detail; to delineate; to describe
list	verb	to tilt or lean to one side
loquacious	adjective	very talkative; garrulous
lubricious	adjective	lewd; wanton; greasy; slippery

lugubrious	adjective	exaggeratedly mournful
meet	adjective	fitting, proper
mellifluous	adjective	sweetly flowing
meretricious	adjective	plausible but false or insincere; gaudy; showy; tawdry; flashy
minatory	adjective	menacing; threatening
nadir	noun	low point
nice	adjective	exacting; fastidious; extremely precise
nonplus	verb	to baffle; to bewilder; to perplex
nugatory	adjective	of little or no importance; trifling; inconsequential
obstreperous	adjective	noisily and stubbornly defiant; aggressively boisterous
ossify	verb	to convert into bone; to become rigid
otiose	adjective	lazy; of no use; futile
panegyric	noun	formal or elaborate praise
parry	verb	to deflect or ward off; to evade or avoid
pellucid	adjective	transparent; easy to understand; limpid
peripatetic	adjective	wandering; traveling continually; itinerant
perorate	verb	to speak formally
plangent	adjective	pounding; thundering; resounding
pluck	noun	courage; spunk; fortitude
prize	verb	to pry; to press or force with a lever
prolix	adjective	long-winded; verbose
propinquity	noun	nearness; proximity
propitiate	verb	to appease; to conciliate
propitious	adjective	marked by favorable signs or conditions
puerile	adjective	childish; immature
puissant	adjective	powerful
pulchritude	noun	physical beauty
pusillanimous	adjective	cowardly; craven
salacious	adjective	lustful; lascivious; bawdy
saturnine	adjective	melancholy or sullen; of a gloomy disposition
sententious	adjective	given to pompous moralizing; preachy; self-righteous
sidereal	adjective	astral; relating to stars or constellations

sinecure	noun	a position requiring little or no work and usually providing an income
stentorian	adjective	extremely loud and powerful
stygian	adjective	gloomy; dark
succor	noun	assistance; relief in time of distress
succor	verb	to give assistance in time of need
sundry	adjective	various; miscellaneous; separate
supine	adjective	lying face upward; offering no resistance
tendentious	adjective	argumentative; biased
turbid	adjective	murky; opaque; unclear
tyro	noun	novice; rank amateur
unctuous	adjective	oily, both literally and figuratively; characterized by earnest insincerity
vagary	noun	whim; unpredictable action; wild notion
voluble	adjective	fluent; verbal; having easy use of spoken language
wag	noun	a wit; a joker

QUICK QUIZ #16
Define the following words.

Apotheosis: _____

_____

Beatify: _____

_____

Captious: _____

_____

Desultory: _____

_____

Essay: _____

_____

Importune: _____

_____

Lachrymose: _____

_____

Limn: _____

_____

Meet: _____

_____

Meretricious: _____

_____

Perorate: _____

_____

Plangent: _____

_____

Prolix: _____

_____

Sidereal: _____

_____

Unctuous: _____

_____

QUICK QUIZ #17

Match the following words to their definitions. The answers are on page 280.

A. Artful   _____ Extremely loud and powerful

B. Salacious   _____ To upbraid or denounce strongly

C. Nonplus   _____ To discriminate or discern

D. Stygian   _____ Uninteresting; childish; immature

E. Corrigible   _____ To make amends for; to atone

F. Excoriate   _____ To bewilder or perplex

G. Expiate   _____ Crafty; wily; sly

H. Dulcet   _____ Lustful; lascivious

I. Propitiate   _____ Various; miscellaneous

J. Descry   _____ Capable of being set right; correctible

K. List   _____ To tilt or lean to one side

L. Jejune   _____ To appease; to conciliate

M. Stentorian   _____ Gloomy; dark

N. Sundry   _____ Melodious; harmonious

Quick Quiz #18

Try the following analogies, antonyms, and sentence completions. The answers are on page 280.

1. CALUMNY : FALSE ::

   ◯ encomium : laudatory
   ◯ celerity : fecund
   ◯ imbroglio : indefatigable
   ◯ pluck : puerile
   ◯ contretemps : voluble

2. WAG : WIT ::

   ◯ bureaucrat : desuetude
   ◯ tyro : inexperience
   ◯ succor : vagary
   ◯ egress : delight
   ◯ dilettante : pulchritude

3. DIFFIDENT : CONFIDENCE ::

   ◯ coeval: nadir
   ◯ ligneous : sinecure
   ◯ turbid : apogee
   ◯ diaphanous : opacity
   ◯ fractious : propinquity

4. LUGUBRIOUS : MOURNFUL ::

   ◯ pellucid : hirsute
   ◯ mellifluous : baleful
   ◯ tendentious : opinionated
   ◯ peripatetic : saturnine
   ◯ diurnal : ecstatic

5. CONTUMACIOUS:

   ◯ hoary
   ◯ fell
   ◯ lubricious
   ◯ generous
   ◯ obedient

6. EXECRATE:

   ◯ parry
   ◯ extol
   ◯ ossify
   ◯ prize
   ◯ adumbrate

7. LASSITUDE:

   ◯ carapace
   ◯ panegyric
   ◯ denouement
   ◯ vigor
   ◯ exegesis

8. PUSSILANIMOUS:

   ◯ intrepid
   ◯ minatory
   ◯ otiose
   ◯ invidious
   ◯ sententious

9. The teacher fortified himself before walking into the room, knowing how difficult it was to control such an _____ class.

   ◯ estimable
   ◯ anodyne
   ◯ obstreperous
   ◯ insouciant
   ◯ artless

10. It was important for the farmers to _____ their resources, as more _____ days could not be counted on with the winter coming.

   ◯ assay : puissant
   ◯ augur : promising
   ◯ abjure : nugatory
   ◯ conserve : bilious
   ◯ husband : propitious

ANSWER KEY

HIT PARADE GROUP 1

Quick Quiz #2

K
L
E
G
B
A
H
I
N
F
C
M
J
D

Quick Quiz #3

1. A
2. B
3. B
4. C
5. C
6. E
7. B
8. D
9. A
10. E

HIT PARADE GROUP 2

Quick Quiz #5

D
L
F
M
B
K
C
A
N
I
G
H
E
J

Quick Quiz #6

1. C
2. B
3. A
4. E
5. E
6. B
7. A
8. C
9. A
10. D

Hit Parade Group 3

Quick Quiz #8

J
E
N
M
I
B
A
H
G
F
C
D
K
L

Quick Quiz #9

1. B
2. A
3. D
4. E
5. D
6. B
7. C
8. E
9. B
10. A

Hit Parade Group 4

Quick Quiz #11

L
J
I
H
K
A
E
C
D
N
M
F
B
G

Quick Quiz #12

1. B
2. A
3. D
4. C
5. E
6. B
7. A
8. D
9. C
10. E

Extra Vocabulary

Quick Quiz #14

F
J
M
I
C
H
D
E
G
A
B
N
L
K

Quick Quiz #15

1. C
2. A
3. E
4. B
5. D
6. A
7. B
8. D
9. C
10. E

Advanced Vocabulary

Quick Quiz #17

M
F
J
L
G
C
A
B
N
E
K
I
D
H

Quick Quiz #18

1. A
2. B
3. D
4. C
5. E
6. B
7. D
8. A
9. C
10. E

More expert advice from
The Princeton Review

Increase your chances of getting into the graduate school of your choice with The Princeton Review. We can help you get higher test scores, make the most informed choices, and make the most of your experience once you get there. We can also help you make the career move that will let you use your skills and education to their best advantage.

Cracking the GRE, 2008 Edition
978-0-375-76615-2 • $21.00/C$27.00

Cracking the GRE with DVD,
2008 Edition
978-0-375-76616-9 • $33.95/C$42.00

Cracking the GRE Biology Test,
5th Edition
978-0-375-76488-2 • $18.00/C$26.00

Cracking the GRE Chemistry Test,
3rd Edition
978-0-375-76489-9 • $18.00/C$26.00

Cracking the GRE Literature Test,
5th Edition
978-0-375-76490-5 • $18.00/C$26.00

Cracking the GRE Math Test,
3rd Edition
978-0-375-76491-2 • $18.00/C$26.00

Cracking the GRE Phychology Test,
7th Edition
978-0-375-76492-9 • $18.00/C$26.00

Verbal Workout for the GRE,
3rd Edition
978-0-375-76573-5 • $19.00/C$25.00

Graduate School Companion
978-0-375-76574-2 • $14.95/C$19.95

Best Entry-Level Jobs, 2008 Edition
978-0-375-76599-5 • $16.95/C$21.95

Guide to Your Career, 6th Edition
978-0-375-76561-2 • $19.95/C$26.95

Available at Bookstores Everywhere
www.PrincetonReview.com

Don't Stop Now...

Get More

More Test Prep—If you're looking to learn more about how to raise your GRE score, you're in the right place. We offer private tutoring, small group tutoring, classroom courses, online courses, and an array of books.

More Books—If you like *Verbal Workout for the GRE*, you might want to check out some of our other titles:

Cracking the GRE

Cracking the GRE with DVD

Word Smart for the GRE

Crash Course for the GRE

Complete Book of Graduate Programs in the Arts & Sciences

Graduate School Companion

More Acceptance Letters—We know more than just tests. We know a lot about graduate school admissions, too. We've got tips for crafting the perfect essay and much more.

To learn more about any of our private tutoring programs, small group tutoring, classroom courses, or online courses, please call **800-2Review** (800-273-8439) or visit **PrincetonReview.com/GRE.**